Henry Keazor (ed.)

We Are All Astronauts
The Image of the Space Traveler in Arts and Media

Henry Keazor (ed.)

We Are All Astronauts

The Image of the Space Traveler in Arts and Media

Neofelis Verlag

Contents

Henry Keazor

"We Are All Astronauts"

The Image of the Space Traveler in Arts and Media

"We are all astronauts" the American architect and thinker Richard Buckminster Fuller declared in his book *Operating Manual For Spaceship Earth*, first published in 1968.[1] Buckminster Fuller thus compared Earth to a spaceship, provided with exhaustible resources while flying through space. Although the metaphor of Earth as a ship had previously been employed by the US-American economist Henry George in 1879 in his book *Progress and Poverty*, where he called our planet "a well-provisioned ship, this on which we sail through space",[2] in Buckminster Fuller's case his comparison was more likely to have been inspired by Yuri Gagarin's words in 1961 about the uniqueness and beauty of Earth,[3] and especially by the view, captured by satellites from 1967 onwards, showing Earth as an isolated 'blue marble' floating through space. This view anticipates the famous image captured by astronaut Harrison Schmitt in 1972 on board Apollo 17[4] – a photograph that not only remains one of the most iconic and most widely distributed images in human history, but was also used frequently in the context of the ecology movement in the 1970s (Colleen Boyle further develops this idea of the astronaut's eye as a "mediator of the human imagination" in her article in this volume).[5]

1 Richard Buckminster Fuller: *Operating Manual for Spaceship Earth*. Mattituck, NY: Aeonian 1969, p. 14.

2 Henry George: *Progress and Poverty*. New York: D. Appleton 1879, p. 173.

3 Meanwhile also communicated to children in books, such as Ben Hubbard: *Yuri Gagarin and the Race to Space*. London: Raintree 2016, p. 43.

4 Don Nardo: *The Blue Marble: How a Photograph Revealed Earth's Fragile Beauty*. North Mankato, MN: Compass Point 2014, p. 8.

5 Ibid., p. 50.

The phrase "we are all astronauts" on the one hand gives us an idea of the phenomenon of the astro-/cosmonaut in public consciousness from the second half of the twentieth century onwards; on the other hand, the wording might also have played a significant role in shaping the symbolic role of the space-exploring human and in shaping an image of humankind in general. However, Buckminster Fuller's phrase also announces a change in the public perception of astro-/cosmonauts, as we will see later. Space travelers were indeed initially presented and conceived as courageous heroes and popular figures to be identified with. They were even presented as representatives of a new step in human evolution (this is, as Ansgar Oswald shows in his article on "The Space Traveler: Ambassador, Cult Figure, and Cultural Icon" in this book, a historical as well as a contemporary phenomenon).
In his articles and in his 2010 book *Maternités Cosmiques*, the French art historian Arnauld Pierre has shown that not only in everyday speech, but especially in artistic representations accompanying the history of space exploration, "the astronaut appeared as the central figure of a modern angelology which dealt with the future cosmic condition of humankind which had succeeded in adapting to space."[6] In his article on the "Angelology of the Astronaut and the Eschatology of Space Travel" from 2014, he also discusses paintings such as those by the artist Robert McCall, today famous for his promotional paintings for Stanley Kubrick's *2001: A Space Odyssey* (a film that Nils Daniel Peiler writes about in his contribution for this volume, where, under the title "Backlash of the Future", he compares Kubrick's original movie with its sequel, *2010: The Year We Make Contact*, directed 16 years later by Peter Hyams, focusing on the image of the astronaut as conceived in each film). McCall's painting of the spacecraft "Orion" and his depiction of the lunar surface with the Moon station "Clavius Base" in the background were both used for the movie posters and for the promotion of the film. Pierre stresses the numinous and religious undertones of some of McCall's paintings, such as the symbol of the cross or the presence of halos, thus making the astronauts appear to be superhuman, angelic beings (Marc Bonner deals with these and similar conceptions of the astronaut as a post-humanistic being in his

6 Arnauld Pierre: Le scaphandrier des nuages: Angélologie de l'astronaute et eschatologie du voyage spatial. In: Christine Poullain / Guillaume Theulière (eds): *Futurs: De la ville aux étoiles: Matisse, Miró, Calder.* Centre de la Vieille Charité, Marseille Exhibition Catalog. Marseille: RMN 2015, pp. 46–53, here p. 52. In the original French: "l'astronaute apparaît comme la figure centrale d'une angélologie moderne discourant de la future condition cosmique de l'homme ayant réussi son adaptation à l'espace" (my translation). See also Arnauld Pierre: *Maternités Cosmiques*. Paris: Hazan 2010.

article on the "The Astronaut as Reciprocal Post-human" in the present volume).[7] This very positive image, however, began to change by the beginning of the 1970s, if not earlier; the fact that paintings such as those done by McCall continued to uphold this positive image is not an argument against this change, but should be seen as a counter-reaction.

In his 2005 book *Moon Dust*, the journalist Andrew Smith relates this change to the classification of epochs that the British historian Eric Hobsbawm defined in his book *Age of Extremes: The Short Twentieth Century 1914–1991*, published in 1994. Hobsbawm distinguishes a "Golden Age" (1945–1972) that encompasses the dawn of "the Space Age" from an ensuing "landslide", leading in turn to the "crisis decades".[8] The first phase, marked by "upheaval, uncertainty, optimism, energy" would then, according to Smith, have reverted into a skeptical and pessimistic era that found itself disappointed by its own hopes, where its former heroes would have lost all their splendor.[9]

Buckminster Fuller's metaphor of humankind as the crew of a spaceship "Earth" now had admonitory connotations: "So, planners, architects, and engineers take the initiative," urges Buckminster Fuller towards the end of his book, in order to tackle the ensuing challenges of caring for this spaceship Earth and to find solutions for the problem of its resources, which he considers – in contrast to George's view from 1879 of the Earth as a still "well-provisioned ship" – exhaustible.[10] A certain optimism towards science may still be implicit in Buckminster Fuller's text, but the image of the astro-/cosmonaut in the arts and in the media has subsequently, right up to this day, tended more towards the negative: astronauts are mostly depicted as deceived, failing or failed characters.

Thus, the astronauts in the works of contemporary photographs such as Bernard Bailly, Hunter Freeman, Jeremy Geddes, and Ken Hermann find themselves on a planet Earth that is apparently abandoned by humans and (judging by the spacesuits the astronauts are wearing) also hostile to life; they wander alone and lonely through empty streets, landscapes and houses (Fig. 1).[11] In his series

7 Pierre: Le scaphandrier, pp. 51–52.

8 Eric Hobsbawm: *Age of Extremes: The Short Twentieth Century 1914–1991*. London: Joseph 1994.

9 Andrew Smith: *Moon Dust*. London: Bloomsbury 2005, pp. 292–293.

10 Buckminster-Fuller: *Operating Manual*, p. 43.

11 For Bailly see http://theinspirationgrid.com/surreal-astronaut-photos-by-bernard-bailly/ (accessed: November 30, 2018); for Geddes who with his photos inspired Bailly for some of his works see https://www.jeremygeddesart.com/ (accessed: November 30, 2018); for Freemann see https://hunterfreeman.com/PROJECTS/ASTRONAUTS/thumbs (accessed: November 30, 2018) and for Hermann see http://kenhermann.dk/portfolio/crash-landed/#e-1 (accessed: November 30, 2018).

Fig. 1a: Bernard Bailly: *Lost Astronaut*, 2007. Photography.

Fig. 1b: Hunter Freeman: *Astronaut Salt Flats*, 2011. Photography.

Fig. 1c: Jeremy Geddes: *The Street*, 2010. Photography.

Fig. 1d: Ken Hermann: *Crash Landed*, 2014. Photography.

Astronaut Suicides from 2011, the photographer Neil DaCosta has drawn his own conclusions from this negative image by showing how seemingly desperate astronauts, still wearing their full outfit, are putting an end to their isolated existence in various ways (Fig. 2).[12] The American artist Scott Listfield interprets similar topics through the medium of painting and depicts the space travelers as they stroll alone through a desolate landscape littered with adverts for consumer goods. These isolated astronauts, according to Listfield, help him to depict the alienation of our present age (Fig. 3).[13]

The iconography of the lonesome astronaut wandering through deserted rooms and buildings, as depicted by Listfield and DaCosta, was transferred into moving images on two occasions in William Eubank's 2011 film *Love*. It tells the story of an astronaut named Lee Miller, who is stranded alone aboard a space station, while on Earth a global war has apparently broken out, which extinguishes all human life. Using various methods, Miller struggles to survive, not only mentally but also physically, as the space station begins to develop technical faults. During a repair mission, in one module Miller finds the journal of a Union soldier, Captain Lee Briggs, who was sent on a mission in 1864 during the American Civil War to investigate an alien, mysterious object. After having read the entries in the journal and following a brief interview section with a modern soldier talking about love being the most important thing in life, Miller apparently fantasizes about making love to a sensuous woman, whose voice can be heard whispering "Are you waiting for someone?",[14] while he is shown sitting alone in his astronaut suit at a bus stop in a situation similar to those depicted by Listfield and DaCosta (Fig. 4a). Later in the movie, when the oxygen system aboard the station begins to fail, Miller decides to commit suicide by leaving the station in his spacesuit and letting himself drift towards Earth in order to burn up in its atmosphere. It remains unclear if he succeeds or if he aborts the attempt and returns to the station – the following sequences could just be his imagination while hurtling towards Earth and dying, but could also be depicting actual events. Years later an unkempt Miller is contacted from outside the station by alien entities, who tell him to dock to their giant vehicle; inside it the astronaut finds deserted rooms containing a server mainframe and, later on, a hotel

12 For DaCosta see http://neildacosta.com/astronaut-suicides (accessed: November 30, 2018).

13 For Listfield see https://www.astronautdinosaur.com/art97.htm (accessed: November 30, 2018). Note his frequent references to sci-fi films such as *The Empire Strikes Back*, *2001: A Space Odyssey* or catastrophes such as the Challenger disaster from 1986.

14 William Eubank: *Love* (US 2011). DVD. Cologne: Splendid Film 2012, 0:44:06.

Fig. 2: Neil DaCosta: *The Astronaut Suicides*, 2011. Photography.

lobby, both moments echoing again the images of Listfield and DaCosta (Fig. 4b). *Love* is, of course, also indebted to Kubrick's *2001: A Space Odyssey*. Not only does Eubank's astronaut resemble Dave Bowman during his passage through the so-called "Star Gate" when Miller finds the diary in the module and colorful lights are reflected by the visor of his helmet,[15] but the hotel lobby he ultimately enters is also an echo of the "Louis-Seize" hotel room, in which Bowman finds himself at the end of Kubrick's movie.[16] The two living areas even seem to serve the same purpose; Miller is told in the end by the aliens that they have built the place as "a scrapbook of sorts, a collection of memories and mementos of mankind's brief existence", which is apparently supposed to make him feel at home in the alien environment.[17] It is likewise assumed that the Louis XVI room in

15 Ibid., 0:41:23 and, as a similar scene, 1:15:11–1:15:33.

16 Ibid., 1:07:50–1:09:00. On the "Louis Seize" room, see Ralf Michael Fischer: *Raum und Zeit im filmischen Œuvre von Stanley Kubrick*. Berlin: Gebrüder Mann 2009, pp. 286–287, 293–296.

17 Eubank: *Love*, 1:14:18–1:14:24.

Fig. 3: Scott Listfield: *Coke Droid*, 2012. Oil on canvas, 9 x 12 inches.

Kubrick's movie is supposed to function as a kind of familiar-looking waiting room for Bowman to die and be reborn in.[18]

Even meetings between astronauts in space often are not sufficient for them to overcome their isolation. The encounter between Hergé's comic character "Tintin", who (as Marc Blancher shows in his article "'Let's discover Space!' Tintin and Other Characters of French-Belgian Comics as Astronauts") is shown planning and making a trip to the Moon as early as 1953/54, and a 'real', contemporary astronaut, as depicted by the Italian artist Tom Colbie in his painting *Close*

18 Fischer: *Raum und Zeit*, p. 293. The "Louis Seize" room in the film corresponds most likely to the (however, modern) hotel room Bowman finds himself in the novel by Arthur C. Clarke: *2001: A Space Odyssey*. Tiptree, Essex: Anchor 1968, pp. 241–249, in the chapter, most tellingly called "Reception". The astronaut himself suspects that the room was built in order to "not [...] deceive but rather – he hoped – to reassure", ibid., p. 243.

Fig. 4a & b: Screenshots from *Love* (US 2011, D: William Eubank).

Encounter from 2015, accordingly takes place in a rather bleak and joyless atmosphere (Fig. 5). One can clearly see the contrast between the spacesuits of Tintin and Snowy with their jolly colors and the strict and severe appearance of the real astronaut, who, moreover, appears alone and isolated unlike Tintin and his dog Snowy (it is almost as if Tintin and Snowy do not even notice the presence of the real astronaut).[19]

The British sculptor David Mach puts all this in a nutshell. In 2000, he created *Spaceman* (today located in the glass foyer of the Space One building in Hammersmith, London: Fig. 6): a figure who not only trudges alone through the surrounding exhibition rooms, but who already seems to be isolated because

19 See http://tomcolbieart.tumblr.com/post/111945822059/close-encounters (accessed: November 30, 2018).

Fig. 5: Tom Colbie: *Close Encounter*, 2015. Print, 11.8 x 11.8 inches.

of his repellent appearance – a myriad of clothes-hanger hooks are poking out of his body, building a cocoon that surrounds and encapsulates him like an armoring whirl of energy.[20]

Given all these depictions, one is reminded of a quote from the American science-fiction author A(lfred) A(ngelo) Attanasio: "Being human is the most terrible loneliness in the universe."[21] The quote was also used in 2011 to powerful effect as a prelude to the music video for the song *Astronaut* by the Canadian rock band Simple Plan, where the iconography of loneliness and isolation associated with

20 See https://www.davidmach.com/gallery/ (accessed: 30.11.2018).

21 A[lfred] A[ngelo] Attanasio: *The Dragon and the Unicorn*. New York: HarperPrism 1996, p. 196.

astronauts is put into moving images, accompanied by the music and matching lyrics, emphasizing the figure of the astronaut as a fitting metaphor. Interestingly, the song was played in December 2012 aboard the orbiting space station ISS by Canadian astronaut Chris Hadfield, who will be discussed further below.[22]

We also encounter the failing or failed astronaut in the genre of the music video, as well as that of film. I am referring here to the video made by Dom & Nic for the 2001 song *What I Mean* by the French house duo Modjo, where an astronaut (as portrayed by the singer Yann Destagnol) is shown as being haunted in outer space by phantasmal images of a woman. The astronaut ultimately gets lost in the depths of space when he, apparently still under the influence of the ghostly vision of the woman, makes a fatal mistake during a repair mission. At the beginning of the video, there is a drop of water in outer space, visible outside the window of the hatch, deliberately placed there to allude to the ghostly appearance of the woman later on, as she seems to materialize out of drops of water. These drops of water then fly towards the astronaut (the images are vaguely in tune with the lyrics, which deal with the loss of a beloved woman). The fatal mistake committed by the astronaut, which unleashes a strong jet of water that blows him into space, is clearly implied to be her doing.

An astronaut (played by lead singer Morten Harket) who is similarly deluded by a woman can be found in the music video for the song *Minor Earth, Major Sky* by the Norwegian group a-ha. The video was directed by Philipp Stölzl a year before the Modjo video. After a successful landing on the Moon and an exploratory walk across its surface, the astronaut is separated from his two companions on the way back to the landing module, being fatally attracted to a "Fata Morgana" that lures him into the phantasmagorical realities of a party on Earth and then into the bedroom of a beautiful and beguiling woman. The deceptive illusion vanishes the moment his colleagues, who have been waiting impatiently for him, head back to Earth in the module, leaving him helpless and alone on the Moon.

This motif of the deluded, seduced, and confused astronaut of course had its predecessor thirty-one years earlier in the video that accompanied an early studio version of the song *Space Oddity* by David Bowie. The well-known song is about Major Tom, who (as the lyrics put it) floats "in a most peculiar way" in his "tin can" through space, observing that "the stars look very different today"

22 See Dominika Marsová: Astronaut Chris Hadfield Played "Astronaut" in Space. In: *Simple Plan*, May 14, 2013. http://www.simpleplan.cz/en/index.php/astronaut-chris-hadfield-plays-astronaut-in-space/ (accessed: November 30, 2018).

Fig. 6: David Mach: *Spaceman*, 2000. Welded and silver nickel plated coat hangers, 88.5 x 43.3 x 43.3 inches, Hammersmith, Space One-Building, London.

and then apparently gets lost (an allusion that was interpreted by director Malcolm J. Thomson in his video – which is in fact an extract from the promotional film *Love You Till Tuesday* – by having his astronaut, portrayed by Bowie, meet two space sirens who lure him into pulling off his protective suit while still in space).

When conceiving their videos for the a-ha and the Modjo songs, Stölzl and Dom & Nic chose to make the fatally alluring females more abstract than Thomson in his Bowie video. The images created by Dom & Nic at times anticipate

the visuals of Alfonso Cuarón's 2013 film *Gravity*, which was received with great public acclaim and deals with failing astronauts. It is the more successful female new astronaut, Dr Ryan Stone, who at the end of the movie appears to be reborn: it is not by chance that her capsule splashes into the sea, since Stone is thus briefly shown floating weightlessly, as before in outer space (Fig. 7a). When leaving the sunken vehicle, she receives a kind of baptism before stepping ashore. Moreover, the scientist turned astronaut appears to be psychologically reborn; during the time she was shipwrecked in space she managed to overcome the trauma of the loss of her daughter. At the same time, when stepping ashore she also re-enacts the evolutionary step from aquatic to terrestrial animal (Figs. 7b–c), thus showing that she is not only reborn as an individual, but in certain way represents a new kind of human, a kind of super-human. This is also why in this sequence she is filmed in such a way that she takes on giant proportions (Fig. 7d). Or, to use Arnauld Pierre's words, she is "a representative of humankind which had succeeded in adapting to and surviving space"[23] (in his article on "Female Space Travelers in Science Fiction Films 1898–2017", Jörg Hartmann not only writes about *Gravity*, but in particular about the tradition it belongs to).
The space vehicles that crash in *Gravity* have a precursor in the 2011 music video for the song *The Commission* by the English band Breton (D: BretonLABS / Stuart Sinclair). In the video, an elderly and lonely astronaut, apparently craving to return home to his family, is shown, by way of contrast, on board a very new and clean-looking space station that is reminiscent of the ISS. He eventually crashes down to Earth with the whole station, partially burning up during the uncontrolled re-entry and then smashing into a residential district. One could moreover refer here to a large group of recent films where other astronauts are shown as victims who fall prey to extraterrestrial life on moons, planets, and space stations (see for example in 2011: *Apollo 18* by Gonzalo López-Gallego, 2013: *Last Days on Mars* by Ruairi Robinson, 2013: *Europa Report* by Sebastián Cordero, 2017: *Life* by Daniél Espinosa).
However, astronauts are not only depicted as victims, but also as culprits. In the 2013 music video, produced by Delo Creative for the song *Ashes in the Air* by the American rock band The Flaming Lips (a collaboration with the American singer-songwriter project Bon Iver), an astronaut is shown first rescuing a baby (surreally shown with the head of an adult) from a crashed space capsule, but then, after having entered his own spaceship, throwing it into a mincer (in

23 Pierre: Le scaphandrier, p. 52. In the original French: "les représentants d' une humanité [...] ayant réussi son adaptation à l'espace."

Fig. 7 a–d: Screenshots from *Gravity* (GB/US 2013, D: Alfonso Cuarón).

his contribution to the present volume "All We Mad Starmen: Contextualizing Barry N. Malzberg's NASA Trilogy and Its Deranged Astronauts", Umberto Rossi analyses the conceptions behind such depictions of astronauts as mad humans).

Such representations are all the more striking if they are compared with the thoroughly positive visual interpretations of astro-/cosmonauts in the East as well as in the West during the 1960s. Norman Rockwell's 1969 painting *Behind Apollo 11* (Washington, National Air and Space Museum; Fig. 8),[24] for example, confronts the viewer with an assembly of portraits in profile of all the people who were crucial for the landing on the Moon, such as the three astronauts (depicted on the left – from left to right: Neil Armstrong, Edwin Aldrin, and Michael Collins), Wernher von Braun (in the center, above the helmeted NASA employee), and the three astronauts' wives (in the lower right). Other persons depicted include the back-up crew of Apollo 11, scientists, government officials and launch-pad workers. The composition describes a soft curve, starting on the right with the Vehicle Assembly Building and a red rocket gantry, gliding over to von Braun (whose visionary staring eye has perhaps the most intense gaze in the whole painting), and from there rising in a slight slope up through the three astronauts. With their helmeted heads, which make them almost appear haloed, at the same time they hint at the objective of the gathered crowd: the Moon. The contrast between the Earth and the Moon is, moreover, evoked by an intense glow behind the launch pad on the right and the darkness into which the three astronauts rise – on Armstrong's visor, the reflection of a white light can be seen which is most likely that of the Moon. The whole composition is also cleverly conceived and full of symbolism in other respects. The astronauts above are 'supported' by the back-up crew below and at the same time 'backed' by all the people standing behind them, while von Braun forms the center, the heart of the group. Profile portraits have always been, from ancient times onwards when coins depicted the profile image of the emperor, associated with nobility and gallantry; the gaze upwards, as displayed here by the characters of the painting, is traditionally associated with heroic afflatus and inspiration. With the profiles all determinedly looking towards the left, the painting not only implies a kind of a journey that starts on the right with the launch pad and ends on the left, where one has to imagine the Moon, but also that all the individuals portrayed here have the same goal and are united in their determination to reach it.

24 James Dean / Bertram Ulrich: *NASA/ART: 50 Years of Exploration*. New York: Abrams 2008, pp. 64–65, no. 55.

Fig. 8: Norman Rockwell: *Behind Apollo 11*, 1969. Oil on canvas, 28 x 66 inches, National Air and Space Museum, Washington.

In East Germany, there are also works such as a mosaic on the exterior of the elementary school in Mellingen, celebrating the cosmonaut Valentina Tereshkova, who became the first woman in outer space on June 16, 1963, as a model for children.[25] The 1969 Soviet Cosmonaut Mosaic on the exterior of the Philharmonic Hall at Lenin Square in Uchaly, Russia aims at visualizing the message that science and heroism are the premises that enable cosmonauts to fly. This concept is also echoed in mosaic murals such as the ones also executed in 1969, entitled *Weltall Erde Mensch* (Space Earth Mankind), by the German artist Otto Schutzmeister in Eisenhüttenstadt (residential complex IV), which express, via a series of correspondences between the depicted scientists on the one side and the cosmonauts on the other side of the mosaicked wall, the conviction that the triumphs of the latter are conditional on the efforts of the former (Fig. 9a & b).[26]

25 The school was built in 1958 and first intended to be named after Tereshkova, which is why the mosaic was executed. Ultimately, however, it was decided to name the school after the communist Albert Kuntz, who was murdered in a Nazi concentration camp – see http://grundschule-mellingen.de/schuljubilaeum-50-jahrfeier/. See also Kevin Anzalone: Soviet Cosmonaut Mosaics. In: *Mid-Centuria*, April 13, 2011. http://www.midcenturia.com/2011/04/soviet-cosmonaut-mosaics.html (accessed: November 30, 2018).

26 See Karl-Siegbert Rehberg / Wolfgang Holler/Paul Kaiser (eds): *Abschied von Ikarus: Bildwelten in der DDR – neu gesehen*. Neues Museum Weimar Exhibition Catalog. Cologne: König 2012, p. 209. *Weltall Erde Mensch* was also the title of a popular volume published between 1954 and 1974 in the GDR by a group of authors. Since it was supposed to present a comprehensive system of nature and society according to Marxist-Leninist thinking, the book was a popular gift to adolescents on the occasion of their "Jugendweihe" (youth dedication). See Heike Acker: *Marxistisches Denken in der Pädagogik: Messianische und prometheische Strukturen*

Fig. 9a & b: Otto Schutzmeister: *Weltall Erde Mensch*, 1969. Mosaic, residence complex VI (close to the Fröbelringpassage), Eisenhüttenstadt.

However, if one looks further back into the past, bearing in mind the aforementioned films *Apollo 18*, *Last Days on Mars*, and *Europa Report*, one discovers a more differentiated image of astro-/cosmonauts; earlier depictions of space travelers can sometimes reveal darker undertones. The only two survivors of the "Rocketship X(pedition)-M(oon)", the space vehicle in Kurt Neumann's eponymous film from 1950,[27] are depicted as heroes whose eventual death is interpreted in the movie as an incentive for further space exploration. Nevertheless, their journey is full of malfunctions and disasters, since their rocket strays from its intended course to the Moon and goes to Mars instead, and ultimately they fall back to Earth in an uncontrolled plunge.

Subsequently, television also explored the less obvious facets of space exploration. The episode "Death Ship" from the series *The Twilight Zone*, directed by Don Medford and first shown in 1963, deals with the ghosts of three astronauts who stubbornly refuse to accept the increasing number of clues that indicate that they are dead. They stoically continue their exploration journey as 'undead' space travelers (their unstoppable sense of duty being one of the traits discussed also in Matthew Hersch's contribution "Redemptive Space: Duty, Death, and the Astronaut-Soldier, 1949–1969" in this volume).

The protagonist of J. G. Ballard's story "The Dead Astronaut", published in 1968, is a similarly 'undead' human. Beyond his physical death, the spaceman develops a demonic afterlife – firstly in the memory of his wife Judith, who desperately wants to recover his space capsule caught in the Earth's orbit, and then because of the atomic cargo the astronaut had on board of his ship and which, with its deadly radiation, is now contaminating Judith.[28] Another deadly freight is brought back to Earth by the astronaut Spencer Armacost in Rand Ravich's 1999 film *The Astronaut's Wife*. During a two-minute-blackout, he and his colleague

einer Erziehungstheorie. Unpublished PhD dissertation, Fernuniversität Hagen, Fakultät für Kultur- und Sozialwissenschaften, Institut für Bildungswissenschaft und Medienforschung, 2010, p. 24. https://ub-deposit.fernuni-hagen.de/servlets/MCRFileNodeServlet/Document_derivate_00000002/Diss_Acker.pdf (accessed: November 30, 2018).

27 For the film see Bill Warren: *Keep Watching the Skies! American Science Fiction Movies of the Fifties*, vol. 1. Jefferson / London: McFarland 1982, p. 11. Since the production of George Pal's ambitious film *Destination Moon* was delayed, *Rocketship X-M* was quickly shot in just 18 days on a low budget. In order to take full advantage of Pal's highly publicized film, *Rocketship X-M* was then rushed into movie theaters 25 days before the premiere of *Destination Moon*. The changed destination of Neumann's film – Mars instead of the Moon – was also due to the constraints in budget and time: Whereas in *Rocketship X-M* Southern California locations could stand in for Mars, for *Destination Moon* the airless and cratered surface of the Moon had to be convincingly created.

28 J. G. Ballard: *Memories of the Space Age*. Sauk City, WI: Arkham House 1988, pp. 67–78.

are infested by aliens who take over their minds and then try to procreate using their bodies. The astronauts in this sci-fi variation of Roman Polanski's 1968 psychological horror movie *Rosemary's Baby* thus become carriers for a devilish seed.

Despite the positive connotations of its ending, Stanley Kubrick's *2001: A Space Odyssey*, also from 1968, deals, in the final analysis, with the failure of a space mission (as implied by the use of the term "odyssey" in the title). Robert Parrish's film *Doppelganger* (aka *Journey to the Far Side of the Sun*), produced a year later and directly influenced by Kubrick's *2001*, ends in a similar fashion to Neumann's *Rocketship X-M*, with a manned, out-of-control spaceship that plunges down to Earth. It destroys the entire ground control on impact and leaves behind an image that resembles the scenery depicted in Ballard's *Memories of the Space Age* stories, which already in the 1960s anticipated the end of the American space program. "The Dead Astronaut", for example, begins with the sentence, "Cape Kennedy has gone now, its gantries rising from the deserted dunes."[29]

Doppelganger also shows the mundane and pedestrian side of an astronaut's private life. Despite the fact that the phenomena of marital breakdowns and increasing divorce rates among astronauts were considered shameful and were accordingly censured and concealed by NASA in the 1960s,[30] the film – perhaps because it was a British and not an American production – shows the failure of an American astronaut's marriage. In one scene, after returning from a mission, he has a fight with his wife, who blames him for no longer being able to have a child with her, since he has been exposed to radiation in space and is therefore sterile – a subject which was only recently tackled again in the American ABC series *The Astronaut Wives Club* from 2015, based on the 2013 book by Lily Koppel.[31]

One can thus see that the astronaut-angels of Arnauld Pierre's "modern angelology"[32] have in these instances been 'grounded', by being placed in the heart of everyday life instead of hovering above it – thus literally confirming Buckminster

29 Ibid., p. 67. For *Doppelganger* see also Henry Keazor: 'A Stumble in the Dark': Contextualizing Gerry and Sylvia Anderson's 'Space: 1999'. In: Alexander Geppert (ed.): *Imagining Outer Space: European Astroculture in the Twenthieth Century*. Basingstoke / Hampshire: Palgrave Macmillan 2012, pp. 189–207.

30 Smith: *Moon Dust*, p. 252.

31 See the voiceover narration at the end of the last episode "Landing" from 2015, where the failed marriages are counted: "Of the thirty space couples of the Mercury, Gemini and Apollo programs only seven marriages survived."

32 Pierre: Le scaphandrier.

Fuller's assertion that "We are all astronauts" (this idea is behind some of the French photographer Vincent Fournier's photographs of cosmonauts, one of which we have therefore chosen for our book cover, but is also behind the concept of the "Protestonaut", conceived by Alexander and Sophia Hauk and explained here in their article "Wall Calendar Journalism: How an Astronaut Gives Journalism New Impetus: The Protestonaut as an Appeal for a Better World").

Even worse, Pierre's "angelology" has been turned here into a 'modern demonology' where the astronaut becomes a kind of empty vessel or a blank canvas, onto which all the fears of the consequences of technology, but also the anxiety of the unknown dangers apparently lurking in deep space, can be projected. Having ventured into outer space, the space traveler becomes, due to their extraordinary experience, a stranger on Earth, but at the same time, they can be considered the epitome of human hubris and are punished for their transgressions.

To some extent, this idea is also behind the music video for David Bowie's *Space Oddity*. Its reinterpretation in 2013 did, however, herald a definite shift in the image of the space traveler towards a more positive one; Canadian astronaut Chris Hadfield not only produced his own cover version of Bowie's song, but also accompanied it with a music video that he broadcast as a farewell to the space station ISS, where he had been working for several months.

The music video immediately caused enormous media interest and in fact, Hadfield's clip is remarkable on several counts. Firstly, because – after a long period of rather negative representations of astronauts as failing, deceived, and confused anti-heroes – he presented a positive counter-image. Even though his video also has (due to the music and the lyrics) some melancholic moments, the beauty of the sequences of Hadfield's 'real' images of zero gravity and views of the Earth at night (i. e. without special effects), the fact that Hadfield had made the clip as a farewell to the ISS, and the general aura of 'coolness' surrounding Hadfield's persona (he went on to pose for the cover of the October 2013 issue of the Canadian magazine *Maclean's* made up as Bowie's Aladdin Sane/Ziggy Stardust)[33] all ensured that the image of the astronaut once again acquired positive features – to

33 Both characters still get mixed up in public perception today: Although the album *Aladdin Sane* from 1973, to whose cover Hadfield's make-up for the *MacLean's* photo session referred to, presented the eponymous character as new, it was nevertheless generally conceived essentially as a development of Ziggy Stardust, in his appearance as well persona. Bowie also performed almost all of the album's tracks on his "Ziggy Stardust Tour" in 1973 and he himself described Aladdin Sane as "Ziggy goes to America". See Roy Carr / Charles Murray / Charles Shaar: *David Bowie: An Illustrated Record*. New York: Avon 1981, pp. 52–56.

the extent that the astronaut was portrayed once more as a role-model who, due to his extraordinary experiences in space, was entitled to give his Earth-bound fellow humans advice on how to get things done.[34]

Secondly, Hadfield's video is interesting inasmuch as it ties in with earlier works, conceptually as well as visually. The images recall moments from earlier music videos, such as Mark Romanek's video for Michael and Janet Jackson's 1995 song *Scream*, which is also set on board a (fictitious) spaceship and among other parallels shows a guitar floating weightlessly through the corridor of a space vehicle. Similarly, the images in Hadfield's video hark back to cover illustrations from science fiction magazines of the 1960s, such as the painting by Virgil Finlay for the cover of *Galaxy Magazine*, published in October 1961 (Figs. 10a & b).

However, the whole idea of the singing or music-making astronaut in fact refers back to an older tradition, which had been referenced at an earlier date, in 2010, by Snoop Dogg and Edwin "Buzz" Aldrin with their rap piece, *Rocket Experience*. The concept had already been discovered and used by the advertising industry during the "Golden Years" of the Space Age: on December 16, 1965, astronaut Walter Schirra, when in radio contact with Earth, played the song *Jingle Bells* on a mini-harmonica that he had smuggled aboard his spaceship Gemini 6. This event inspired Hohner, the company that produced these instruments, to publish an ad that read: "Buy a Hohner harmonica. Learn to play 'Jingle Bells'. And three billion people just might look up to you"[35] (Martin Butler's contribution to this volume "The Future that Never Was: Analogue Nostalgia and the Ambivalent Astronaut in the Songs of Man ... or Astro-man?" talks more about the connection between space flight and music).

Hadfield's activities on board the ISS and after his return on Earth led to a great increase in the popularity of other astronauts (such as Alexander Gerst in Germany) and he thus encouraged his colleagues to perform similar tributes to popular culture aboard the space station ISS (for example, Samantha Cristoforetti who tweeted a photo of herself wearing a costume from the science fiction series

34 Chris Hadfield: *An Astronaut's Guide to Life on Earth: Life Lessons from Space*. London: Pan Macmillan 2015.

35 See for example the advert in *Billboard*, March 26, 1966, p. 36 with the slogan: "On December 16, 1965, the Hohner harmonica became the first musical instrument to be played in outer space." The crew of Apollo 11 also took music with them on a tape recorder: Neil Armstrong choose Antonin Dvořák's *The New World* symphony and the album *Music Out of the Moon* with pieces by the composer Harry Revel, interpreted by Theremin player Samuel Hoffman and a band conducted by Les Barker. See David Michael Harland: *The First Men on the Moon: the Story of Apollo 11*. Chichester: Springer 2007, p. 174.

Fig. 10a
Screenshot from
Space Oddity (US 2013,
D: Chris Hadfield).

Fig. 10b
Virgil Finlay:
Illustration for cover
of *Galaxy Magazine*,
October 1961, 20:1,
illustrating at the same
time the there contained short story
"The Beat Cluster" by
Fritz Leiber.

Star Trek: Voyager,[36] or her colleague Terry Virts, who, a few weeks earlier, as a tribute to the recently deceased *Star Trek* actor Leonard Nimoy, photographed his hand doing the Vulcan salute).[37]

It is perhaps no wonder that recent films such as *Interstellar* (US/GB/CA 2014; D: Christopher Nolan) or *The Martian* (GB/US 2015; D: Ridley Scott) feature astronauts who apparently fail, but ultimately take on their challenges in order to prove themselves as successful and even more heroic than before. We can also witness here a return of previously expressed ideas: The motto of *Interstellar* – "Mankind was born on Earth. It was never meant to die here" – sounds a bit like a rephrasing of the famous quote from the Russian rocket scientist and pioneer of astronautic theory, Konstantin Tsiolkovsky: "This planet is the cradle of human mind, but one cannot spend all one's life in a cradle [...] Humanity will not always remain on Earth."[38]

The success of *The Martian* can be explained partly by the fact that the path of the film (based on the 2011 novel by Andy Weir) into popular culture was clearly paved by computer game adaptations. One example is the app *Lifeline* from Spring 2015, where the player has to help a frightened astronaut named Taylor, who has crashed on an alien moon and is now desperate to make contact with somebody who can help him to survive by giving him the right recommendations for his decisions (in their article "Astronaut and Avatar: Some Remarks about the Video Game as Outer Space" Marc Bonner and Thomas Hensel further explore this connection between outer space and the space of computer games).

In more recent times, the image of the astronaut is one of a well-balanced individual. A film such as Damien Chazelle's *First Man* from 2018 no longer presents its protagonist, Neil Armstrong, the first man on the Moon, as a superhero, but rather as a hardworking, resilient, modest, and steadfast individual who is ultimately rewarded for his strong nerves, calmness, and the stoicism with which he endures the challenges posed by technology as well as fate. Armstrong may thus appear to be indestructible, but in the film he also shows emotions which appear to be even more intense and deeper since he expresses them only while alone and unseen, or through small gestures. After his successful return

36 https://twitter.com/astrosamantha/status/589035429879513088 (accessed: November 30, 2018).

37 https://twitter.com/astroterry/status/571700996360970241 (accessed: November 30, 2018).

38 Arkadii Aleksandrovich Kosmodemyansky: *Konstantin Tsiolkovsky His Life and Work*. Honolulu, HI: UP of the Pacific 1956, p. 95.

from the Moon, when he receives a visit from his wife Janet, she and the quarantined Armstrong do not attempt to talk. They take their time instead to slowly overcome the estrangement and separation they have had to endure, due to the emotional strain of the mission on both of them, and due to their disagreement over Armstrong's decision not to inform their children about the mission before his departure. The pane of glass between them, which initially symbolizes the gulf between them that they must overcome with eye-contact and gestures, ultimately becomes the sign of their reunification when Janet's face is mirrored in the glass, blending with Neil's face (Fig. 11a). Armstrong is depicted as similarly speechless earlier in the film, when he lets go of his daughter, who dies of cancer at the beginning of the film. After having successfully landed on the Moon, he symbolically buries her in a crater by letting go of her name bracelet, which he has smuggled on board with him. He thus might be unable or unwilling to talk about the death of his child throughout the film, but he nevertheless obviously harbors deep affection for her, which he can only display in the isolation of the lunar surface. In this way, Chazelle and his script author Josh Singer not only connect Armstrong's personal issues with the mission of the Moon landing, but also present space flight as a kind of liberation from the limited perspectives each human has on Earth. Throughout the film, the camera is either very close to the individuals being shown or it depicts them as being almost confined by the rooms they are in, which are often framed in a triptych structure, inducing a sense of almost claustrophobic narrowness. It is only during the scenes of flight throughout the film that the camera angle increasingly widens; in the first scene, we see Armstrong flying an X-15 rocket plane that he is barely able to control. Despite all the heavy shaking and shrill noise its pilot has to endure, there is the apparent compensation of a sudden moment of calm and quietness, when Armstrong gets a view into the infiniteness of the frontier between the blue sky and black space in front of him. Tellingly, what he sees through the windows is mirrored on the visor of his helmet in such a way that his eyes seem to blend into this image on his visor, the same way that at the end of the film the two faces of Neil and Janet Armstrong blend into each other via the windowpane between them (Fig. 11b). This synthesis between the pilots as humans and astronauts, the technology they use, and the broad spaces it opens up to them is further enhanced when the Saturn V craft of the Apollo 11 mission takes off. For the first time in the entire movie, the camera angle fully widens – first onto a panoramic view of the landscape out of which the rocket soars into the sky (Fig. 11c), later onto an equally panoramic and majestic vision of the lunar

Fig. 11a–d: Screenshots from *First Man* (US/JP 2018, D: Damien Chazelle).

landscape, which is approached in the far distance on the left by the tiny lunar landing module.[39] Once again, as at the beginning of the film, it is made clear that such experiences are only achieved via the craft that appear in the movie as the proverbial 'Bowiean' "tin cans", rattling and shrieking under the strain of the booming explosions that catapult these ramshackle contraptions into and through the sky. The humans inside, as much as they might get shaken and churned up inside during their journey, are thus ultimately given the chance to experience the harmony between themselves and the vastness they witness, be it in space or on the Moon. As in the opening sequence of the film, the bonding between Armstrong and his lunar surroundings becomes visually apparent via the visor of his helmet. After having symbolically buried his daughter in the moon crater, the astronaut pulls the golden protective shield over his visor, in which, instead of his face, the mirrored image of the lunar surface with the funeral crater becomes visible (Fig 11d).

Given such repeatedly changing conceptions and perceptions of the image of the space traveler one could consider them to be what has been dubbed a "figure of discourse, thinking and agreement" (in German a "Verständigungsfigur"), meaning a phenomenon through which central questions of human self-conception can be demonstrated and discussed by tracing, contextualizing, and analyzing their dynamics as well as their motivations.[40] Since the "image" (be it literary or a visually interpreted image) thus plays a central role, it appears that the theme of the "Image of the Space Traveler in Arts and Media" is one where art history and the visual studies play a particularly strong role whenever a work of art or film is examined. However, the contributions of history, literature, film, media studies, music history, and popular culture are equally essential. In other words, the topic, perhaps more than any other, calls for an interdisciplinary approach where the different disciplines complement each other.

39 Chazelle and his team therefore also used different lenses and film stock, such as for example 16mm film and a Canon 6.6-66mm T2.7 lens for the X-15-sequence in order to give it a "raw, gritty feel" and to draw the viewers closer, whereas the exterior aircraft scenes were filmed on 35mm with a Fujinon ZK19-90mm T2.9 lens which, among other, makes the scenes appear wider. Ultimately, with the outdoor scenes on the Moon the format changes to 70mm IMAX 1.43:1, thus enormously opening up the visual field: "16mm connected the raw truthfulness, 35mm drove the pretend good life in Houston, and IMAX created scale and separation", as Daron James comments in an article on cinematographer Linus Sandgren's work for *First Man*. See Daron James: How Cinematographer Linus Sandgren Used Format to Change Visual Tone in 'First Man'. In: *No Film School*, October 16, 2018. https://nofilmschool.com/2018/10/cinematographer-linus-sandgren-first-man (accessed: March 2, 2019).

40 See for example Oliver Müller: *Selbst, Welt und Technik: Eine anthropologische, geistesgeschichtliche und ethische Untersuchung*. Berlin / Boston: de Gruyter 2014, p. 28.

The texts in this book are partly based on the papers presented during a conference, held at the Heidelberg University in October 2015.[41] I would therefore like to thank the University of Heidelberg and the Institute for European Art History for hosting the conference – a special thank you here goes to the Institute for Psychology, which let us use their lecture hall and the surrounding facilities as the conference's venues.

The Deutsche Forschungsgemeinschaft (DFG) made the conference possible in the first place, thanks to its financial support, while the Verein zur Förderung von Lehre und Forschung at the Institut für Europäische Kunstgeschichte at Universität Heidelberg e. V., represented by its chairman Dr. Benno Lehmann, gave additional help.

My thanks also go to the European Space Agency (ESA), which followed the conference with great interest and to the Technik Museum in Speyer, which invited the speakers of the conference to the opening of the new exhibition space dedicated to German astronauts, an event which gave us the chance to not just talk about astronauts during the conference, but to also speak with German astronauts such as Ulf Merbold, Ernst Willi Messerschmid, Hans Wilhelm Schlegel, and Ulrich Walter.

Susann Henker designed the conference's poster, flyer and the logo. The cover of this book is based on a photo by the French photographer Vincent Fournier, who was kind enough to let us use his picture of General Boris V. at the Yuri Gagarin Cosmonaut Training Center (GCTC) at Star City (Zvyozdny Gorodok) in Russia. In 2015, Katharina Lau worked tirelessly as a Liaison Manager in order to give the conference its touches of perfection at every corner. My thanks also go to those who, although scheduled, could not participate in the conference (Alexander Geppert, Shanghai/New York, and Michael Iwoleit, Wuppertal) and to those who presented a paper during the conference, but are not among the authors of this book (Bettyan Kevles, Yale, and Monika Rüthers, Hamburg).

My most heartfelt thanks go, last but not least, to Erica Foden-Lenahan (Karlsruhe) and Graham Hogg (Edinburgh) for their highly dedicated and dependable proofreading as native speakers. If there are any errors in the texts, these are entirely the responsibility of the authors or the editor.

41 For the biographies of the authors of the contributions in this book see also the conference link: https://www.uni-heidelberg.de/fakultaeten/philosophie/zegk/iek/astronauts/abstracts/ (accessed May 20, 2019).

Matthew H. Hersch

Redemptive Space

Duty, Death, and the Astronaut-Soldier, 1949–1969[1]

The captions accompanying the images in the 1949 *Life* magazine article "Rocket to the Moon: Man May Travel to Earth's Satellite within 25 Years" (Figs. 1 & 2) may have dated the illustrations to the distant future of the year 1974, but to *Life*'s readers, what the images depicted was every bit as believable as the rockets and computers that had already become household words in the years immediately following the Second World War. Right now, the article declared, the United States Department of Defense was improving upon German wartime technology to build vehicles capable of traveling into space; within 25 years these machines would carry people to the Moon.

Looking closely at the artist's visualisations, there appeared to be little doubt these efforts were plausible and would be successful. Rather than imagining fanciful new technological regimes, *Life* artist Noel Sickles combined the real American technology and industrial design of 1949 to craft a convincing visual representation of what spaceflight would look like in 1974. If anything, his vision was conservative: few, if any of the technologies depicted in the images were not already in existence in 1949, and the fashions and even the hairstyles of the men seem similarly frozen in time, to a period just following World War II. The

1 This essay was presented as the keynote address at "'We Are All Astronauts': The Image of the Space Traveler in Arts and Media", Heidelberg University, October 22, 2015. The comments draw from and expand upon several of the author's previous publications and the research cited therein, including *Inventing the American Astronaut*. New York: Palgrave Macmillan 2012; Space Madness: The Dreaded Disease that Never Was. In: *Endeavour* 36:1 (2012), pp. 32–40; and Return of the Lost Spaceman: America's Astronauts in Popular Culture, 1959–2006. In: *The Journal of Popular Culture* 44:1 (2011), pp. 73–92.

IN TAKE-OFF ROCKET GETS ADDED BOOST FROM EARTH'S ROTATION AND SPINS AROUND PLANET. LATER IT WILL REVOLVE ABOUT MOON WHILE IT SLOWS BEFORE LANDING

ROCKET TO THE MOON

MAN MAY TRAVEL TO EARTH'S SATELLITE WITHIN 25 YEARS

Earth-bound man, watching the pale sphere of the moon swing across the night sky, has long dreamed of visiting this nearest of heavenly bodies. Long the subject of fantasy, travel to the moon is now, as a result of recent scientific developments, not only a possibility but a probability. From tests made with the V-2 rocket engineers believe that a similar rocket, adapted to carrying humans, could make the 238,000-mile trip in about 48 hours. Fuels exist which are theoretically (but only theoretically) powerful enough to enable a rocket to break out of the gravitational grip of the earth (*next page*). Radar, which has already been used to contact the moon, would be an aid to navigation. Complex engineering problems are yet to be solved, but the U.S. government, at the request of Defense Secretary Forrestal, is planning an unmanned spaceship which would circle the earth like the moon itself and automatically radio back information which may solve them. Considering both progress made and problems ahead, some hardheaded engineers believe that a manned rocket, like the one in the drawing above, may get to the moon within the next 25 years.

There are practical as well as romantic reasons behind man's desire to reach the earth's satellite. Forward-looking military leaders are considering it as a base from which rockets could be launched to control the world. Astronomers would like very much to construct observatories there because unlike earth the moon has almost no atmosphere to interfere with study of the sun and the other stars. Most important, a successful trip to the moon would mean that man was no longer bound to his own planet but would be free to visit other worlds and to explore the regions outside the boundaries of the solar system.

Fig. 1: This 1949 *Life* magazine article imagined a human voyage to the Moon employing technology developed for the United States Army Air Forces during World War II.

Fig. 2: American astronauts exploring the Moon wear pressure suits similar to those developed for United States Army Air Forces bomber crews for missions over Germany during World War II.

aesthetic vision of the *Life* images was of a particular form of American military style, found everywhere from Pentagon offices to battleships in 1949: the gray office chairs with green vinyl padding, steel sleeping berths, war-surplus radar displays, and a design vocabulary reminiscent of austere wartime life, not the utopian fantasies of pre-war science fiction. Aviation enthusiasts could instantly recognize the spacemen's pressure suits as actual military prototypes, developed in 1943 by American tire-maker B. F. Goodrich, for the high-altitude bomber crews of the United States Army Air Forces.[2]

In dress, in manner, even in grooming, the visions of the space explorer that date from 1949 through the late 1950s share a visual vocabulary of wartime American militaria, and in particular, the image of the American combat aviator. Of all the

2 Rocket to the Moon: Man May Travel to Earth's Satellite within 25 Years. In: *Life*, January 17, 1949, pp. 67–73.

Fig. 3: The "Original Seven" astronauts of Project Mercury – Malcolm "Scott" Carpenter, Leroy "Gordon" Cooper, John Glenn, Virgil "Gus" Grissom, Walter "Wally" Schirra, Alan Shepard, and Donald "Deke" Slayton – pose in 1961 in front of a Convair F-106B fighter jet loaned to the men for training. Astronaut Donald "Deke" Slayton stands at far right.

images of American space travelers present in the popular culture of the 1940s, 1950s, and 1960s, few were more persistent than that of the cosmic explorer as combat pilot. Looking as if they had only just recently returned from the skies over Germany, the leather jacket-clad space pilots of postwar American science fiction film were immediately recognizable to audiences as military veterans for whom duty and death were inextricably linked. In Hollywood movies like 1950's *Rocketship X-M*, it is former military pilots who helm the space vehicles within which Americans explore the cosmos. The distinctive dress and puzzling detachment of the men themselves hint that they are war veterans (Fig. 3) and that blasting to the Moon in a rocket ship is only slightly more dangerous than the work to which they are already accustomed.[3]

The image of the astronaut as military pilot has become so entrenched in the mythology of spaceflight that it may be difficult for one to imagine an era in

3 *Rocketship X-M* (US 1950, D: Kurt Neumann).

which anyone doubted whether military personnel would occupy a central role in the endeavor. The earliest assessment of who would make an appropriate space traveler is that of Johannes Kepler, who, in *Somnium* (1634), determined that professional sailors likely possessed the requisite fortitude, including the ability to eat abhorrent food, a requirement of space travelers that proved eerily prescient:

> We admit to this company nobody who is lethargic, fat, or tender. On the contrary, we choose those who spend their time in the constant practice of horsemanship or often sail to the Indies, inured to subsisting on hardtack, garlic, dried fish and unappetizing victuals. [...] No men from Germany are acceptable; we do not spurn the firm bodies of the Spaniards.[4]

Also suited to cosmic travel, incidentally, were older women, who seemed to Kepler to be inured to hardship. Least suitable, Kepler wrote, were his own countrymen – he wasn't sure that anybody in Germany was suitable.[5]

Through the early 1940s, the role of military pilots in fictional spaceflight had often been secondary to that of explorers, engineers, and scientists. Cinematic and television space crews required astronomers to make discoveries and engineers to keep the craft in working order, as well as colorful, clashing personalities to ensure drama. The addition of a female scientist could provide much needed sexual tension, a child acted as an audience surrogate to whom plot points could be explained, and an elderly professor represented a know-it-all to provide exposition and technical explanations. Although a token aviator, navigator, or naval officer was commonplace aboard fictional spacecraft before 1945, crews consisting solely of such men were not. Even many postwar concepts for future spacecraft, like those of Wernher von Braun and Willy Ley, described automated spaceships that required little hands-on piloting.

The enormous spacecraft of these fictional works, however, bore little resemblance to the actual craft Americans were preparing to fly into space in the 1950s: vehicles so small that they would likely accommodate only a single, highly trained occupant. Who that individual should be was a question that attracted substantial Air Force interest long before NASA's creation in 1958. When it came time to select men for service in NASA's astronaut corps, however, any

4 Johannes Kepler: *Somnium: The Dream, or Posthumous Work on Lunar Astronomy,* transl. from the Latin by Edward Rosen. Madison: UP of Wisconsin 1967, p. 15.

5 The experiences of Reinhold Ewald, Klaus-Dietrich Flade, Reinhard Furrer, Alexander Gerst, Sigmund Jähn, Ulf Merbold, Ernst Messerschmid, Thomas Reiter, Hans Schlegel, Gerhard Thiele, and Ulrich Walter offer interesting counter-examples.

idea that the individuals chosen would be children or college professors had been tossed out. Instead, NASA's first call for applications solicited technical and scientific specialists with combat experience, especially veterans of World War II and the Korean War, whose ages would correspond perfectly with the upper and lower margins of the desired age range of applicants (aged 25 to 39):

> *NATIONAL AERONAUTICS AND SPACE ADMINISTRATION*
> *Washington 25, D. C.*
>
> *NASA Project A*
> *Announcement No. 1*
> *(December 22, 1958)*
>
> *Invitation to Apply for Position of*
> *RESEARCH ASTRONAUT-CANDIDATE*
> [...]
>
> III. QUALIFICATION REQUIREMENTS
> [...]
> D. Hazardous, Rigorous, And Stressful Experience
> [...]
> These three characteristics may have been demonstrated in connection with certain professional occupations such as test pilot, crew member of experimental submarine or arctic or antarctic explorer. Or they may have been demonstrated during wartime combat or military training.[6]

Permitted applicants would have ranged in age from 12 to 27 in 1945, or from 19 to 34 in 1952, placing well within the demographics of World War II and Korean War veterans. NASA's Space Task Group cancelled the announcement weeks later, however, choosing instead, at the insistence of President Eisenhower, from the all-male ranks of existing military test pilots.

Despite efforts by elite government image-makers to define for the American public what scientific goals spaceflight would accomplish, the public ultimately proved a challenging target for manipulation. The earliest NASA promotions of its new astronauts (including NASA-sanctioned spreads in *Life* magazine) depicted them in suits and ties, but the public favored a slightly more militant

6 NASA Project A, Announcement 1, December 22, 1958. NASA Historical Reference Collection, NASA Headquarters, Washington, D. C., Folder 013880, pp. 1–4.

Fig. 4: Future astronaut and U. S. Army Air Forces pilot Deke Slayton (left) stands with first Lt. Ed Steinman beside a Douglas A-26 attack aircraft in 1945, most likely in Okinawa, Japan, where Slayton was stationed after his tour in Europe.

image (Fig. 3) and tended to view the space race as what Lewis Mumford, in the *New York Times*, disparagingly called a "symbolic act of war".[7] Within NASA's astronaut corps, a military piloting culture quickly took root and bled into the public sphere through press reports about the men.

Many of the new "astronauts" wore the new label comfortably (Fig. 3): they had spent much of their professional careers either training for war or, in the cases of former fighter pilot John Glenn and bomber pilot Donald "Deke" Slayton (Fig. 4), had each fought in them. Marine Corps aviator John Glenn learned to fly in college in 1941, but left school after the Japanese attack on Pearl Harbor and spent the next two years trying to find a military branch that would commission him immediately as a pilot. Glenn eventually flew 59 missions as a fighter pilot in the Pacific, mostly attacking ground targets. After the War, Glenn served as an instructor, but the Korean Conflict brought Glenn back into the seat of fighter plane, where he eventually flew 163 missions.

7 Lewis Mumford: No: 'A Symbolic Act of War …' In: *The New York Times*, July 21, 1969, p. 6.

His jet returned from the skies over North Korea filled with so many holes that other aviators nicknamed him "magnet ass" for his propensity to attract steel-jacketed bullets. On one mission, Glenn's F9F Panther was shot 250 times. During later missions in an F-86 Sabre, Glenn shot down three Soviet-built MiG-15s, earning the "MiG Mad Marine", a substantial reputation that he further bolstered as a test pilot after Korea, by undertaking the first supersonic transit of the continental United States.[8]

For astronaut Deke Slayton, who graduated from high school in 1942, wartime service was not an "if" or a "when", but a "how": like many recruits who sought assignment to flight school, he had taken civilian flying lessons before his induction and found flying opportunities in an Army Air Corps that was rapidly expanding and desperate for capable young men. Assigned to fly B-25 and A-26 bombers over Italy and Japan, Slayton found himself on the receiving end of a German bombing raid before flying his own terrifying missions over Italian cities well-defended by German anti-aircraft artillery and fighter planes (Fig. 4). Among the more careless American bomber pilots, fear and boredom gave rise to false bravado and gallows humor as the men struggled to find meaning in their uncomfortable work. For some, that meant painting the name of the notorious Italian-Jewish organized crime syndicate – "Murder Inc." – on their airplane and flying jackets and inadvertently handing the Nazis a minor propaganda victory when one member of the crew was captured after bailing out over Germany. About those whom he bombed, Deke Slayton knew and felt little. The bombs he dropped were not aimed at any particular person, even if they often seemed that way from the ground. Speed and altitude reduced people to abstractions and he never delighted in the work. Slayton had wanted, instead, to be a fighter pilot, flying in solo combat against individuals like himself who had chosen to embrace the same risks and dangers. Instead, he found himself unloading explosives on cities and bridges he could never quite see.

The chief concern on Slayton's mind was German artillery, included the dreaded 88mm high-velocity guns whose explosive shells could tear bombers apart at their cruising altitudes. Often, Slayton recalled, pilots could see the weapons' muzzle flashes below them and counted the ten seconds until the shells reached altitude. Pilots could swerve left or right to avoid the arriving shells, but chose wrong half the time, and the bravest simply resigned themselves to their own powerlessness,

8 E.g. John Glenn / Nick Taylor: *Nick John Glenn: A Memoir*. New York: Bantam 1999.

steering straight ahead and hoping for the best.[9] Five years later, American actor Gregory Peck explained the fatalism expected of wartime bomber crews in the 1949 film *Twelve O'Clock High*. Addressing the pilots of a bomber group suffering faltering morale early in the film, Peck dismisses their fears and explains to them that the cause of their suffering is not the danger they face, but their foolish attachment to their own lives. The sooner they "stop making plans", the better. As the thousands of American college students who later saw this film in their psychology classes will attest, however, Peck's Spartan philosophy is eventually too much for even him to bear and he cracks under the strain of wartime leadership.[10]

Likewise, the emotionless, crew-cut space pilots of 1950s and 1960s television and film are recognizable caricatures, not of the fictional adventurers of 1930s space movies, but of the kinds of taciturn pilots with whom American audiences had become familiar thanks to a steady postwar diet of combat films. For these unflappable aviators, spaceflight is less an adventure than a solemn duty and one likely to require great sacrifice. Astronauts need not fear death, though, because they, like the bomber pilots Peck's character commands in *Twelve O'Clock High*, are "already dead": engaged in too perilous a pursuit to even contemplate surviving. Exactly 20 years later, Peck reprised his role in *Twelve O'Clock High* in the 1969 film *Marooned*, playing not a grizzled Army Air Forces general, but the director of NASA's human spaceflight program. He informs the men under him that the three astronauts stranded in Earth's orbit are, effectively, already dead and that there is little to be done but finish a press release that honors their sacrifice and assuages public grieving. In the space business, he notes, death is inevitable. It is one thing to talk of dying, however, and quite another to do it. Confronted with the prospect of a meaningless death, the astronauts in *Marooned* show the first cinematic glimmers of rebellion as they desperately fight to live.[11]

Popular depictions of astronauts in the 1960s emphasized the astronauts' competence, rugged masculinity, and unique fortitude of character, finding duty and nihilism in their quiet resolve. Characters ignoring their own mortality were a fixture of Rod Serling's innovative 1960s television series *The Twilight Zone*. A combat veteran strongly influenced by his experiences in the Philippines during

9 See e.g. Donald K. Slayton / Michael Cassutt: *Deke! U. S. Manned Space: From Mercury to the Shuttle*. New York: St. Martin's 1994.

10 *Twelve O'Clock High* (US 1949, D: Henry King).

11 *Marooned* (US 1969, D: John Sturges).

World War II, Serling wrote or produced dozens of scripts featuring military men who heroically resist an inevitable death. Not surprisingly, *The Twilight Zone* featured some of the most thoughtful investigations of the astronaut psyche, finding it somewhat akin to that of a war-hardened combat pilot. Although death is an ever-present menace, alienation is the astronaut's worst enemy: spaceflight brings a separation from loved ones, human society, familiar places, and the expectations of a full, happy life. On distant planets and asteroids, astronauts can expect not warm welcomes, but privation, murder, and imprisonment at the hands of extraterrestrials.

The lonely, mournful men packed away in Serling's spaceships are literally not long for this world. In a 1959 episode entitled "And When the Sky Was Opened", the three astronauts who return to Earth after flying their X-20 rocket plane (an Air Force program under development at the time) feel so alienated from society that they slowly disappear, consumed by the sense that they no longer belong on Earth.[12] Like veterans grappling with the after-effects of wartime service, Serling's spacemen have no place in the world they left behind. Indeed, only spaceflight's public visibility made it unlike combat: in one conversation with President Kennedy, astronaut Glenn is said to have likened astronauts to soldiers who must accept, in addition to the dangers of public service, the indignities of an awkward kind of public notoriety.[13]

In later episodes, *The Twilight Zone* spacemen encounter parallel universes, nuclear wars, and worse: the astronauts in 1963's "Death Ship" soldier on in the face of incontrovertible evidence that they are already dead, including hallucinations of deceased loved ones and the sight of their own corpses. The script by Richard Matheson ended with Serling's narration distilling the psyche of the episode's astronaut hero, "a man of such indomitable will that even the two men beneath his command are not allowed, by him, to see the truth ... that they are no longer among the living."[14] Gregory Peck might have told the astronauts to accept their fate and die with dignity, but it is not clear whether the men's stubborn attachment to their own lives is their greatest strength or their worst weakness. In either case, their indomitable will moves the audience and makes the astronauts objects of sympathy as well as admiration. It was precisely this kind of self-control, rather than raw piloting ability, that NASA noted with

12 "And When the Sky Was Opened". In: *The Twilight Zone* (US 1959, D: Douglas Heyes).
13 Walter Cunningham: *The All-American Boys.* Rev. Ed. New York: ibooks 2003, p. 194.
14 "Death Ship". In: *The Twilight Zone* (US 1963, D: Don Medford).

favor in its real-life space crews. "Central in their personalities", NASA psychiatrists wrote of America's first astronauts, was a "striking resilience in the face of frustration."[15]

Few media products dealt with astronaut's inner lives as effectively as did *The Twilight Zone*. Even in comedies, astronauts usually appeared instead as simple-minded, Spartan warriors. Larry Hagman's Major Nelson, from the television comedy *I Dream of Jeannie* (1965–70), is a capable Air Force pilot who manages to do his duty despite good-natured interference from Jeannie, a temptress he found in a bottle on a beach after returning from space. *Jeannie* is a particularly good example of the voluntary cooperation between media and government in astronaut image-making: NASA vetted scripts for the series and collaborated with associate producer Sidney Sheldon to ensure accuracy and keep the show "on message". NASA, for example, was desperate to reduce the number of military uniforms depicted in the series; the space agency forbade its astronauts from wearing them in public and encouraged Sheldon to limit their appearance in the show.[16]

Images of the stolid, military astronaut persisted well into the mid-1970s, by which time the astronauts on which these characters had been based had retired. Colonel Steve Austin (Lee Majors), from *The Six Million Dollar Man* (1974–1978) was an astronaut who had nearly been killed in the crash of an experimental vehicle. Government scientists reassemble him as a cyborg who serves his country secretly, with unique courage and superhuman strength. Astronauts, these media products declare, are, unlike their real-life counterparts, either too busy for women or, due to their risky work, not meant to find love. For the frightened, isolated astronauts of *The Twilight Zone*, wives and girlfriends are distant memories. To the stolid Major Nelson, women are a distraction. His single-mindedness proved part of his appeal; Nelson's eventual marriage to Jeannie in the show's fifth season received poor ratings and presaged the end of the series months later. And for Colonel Austin, no "normal" woman could be a proper mate. The astronauts in these media products espouse a "virginal ideal" intimately connected to their elite professional world.

15 Sheldon J. Korchin / George E. Ruff: Personality Characteristics of the Mercury Astronauts. In: George H. Grosser / Henry Wechsler / Milton Greenblatt (eds): *The Threat of Impending Disaster: Contributions to the Psychology of Stress*. Cambridge: MIT 1964, pp. 197–207, here pp. 204–207.

16 Stephen Cox: *Dreaming of Jeannie: TV's Prime Time in a Bottle*. New York: St. Martin's Griffin 2000, pp. 58–61.

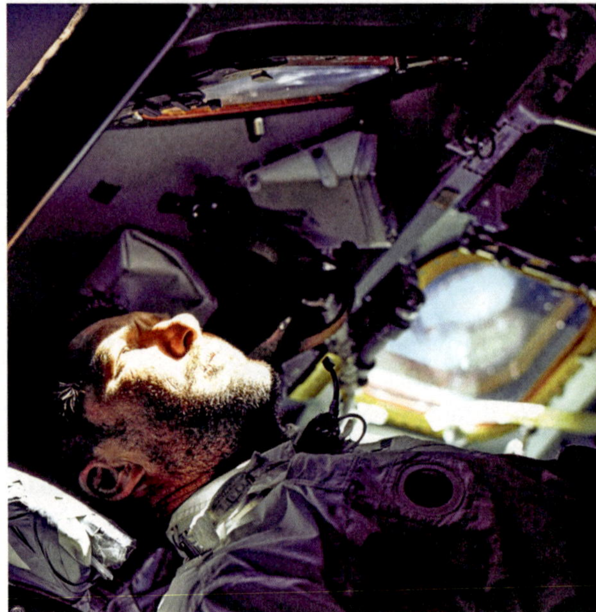

Fig. 5
Apollo 7 Commander Wally Schirra in Earth orbit (1968).

As Vivian Sobchack writes in "The Virginity of Astronauts: Sex and the Science Fiction Film":

> These virginal astronauts [...] tend to be more corporate than corporeal. Indeed, it is their interchangeable blandness, their programmed cheerfulness, their lack of imagination, their very banality [...] that makes them heroes, that gives them that aura of mechanical competence which insists that nothing can go wrong, that everything is A-OK. [...] Offscreen or on, these men who figure in our public myths neither appeal to prurient interest nor really seem to have any.[17]

The spaceman cannot love, but he can fight. The theme of astronaut as stolid, mythic warrior continued to be a common one from the 1960s through the 1980s; motion picture depictions of astronauts often ascribed to them military skills no real astronaut was expected to possess. The astronauts in the 1967

17 Vivian Sobchack: The Virginity of Astronauts: Sex and the Science Fiction Film. In: Annette Kuhn (ed.): *Alien Zone: Cultural Theory and Contemporary Science Fiction Cinema.* London: Verso 1990, pp. 103–115, here p. 108.

James Bond spy thriller *You Only Live Twice* fight their captors with expert hand-to-hand combat.[18] Later, in the 1979 Bond film *Moonraker*, Shuttle astronauts are laser-armed space warriors who help capture an enemy orbital outpost.[19] And in 1982's *Firefox*, an advanced Soviet fighter plane is stolen by a punch-throwing, tough-as-nails American pilot (actor/director Clint Eastwood) so skilled that Soviet intelligence personnel conclude that the thief must be a "NASA Astronaut".[20]

Like all of the images fabricated of the astronauts, the astronaut as soldier was an imperfect mask that concealed the diverse and often conflicted emotions of the men that flew into space. Had they not joined NASA, America's first astronauts would have likely pursued solid careers as military test, instructor, and tactical pilots. Astronauts Michael Collins and Eugene "Gene" Cernan, in David Sington's 2007 documentary *In the Shadow of the Moon*, speculated with some ambivalence that they would have flown combat missions over Vietnam, as had many of their friends in military service. While pleased to have survived the period, Cernan later resented having missed an opportunity to apply his training in combat alongside his colleagues.[21] Astronauts William Anders and Frank Borman, too, reflected with some guilt upon on the relative safety of their NASA assignments and the wartime dangers they avoided through their participation in the space program.[22] To be sure, flying in space had exposed the men to tremendous dangers, but it had also spared them the fate of killing and dying in another war, a gift that many astronauts struggled to accept. Simply resigning from NASA and joining their friends in the field, however, was not an option; many military-trained astronauts gained access to classified information in the space program and could no longer be deployed overseas, lest they be captured and interrogated. Spaceflight, simply put, had ruined the men professionally.

It also took their lives in alarming numbers. Of the 26 American astronauts on active duty in 1964, 27 % were dead three years later:

18 *You Only Live Twice* (GB 1967, D: Lewis Gilbert).

19 *Moonraker* (GB 1979, D: Lewis Gilbert).

20 *Firefox* (US 1982, D: Clint Eastwood), 1:12:10, et seq.

21 *In the Shadow of the Moon* (US 2007, D: David Sington), 0:21:17, et seq.

22 Frank Borman / Jim Lovell / Bill Anders: *John H. Glenn Lecture: An Evening with the Apollo 8 Astronauts*. Washington, D. C.: Smithsonian Institution, National Air and Space Museum, November 13, 2008. https://airandspace.si.edu/events/evening-apollo-8-astronauts (accessed: August 3, 2017).

TABLE 1
NASA ASTRONAUTS, 1964,
WITH FATALITIES THROUGH 1967 IN BOLD

Virgil Ivan (Gus) Grissom	William A. Anders
Walter Marty (Wally) Schirra Jr.	**Charles A. Bassett, II**
Leroy Gordon Cooper Jr.	Alan L. Bean
Neil A. Armstrong	Eugene A. Cernan
Frank F. Borman, Jr.	**Roger B. Chaffee**
Charles Conrad, Jr.	Michael Collins
James A. Lovell, Jr.	R. Walter Cunningham
James A. McDivitt	Donn F. Eisele
Elliot M. See, Jr.	**Theodore C. Freeman**
Thomas P. Stafford	Richard F. Gordon, Jr.
Edward H. White, II	Russell L. Schweickart
John W. Young	David R. Scott
Edwin E. Aldrin, Jr.	**Clifton C. Williams**

None of these fatalities, though, occurred in space. Rather, astronauts, as military test pilots, died in the ways that military test pilots always had: routine airplane crashes and bizarre training accidents:

TABLE 2
FATALITIES AMONG ASTRONAUTS ABOVE, 1964–1967,
WITH CAUSE OF DEATH

Theodore Freeman (1964)	**Bird strike, low altitude-ejection, T-38 aircraft**
Elliot See (1966)	**Controlled flight into terrain, T-38 aircraft**
Charles Bassett (1966)	**Controlled flight into terrain, T-38 aircraft**
Gus Grissom (1967)	**Launch pad fire**
Edward White, II (1967)	**Launch pad fire**
Roger Chaffee (1967)	**Launch pad fire**
Clifton "C. C." Williams (1967)	**Mechanical failure, T-38 aircraft**

This casualty rate was not unexpected. In one oft-cited statistic, test pilot work killed more than one quarter of those undertaking it; for such men, death in the line of duty, however dreaded, was unremarkable. The work of the astronaut required daily contact with potentially life-threatening machinery and the virtual certainty of casualties. However, not every astronaut wanted to fight and die for an organization, especially in the 1960s, when blind obedience to duty or country was becoming increasingly problematized.

Like other organization men of the 1950s, some astronauts were driven to embrace the counterculture of the 1960s, including its rejection of the nation state and embrace of progressive politics. In his 1970 bestseller, *The Greening of America*, Charles Reich defined the social convulsions of the late-1960s as a counter-attack against a society in which unfeeling institutions increasingly controlled every aspect of civic life.[23] For astronauts, NASA often seemed like such an entity. Dismayed by their declining autonomy, some astronauts even rebelled against government authority over their missions of exploration. "By 1968 there was a bureaucracy developing", veteran astronaut Wally Schirra later wrote, "the fun days were over."[24] Unwilling, literally, to play ball, some astronauts were transformed sooner than others.

Original Seven astronauts Malcolm "Scott" Carpenter and Leroy "Gordo" Cooper exhibited behaviors incompatible with a space career and departed from NASA prematurely. Carpenter was given to philosophical musings about spaceflight and aggravated colleagues by preferring the company of his wife to that of drunken astronauts. He also spurned competitive sports, choosing to fence with an instructor instead of playing handball with his peers. When orbiting Earth in 1962, Carpenter was so enthused by the experience that he ran his spacecraft out of fuel and landed hundreds of miles off-course. While Carpenter continued to work with NASA through 1967, injuries sustained in a motorcycle accident ended his flying career. He spent much of the mid-1960s occupied with deep-sea research and, according to one fellow astronaut, "letting his hair grow long" and taking up "music."[25]

Cooper, meanwhile, boasted, rebelled against authority figures, made indelicate remarks to the press, raced cars illegally, and flew recklessly. The day before Cooper's first scheduled lift-off in 1963, he attacked a NASA administrator with a fighter jet. Flight Director Eugene "Gene" Kranz described Cooper as a "loner" and a "rebel"; Cooper later accused a "government bureaucracy" of hamstringing him. Both Carpenter and Cooper, combined rebellion against authority with a sense of adventure, embracing spaceflight's metaphysical implications.[26]

Other astronauts described themselves as transformed by their experiences, and returned to Earth expressing what appeared to be newfound interests in subjects that would have been regarded as taboo only a few years earlier.

23 Charles A. Reich: *The Greening of America*. New York: Random House 1970.

24 Francis French / Colin Burgess: *Into That Silent Sea: Trailblazers of the Space Era, 1961–1965*. Lincoln: Nebraska UP 2007, p. 186.

25 Cunningham: *All-American Boys*, pp. 96–97.

26 Francis French / Colin Burgess: *In the Shadow of the Moon: A Challenging Journey to Tranquility, 1965–1969*. Lincoln: Nebraska UP 2007, pp. 50–52.

Above all, astronauts soon reveled in what psychologists would later describe as the "overview affect", looking out upon the Earth as a privileged oasis undivided by geographic borders and united in the same concerns for peace and environmental protection. Indeed, often, astronauts of the late 1960s returned to Earth with what appeared to be genuine concern for Earth's habitat. Apollo 7's Commander, the seldom-shy Walter "Wally" Schirra, is reported to have been so incensed by the smog covering California that he sent photographs of it to Governor Ronald Reagan upon his return (Fig. 5). Coasting around the Moon in December 1968, Apollo 8 astronauts Borman, James "Jim" Lovell, and William "Bill" Anders had conveyed their blessings to everyone "on the good Earth" and snapped unplanned photographs of a crescent Earth rising above a desolate lunar horizon against an inky black sky. "Earthrise" soon became an iconic fixture of the environmental movement, described, in 1971's *The Last Whole Earth Catalog*, as the photograph "that established our planetary facthood and beauty and rareness ... and began to bend human consciousness."[27]

Apollo 9 astronaut Russell "Rusty" Schweikart returned from his 1969 Earth orbital flight describing his spacewalk as a metaphysically transcendent experience that introduced him to the majesty of the cosmos. "Many of us, on returning home from space," Schweikart wrote, "brought back the perspective of a lonely and beautiful planet crying out for a more responsible attitude from its most prolific partner."[28] In fact, more often than not, the interests astronauts expressed upon their return to Earth were the same ones they had when they left. Having completed their missions, however, they could now express these interests openly. To an increasingly unmoored and confused public, what marked astronauts as heroes in the 1960s – their isolation and personal assumption of risk – seemed to make them true rebels who, in their cosmic loneliness, could realize truths hidden to terrestrial men.

While some segments of the American public during the late 1960s continued to view space travelers as soldiers heroically battling communism in space, they themselves hoped that the space environment would be – and, indeed, they sometimes found it to be – something entirely different. Instead of viewing space as the next battleground, spacemen increasingly began to see it as a place of redemption: a realm with borders and armies, where they could make peace with themselves and live free of others' expectations. Increasingly in the late 1960s

27 Portola Institute: *The Last Whole Earth Catalog: Access to Tools.* New York: Random House 1971, p. i. On "Earthrise" see also Colleen Boyle's contribution "Through the Eyes of the Astronaut. Mediator of the Human Imagination" in this volume.

28 Russell Schweickart: Letter Re: Space Colonies. In: *Coevolution Quarterly* 3:2 (1976), p. 6.

Fig. 6: Lowell Freeman (Bruce Dern) tends to his garden with the help of his robotic assistants in the 1972 film *Silent Running.*

and early 1970s, American popular culture portrayed spacemen as progressive, dissenting voices in societies losing their connection to the organic. Often, these Hollywood portrayals reinterpreted stock literary archetypes, rather than inventing new characters. In Douglas Trumbull's *Silent Running* (1972), space botanist Freeman Lowell (played by Bruce Dern) is neither taciturn nor fearless while ferrying the last remnants of Earth's forests aboard the space freighter Valley Forge. Clad in his flowing space robes and finding solace in the company of the robots who tend his space garden, Lowell, to a soundtrack by Joan Baez, becomes a paranoid voice for a peculiar form of American environmentalism. (The screen portrayal – Fig. 6 – oddly resembles earlier publicity photographs of astronauts in survival training during the 1960s, wearing robes made from parachutes: Fig. 7.) Lowell, in fact, serves as a thinly veiled version of nineteenth-century Massachusetts author, naturalist, transcendentalist, abolitionist, and political dissenter Henry David Thoreau – a space poet surrounded by liberated mechanical slaves, tending a synthetic *Walden* for which no one else seems to care.[29]

29 *Silent Running* (US 1972, D: Douglas Trumbull).

Fig. 7: Astronauts Gordon Cooper, Scott Carpenter, John Glenn, Alan Shepard, Gus Grissom, Wally Schirra, and Deke Slayton pose during desert survival training in Nevada in 1960.

Incidentally, the same year Trumbull resurrected a nineteenth-century American naturalist, Andrei Tarkovsky conjured up a similar conception of the space traveler in the Soviet Union, reveling in the literary depressions of the nineteenth-century Russian intelligentsia. In *Solyaris*, a brooding adaptation of Stanislaw Lem's science fiction novel, Russian space authorities send morose psychologist Kris Kelvin to a distant planet to encounter a telepathic alien intelligence. Kelvin is a deep thinker expert in the various forms of human suffering; a widower pained by memories of lost love and a naturalist humbled by modernity. The closest thing to heaven he can imagine is to be alone with his thoughts in the Russian countryside. In both *Silent Running* and *Solyaris*, spacemen cross from national protectors to countercultural icons, expressing their distrust of the technologies that have brought human beings into conflict and isolated humanity from the organic world.[30]

30 *Solyaris* (SU 1971, D: Andrei Tarkovsky).

By 1973, even real astronauts were finally rebelling. During NASA's Skylab 4 mission, astronauts overwhelmed by brutal work schedules aboard America's first space station most likely turned off their radio on purpose for several hours. Panicked NASA ground controllers relented on their micromanagement of the astronauts' lives, gave them free time to work on their own or just look out of the window, and acknowledged that in space, it was the astronauts who should be in charge, not the people back on Earth. The astronaut-soldier had not quite disappeared, but he was no longer following orders.

Umberto Rossi

All We Mad Starmen

Contextualizing Barry N. Malzberg's NASA Trilogy and Its Deranged Astronauts

> Little information has been released about the psychological effects of space travel. [...] But it is clear from the subsequently troubled careers of many of the astronauts [...] that they suffered severe psychological damage.
> J. G. Ballard[1]

Far from being an objective reality, Barry N. Malzberg's NASA Trilogy is an interpretive construct I have devised based on common elements found in three novels by the American author, *The Falling Astronauts* (1971), *Beyond Apollo* (1972), and *Revelations* (1972), which were not meant to be read as parts of a whole. Hence I take full responsibility for having grouped these three texts together, as they present us with an original treatment of the figure of the astronaut in English-language science fiction, also allowing us to outline more traditional depictions of spacemen in the genre and the complex relations tying those depictions to their historical counterparts.

The publication years of these three novels place them during the final phase of the Apollo Program. It is difficult to understand how subversive these novels were when they were published, if we do not understand what the expectations surrounding the US Space Program were in the science fiction community, especially because Barry N. Malzberg had been a science fiction columnist

1 J. G. Ballard: *The Atrocity Exhibition*. San Francisco: RE/Search 1990, p. 43.

and editor[2] with a wide knowledge of the genre since the late 1960s, and was well aware of those expectations. Malzberg, in addition, is a renowned member of the iconoclastic and transgressive science fiction trend known as New Wave – though neither as celebrated and successful as James G. Ballard, nor as circumfused with myth as Philip K. Dick – so much so that Roger Luckhurst mentions him (with Ballard) as an emblematic representative of New Wave's dislike of outer space and the space race,[3] even though Luckhurst sees the New Wave as a fundamentally British movement and is skeptical about the idea of an American counterpart.[4] The New Wave was above all a movement that rebelled in the 1960s against the tradition of science fiction as it had been defined during the Golden Age (late 1930s to early 1940s), so that Malzberg's works should be always read as deliberately and aggressively demolishing the myths of that tradition, which was characterized by an almost religious faith in science and technology. Among those myths is the archetypal hero of science fiction: the spaceman, the space traveler, as Thomas M. Disch has persuasively posited the starship as the "primary icon" of the genre, and the man (or woman) travelling on and piloting a starship must necessarily be the primary hero of science fiction.[5]

Malzberg's NASA Trilogy presents readers with mad astronauts in a very irreverent and sarcastic fashion. He was not the first science fiction author whose spacemen go insane, but the treatment of madness and space flight by previous authors was quite different. Let us begin with a paradigmatic science fiction narrative focusing on the endeavors of astronauts, James E. Gunn's 1957 novelette *Space is a Lonely Place*: here madness is represented in a dignified, tragic, even epic fashion. Gunn tells of the ordeal of the crew of the Santa Maria, the first space ship flying to Mars, whose five crew members go insane, one by one, and ultimately kill each other or commit suicide before reaching the Red Planet. Gunn depicts the gradual deterioration of the astronauts' minds in a rather effective way, despite the fact that many of the scientific and technological details sound quite outdated today.

2 He edited the science fiction magazines *Amazing Stories* and *Fantastic*, and co-wrote (with Mike Resnick) an advice column for writers in the Science Fiction and Fantasy Writers of America's magazine, the *SWFA Bulletin*.

3 Roger Luckhurst: *Science Fiction*. Cambridge: Polity 2005, p. 143.

4 Ibid., pp. 160–166.

5 Thomas M. Disch: *The Dreams Our Stuff Is Made Of: How Science Fiction Conquered the World*. New York: Free Press 1998, p. 57.

However, Holloway, Craddock, Burr, Jelinek, and Migliardo, the astronauts on the Santa Maria, are depicted as heroes overwhelmed by an exceedingly long confinement and the strain of the space mission; they are martyrs dying for a good cause. The space ship eventually reaches Mars and one of the managers of the Mars mission explains that it "will be sending back telemetered reports from its telescopic examination of the surface, from its sounding missiles" and "conduct geological explorations, [...] analyze samples and telemeter back their findings". The ship itself is the astronaut, but with "[n]o neuroses, [...] no weakness, [...] no space-madness". Of course, as another character objects, "Man's representatives [...] must be living, breathing, fearful men like themselves":[6] one day the Red Planet must be reached by men, not only machines. But in the meantime, the death of the astronauts notwithstanding, the mission is seen as a technological success, because the Santa Maria worked perfectly. The sacrifice of the five spacemen is therefore not in vain; theirs is a dignified, somewhat heroic madness: "Men died for the Western Hemisphere, to tame the Antarctic, to develop atomic power, to build skyscrapers and roads. Men died to build the Little Wheel and the Big Wheel. Space is hungry, too. And men stick their heads in its mouth because they're men."[7]

The ending of the story reveals that there will be spacemen able to reach the other planets of the Solar System and come back: it will be the sons of commander Lloyd (the mastermind of the Mars expedition, who follows the flight of the Santa Maria from a space station orbiting Earth), because they were born in the space station and have grown up there. They therefore consider space their natural environment and confinement in an orbital station (or a space ship) their natural condition. The sacrifice of the unfortunate crew is thus is a step forward – "one giant leap for mankind", like the one announced by Neil Armstrong twelve years later. Remarkably, Sputnik 1 was launched on October 4, 1957 – the same year that Gunn published his novelette in the May issue of the science fiction magazine *Venture*.

Such a heroic representation of astronauts was not limited to the science fiction ghetto of pulp magazines and paperbacks. "Where is Everybody?", the first episode of the celebrated TV series *The Twilight Zone* – aired on October 2, 1959 – features an insane astronaut, Mike Ferris, who has entered a frightening

6 James Gunn: Space Is a Lonely Place. In: J. G.: *Station in Space*. New York: Bantam 1958, pp. 112–156, here p. 156.
7 Ibid., p. 144.

hallucination, in which he is the only person in an empty world, due to the stress of training (he has been kept in isolation for 484 hours on Earth), not as a consequence of a real space flight. The story implies that the plight of the astronaut is so extreme that madness – albeit temporary – can affect spacemen even *before* they are launched. Despite Ferris' delusional experience, the episode ends in an optimistic tone, because he recovers his sanity and tells the Moon: "Hey! Don't go away up there! Next time it won't be a dream or a nightmare. Next time it'll be for real."[8] There may be momentary insanity, but reason, good will, and courage ultimately prevail.

A somewhat similar mentality is expressed in the third chapter of John Wyndham's *The Outward Urge* (1959), "Mars – A. D. 2094". It tells the story of the first landing on Mars, which is reached by a Brazilian ship with a crew of three astronauts. Unusually, it is not an American ship, as the nations of the Northern hemisphere have been annihilated by a nuclear war and Australia and Brazil are competing in a counter-historical space race. The Brazilian starship topples over soon after landing: Captain Geoffrey Montgomery Trunho, the narrator, is unscathed, but the ship commander, Raul Capaneiro, is killed, and the third member of the crew, Camilo Botoes, electronics officer and geologist, suffers a cranial shock that drives him insane. Camilo thinks Geoffrey is not a man, but a Martian in disguise, and ultimately tries to leave the planet despite the damage suffered by the starship, which is then destroyed. Thus Geoffrey is stranded on the Red Planet facing death, even though he has enough food for nearly three years: "[f]ood enough", he writes on his diary (which is the text of the chapter) "but not, I fear, spirit enough".[9] Geoffrey is affected by amnesia, in the form of a "long gap" in his memory after the destruction of the starship, probably caused by the shock that occurs when he realizes he has no hope of getting back to Earth. His predicament is so desperate that he is understandably afraid that madness may overwhelm him soon.

Another mad astronaut is George Montgomery Troon, whom we meet in "The Emptiness of Space: The Asteroids – A. D. 2194", the fifth and last chapter of this destructured novel. He believes he has died and lost his soul in space. Compared to the characters of the previous narratives, George is harmless and pathetic, but his words bespeak a severe mental disorder: "Without [my soul] I am a sham. A man who has lost a leg or an arm is still a man, but a man who has lost his soul is nothing – nothing – nothing…"[10] We ultimately find out, however, that George

8 "Where is Everybody?" In: *The Twilight Zone* (US 1959, D: Robert Stevens).
9 John Wyndham [Lucas Parkes]: *The Outward Urge*. Harmondsworth: Penguin 1971, p. 129.
10 Ibid., p. 176.

was involved in a space accident and only survived thanks to a primitive and unreliable resurrection device, the Hapson Survival System. When a collision with a meteorite took place, he activated the survival system, which put him in a state of suspended animation, a sort of artificial death – hence the psychological problems when, after a long time, George is accidentally rescued and then reanimated.

These stories more or less overtly imply that if humankind wants to conquer space there is a price to be paid; people will go insane, die, be crippled, but their sacrifice will pave the way to the stars. Such a moral is also suggested by a short story published the same year as *The Outward Urge*, Theodore Sturgeon's "The Man Who Lost the Sea", where a failed mission to Mars is told through flashback and a moderately destructured stream-of-consciousness technique, combined with a rare second-person narrative. This stylistically sophisticated story culminates in the moment when the dying protagonist realizes that "the satellite fading here is Phobos, that those footprints are your own, that there is no sea here, that you have crashed and are killed and will in a moment be dead". The gloomy ending is however redeemed by the feelings of joy that overwhelm the fading consciousness of the dying astronaut when "he takes his triumph at the other side of death". Because, after all, the enterprise managed to carry humans to another planet, so it was a success from a scientific and technological point of view. Hence the final cry of the protagonist, "God, we made it!"[11]

The sacrifice of the hero has always been part of epic narratives and these stories belong to an epic of space conquest that highlights the human cost of that conquest, and accepts it. We no longer have the escapist fantasies of the 1920s and 1930s, with its space heroes and superheroes,[12] which may have to do with the fact that by the end of the 1950s, space seemed much closer than ever before. Moreover, one may well suspect that the context of the Cold War has a lot to do with the recurrence of astronauts' heroic sacrifice; in fact, nuclear war features in both Gunn's *Station in Space* (the 1958 collection including *Space Is a Lonely Place*) and Wyndham's *The Outward Urge*. It is actually more of a hindrance for both writers, as the ultimate destination of humankind is outer space: astronauts

11 Theodore Sturgeon: The Man Who Lost the Sea. In: *The Man Who Lost the Sea: The Complete Stories of Theodore Sturgeon*, vol. 10. Berkeley, CA: North Atlantic 2005, pp. 155–166, here p. 166.

12 E.g. John W. Campbell's Aarn Munro, space explorer, scientist, engineer, and adventurer, who is the protagonist of a diptych of novels that may be taken as representatives of Golden Age science fiction's take on the figure of the spaceman: *The Mightiest Machine* (1934–35) and *The Incredible Planet* (published in 1949, but made up by three novelettes probably written in the late 1930s).

cannot be bothered with megadeath and fallout. Yet World War Three is part of the picture of future history Gunn and Wyndham present to readers, and such an ethic of sacrifice seems to me to be connected with the logic of sacrifice Adam Piette detected in several Cold War narratives.[13] However, when the US space program actually started, such images of the dangers of space missions are not the ones NASA wanted circulating in the media. Fabienne Collignon has persuasively argued that Cape Canaveral, the launching site of the space missions, embodies "a terminal, bleached dreamworld of absolute security, tranquility".[14] Security seems to be the main concern of the US space program, which Collignon reads in the wider context of Cold War. Her analysis of technology and above all technological imagination and discourses shows how NASA's rhetoric pivots on the implementation of safe and predictable systems. There is no room in such discourses (or in the actual space missions NASA carried out) for the tragic, heroic figure of the astronaut as depicted in Wyndham's, Gunn's, and Sturgeon's stories – and there is no place at all for the mad astronaut.

Ideally, the astronaut should have been a cyborg, as suggested by two scientists, both researchers at the Rockland State Hospital, Manfred E. Clynes and Nathan S. Kline, in their 1960 essay *Cyborgs and Space*. They maintain that reproducing the natural environment in space is too expensive and too complicated; what should be done instead is to modify human beings to make them adapted to space: "If man attempts partial adaptation to space conditions, instead of insisting on carrying his whole environment along with him, a number of new possibilities appear."[15] Once adapted, the human being will become like the components of the weapons systems that were developed in those years, where the key factor was "the integration of individual subsystems to produce a total-system technical design".[16] The space program and the weapons race were, after all, two sides of the same coin. The same man who was managing the construction of the Saturn V rocket that brought men to the moon, Wernher von Braun, was the father of the PGM-11 Redstone, the first US large-sized ballistic missile (first

13 Adam Piette: *The Literary Cold War: 1945 to Vietnam*. Edinburgh: Edinburgh UP 2009, pp. 11–14.

14 Fabienne Collignon: *Rocket States: Atomic Weaponry and the Cultural Imagination*. London: Bloomsbury 2014, p. 74.

15 Manfred E. Clynes / Nathan S. Kline. Cyborg and Space. In: Chris Hables Gray / Steven Mentor / Heidi Figueroa-Sarriera (eds): *The Cyborg Handbook*. New York / London: Routledge 1995, pp. 29–34, here p. 30.

16 Robert L. Perry: The Atlas, Thor, and Titan. In: *Technology and Culture* 4:4 (1963), pp. 466–477, here p. 472.

launched in 1953) – the Redstone was also used to launch Alan Shepard and Gus Grissom to their sub-orbital flights in 1961. Intercontinental ballistic missiles were very complex and sophisticated weapon systems, "designed to insure that all major factors in the [...] effort were traced in terms of their complex interrelationships and not in isolation".[17] If the evidence I have quoted represents the prevailing mentality in the US space program, it is clear that there is no place for heroic individuals: here astronauts are just cogs in a machine, "factors" whose behavior must be predictable and dependable.[18]

Collignon stresses the passivity of astronauts: not aviator-aces (or enterprising captains or spacemen on space ships), but passive subjects in a pod, or to put it in Tom Wolfe's words, "laboratory animal[s] wired up from skull to rectum with medical sensors".[19] Instead of the atmosphere of cosmic adventure – albeit more "adult" and mature than the Space Opera of the 1930s and 1940s – found in Gunn's, Wyndham's and Sturgeon's stories, we have a carefully programmed routine, a clockwork mission where everything is under control and takes place at the right moment in a predictable schedule. Only Apollo 13 injected some elements of drama in the program: no wonder that the unlucky Apollo mission with Lowell, Swigert and Heise seems to be the only one that has managed to survive in the collective memory after the triumphal flight of Apollo 11.

To quote Ballard once more: "Even before the Space Age had begun I had a hunch it would be short-lived – basically because NASA and the Russians had left the imagination out of space, one mistake the S-f writers never made."[20] Yet such a skeptical approach to the space race of the 1960s and early 1970s cannot be said to be typical of science fiction readers, writers and critics. Armstrong, Collins and Aldrin's 1970 celebratory book *First on the Moon* had an epilogue written by a science fiction author as popular as Arthur C. Clarke. Many shared the stance expressed by science fiction scholar Gary Westfahl:

> Like many science-fiction readers of my generation [...] I long considered myself an advocate of human space exploration. I attentively followed the American space program in

17 Ibid., p. 472.

18 See also Matthew H. Hersch's contribution, "Redemptive Space: Duty, Death, and the Astronaut-Soldier, 1949–1969" in this volume.

19 Tom Wolfe: *The Right Stuff.* New York: Farrar, Straus & Giroux 1979, p. 60.

20 James Graham Ballard: Foreword to The Cage of Sand. In: *The Best Fiction of J. G. Ballard.* London: Futura 1977, p. 310.

> the 1960s, cheered when Spiro Agnew proposed a manned Mars expedition during the Apollo 11 flight, and lamented the stagnation and hesitancy of American space activities after the Apollo program.[21]

Westfahl went so far as to write a critical study, *Islands in the Sky*, in favor of an extensive space program.[22]

And yet there was malcontent among the science fiction writers. One of them, as we have already seen, was J. G. Ballard, whose depiction of an abandoned Cape Canaveral in his 1962 short story "The Cage of Sand" is the turning point in the treatment of astronauts in science fiction: they become "troubled anti-heroes, locked in psychotic delusion or – in a characteristically perverse twist – stupefied with nostalgia for the glory days of space that had long since passed away".[23] However, in Ballard's fiction of the 1960s, astronauts are more often dead than insane, thus becoming even more disquieting and uncanny figures, as I have already argued.[24]

Ballard's provocative take on astronauts inspired other science fiction writers, such as Robert Silverberg, whose 1972 novella *The Feast of St. Dionysus* also features captain Oxenshuer, an astronaut who may be deranged – or on the verge of insanity. He is the only survivor of a catastrophic mission to Mars in which the rest of the three-man crew perished in a sandstorm. He is afflicted by a sense of guilt for the death of his companions, Richardson and Vogel, and for having left their bodies on Mars. Moreover, he is tormented by his love for Claire, the widow of his friend and crewmate Vogel. Oxenshuer is so racked by remorse that he ventures into the Mojave Desert on foot, looking for a strange sort of atonement:

> That gray, pervasive sense of guilt, heavy on him since his return from Mars, held less weight here beyond civilization's edge. This wasteland was the closest he could come to attaining Mars on Earth. Not really close enough [...]. But it was as close [...] as he could manage.[25]

21 Gary Westfahl: The Case against Space. In: *Science-Fiction Studies* 24:2 (1997). http://www.depauw.edu/sfs/essays/westfahl%20case.html (accessed: June 22, 2017).

22 Gary Westfahl: *Islands in the Sky: The Space Station Theme in Science Fiction Literature*. San Bernardino, CA: Borgo 1996.

23 Rob Latham: The New Wave. In: David Seed (ed.): *A Companion to Science Fiction*. Oxford: Blackwell 2005, pp. 202–216, here p. 208.

24 Umberto Rossi: A Little Something about Dead Astronauts. In: *Science-Fiction Studies* 36:1 (2008), pp. 101–120.

25 Robert Silverberg: The Feast of St. Dionysus. In: R. S.: *The Feast of St. Dionysus*. New York: Berkley 1979, pp. 3–60, here p. 8.

Oxenshuer is looking for a sort of inner Mars, which only exists in his tortured mind. What he finds instead is a strange community of Dionysus worshippers living in the desert and performing mysterious rituals involving wrestling and wine drinking. The former astronaut joins the community and is told that Dionysus is also Christ, so that he "will enter the ocean of Christ"[26] – right in the middle of the Mojave Desert. When the moment of Oxenshuer's initiation comes, he is thrown into a sort of hallucination: he is on Mars right after the disaster that killed his crewmates and manages to retrieve the corpses of the two dead astronauts, so that they can return to Earth. Is this mere wish-fulfilment, a sort of psychedelic trip triggered by wine, or a journey into inner space? When Oxenshuer tries to return to the village of the St. Dionysus worshippers – this time not alone but with Claire – he cannot find the community in the desert, suggesting that it was all in fact a delusional experience, which nonetheless managed to heal his psychological wounds.
Even more interesting is the fact that while the US space program was somewhat under the aegis of Apollo, the solar god of reason (as suggested by David A. Lanyon in his reading of Barry Malzberg's science fiction[27]), Oxenshuer must resort to the worshippers of Dionysus, who, according to Nietzsche, was Apollo's complementary opposite: the god of drunkenness, ritual madness, and religious ecstasy.[28] If, as we shall see, Malzberg takes us *beyond* Apollo, in his demolition of the rationality of the space program, Silverberg places himself and his deranged astronaut *against* Apollo, on the side of Dionysian madness.
Seen in this light, Oxenshuer's two fellow astronauts were evidently killed by the very pinpoint precision of the mission schedule. Vogel proposes to change the plan and go to the Gulliver site (90 kilometers away) at the beginning of their stay on Mars, not on day twenty, as decreed by the mission timetable. By doing this, he is trying to overrule the inflexible order imposed by Mission Control and regain at least some autonomy, to stop being an individual subsystem integrated in the great clockwork machine of the Mars mission. But Oxenshuer hesitates "to deviate from the schedule".[29] He and Richardson accept the passive role devised for them by NASA, the EVA takes place on day twenty as planned and the two astronauts head towards their death. No wonder that, after such a failure of rationality, Oxenshuer feels he has to forsake Apollo and join a Dionysian cult.

26 Ibid., p. 4.

27 David A. Lanyon: The Barriers of Inner and Outer Space: The Science Fiction of Barry N. Malzberg. In: *Science-Fiction Studies* 18:1 (1991), pp. 71–90, here p. 83.

28 Friedrich Nietzsche: *The Birth of Tragedy Out of the Spirit of Music*. London: Penguin 1993.

29 Silverberg: *Feast*, p. 9.

Here the madness of the astronaut is both the product of an over-rationalized and alienating space program, and an escape from the clockwork machinery of the Apollo program.

It is not the only contradiction we find in this novelette. Istvan Csicsery-Ronay Jr. maintains that "astronauts are the quintessential Handy Man",[30] one of the most recent embodiments of a figure with an archetypal value, someone "usually male, who possesses skill in the handling of tools".[31] The genealogy of such a character stretches back to Odysseus, who is usually defined in Homer's poem as "polymechanos" (πολυμήχανος), meaning full of resources, inventive, ever-ready. Csicsery-Ronay examines the heroic astronauts à la Gunn, Wyndham and Sturgeon, and their forerunners in Golden Age science fiction, who were larger than life, however, there is a contradiction that his analysis only begins to describe. He notes that the astronauts "are even viewed as disorientingly automatic"; that they "are shown lacking poetic imagination, [...] but they are the perfect, austere, self-sacrificing subjects of Enlightenment"; and, as Handy Men, they should "demonstrate their handiness",[32] their skills in the handling of extremely advanced tools. Yet the space capsules and the Saturn rockets are controlled by Mission Control: it is only when something goes wrong, as on Apollo 13, that astronauts can "demonstrate their handiness in very Crusoe-like ways, constructing life-saving devices out of the scraps left in the shipwreck".[33] The tradition of science fiction that depicts astronauts as active individuals, heroic actors of a dangerous enterprise, therefore clashes with the reality of the US space program, in which the stress is on predictability, subordination of components (including the crews of space capsules) to the overall system and ultimately passivity. As in Silverberg's novelette, it is Mission Control that ultimately makes the decisions.

This contradiction is exposed with remarkable results by Barry N. Malzberg in his *The Falling Astronauts*, a novel published just two years after the first Moon landing and a year after the troubled Apollo 13 mission. Though the acronym NASA and the word "Apollo" never appear in the text, the anonymous agency in the novel and the nameless program clearly mirror historical reality: what has already happened when the novel begins, though, and is slowly revealed through

30 Istvan Csicsery-Ronay Jr.: *The Seven Beauties of Science-Fiction*. Middletown, CT: Wesleyan UP 2008, p. 241.

31 Ibid., p. 227.

32 Ibid., p. 241.

33 Ibid.

a series of flashbacks is definitely imaginary. While orbiting the Moon, the protagonist, Colonel Richard Martin, suffers a nervous breakdown. He obsessively keeps asking himself what would they do to him if he pressed the retrofire button and returned to Earth, leaving his two crewmates to die on the surface of the moon. This obsession reaches its climax when Martin hears the retrofire button talking to him "in a small but manic voice", tempting him to do the deed, to "TAKE A CHANCE", and justifying the insane act: "THEY'LL CALL IT TECHNICAL MALFUNCTION ANYWAY AND YOU'LL BE CALLED TWICE A HERO FOR MANAGING TO ESCAPE WITH YOUR LIFE."[34]

Martin begins to rave and Mission Control strives to bring him back to reason, not an easy task when all they can do is talk to him. Ultimately, Mission Control manages to avert the disaster, but only barely. Of course, Martin's career as an astronaut is over, yet to cover up the accident he is not expelled from the Agency, but assigned a symbolic position as information officer. This is a very easy job as the reporters he has to meet are "docile, cooperative, amenable", and Moon landings are no longer big news. As Martin keeps telling them: "Everything is on schedule [...]. Everything is go-normal [...]. Everything is great."[35]

It is very clear, however, that Martin's moment of madness has much to do with the fact that everything in the vast machinery of the space program is totally, absolutely under control. In its own deranged way, his is an act of rebellion, as the retrofire button tells him: "SHOW THEM THAT YOU ARE A MAN AND NOT A ROBOT. SHOW THEM THAT THEY CAN'T PUSH A MAN LIKE YOU AROUND WITH THEIR GODDAMNED SILLY ORDERS AND ARROGANCE BUT THAT YOU'VE GOT A MIND OF YOUR OWN AND YOU CANNOT BE TRIFLED WITH."[36]

We can thus apply to *The Falling Astronauts* something Layton said about a later novel by Malzberg, *Beyond Apollo*: "the type of [...] machine mind astronauts are supposed to have is somehow sick and insane."[37] But madness in this novel is not caused, as in Gunn's, Wyndham's, and even Silverberg's stories, by the stress of space flight or traumatic experiences in space or on other planets. It is *the space program itself* that has driven Martin insane. This is said quite clearly when, during the humiliating meeting with the Director in chapter 13, the former astronaut gives vent to his feelings:

34 Barry N. Malzberg: *The Falling Astronauts*. Grand Rapids: Anti-Oedipus 2017, p. 70.

35 Ibid., pp. 26–27.

36 Ibid., p. 73.

37 Lanyon: Barriers, p. 84.

> Do you know what it's like to be locked up in a training mission? [...] Do you know what it's like to spend six weeks living in a cubicle with two other men, two adult males: [...]? Do you know what it's like in a simular? [...] When you get ten gravities on you the eyeballs feel like you're imploding, just dropping into the sockets and draining into the mouth cavity. Ten gravities also does interesting things to your balls if you get it three times a week for a month [...].[38]

Martin is not the only astronaut who shows signs of being unbalanced: Busby, a member of the next crew that will soon fly to the moon, attracts Martin's attention, because "there was some talk of Busby dropping out of the project when his wife died".[39] Then his daughter is killed in an accident and though it does not seem to have upset him, his lack of visible emotions strikes Martin. Throughout the novel, Martin is increasingly fascinated by Busby and thinks that "he should get to know Busby; of all the men in the project, Busby may be the one to whom he has the most to say at this time".[40] The reason for this attraction emerges for the first time when Busby overreacts to the remarks of a reporter during a press conference, then, once in space, he kills one of his crewmates, and takes control of the capsule; Allen, the commander, is paralyzed by fear and totally unable to stop the mad astronaut.

This time the disruption of the schedule is much worse, as the ship is carrying a huge cargo of nuclear ordnance: a government official admits that "[t]here's a good deal of armament on that ship, more even than we conceded".[41] The official explanation is that the nuclear bombs are to be used in a seismic experiment, but one might suspect a military purpose as we are told that the Agency is under the direct control of the Department of Defense. Once Busby has taken over the capsule, the overwhelming question is what he is going to do with those weapons.[42]

In a desperate last minute move, Oakes, a high-ranking member of the administration who has superseded the Director of the Agency, asks Martin to talk to Busby: "After all, if you can't talk to the man, who can? There are so many similarities. [...] He might be, uh, less resistant to you than to anyone else."[43] The

38 Malzberg: *Falling*, p. 103.

39 Ibid., p. 49.

40 Ibid., p. 51.

41 Ibid., p. 179.

42 Curiously, David Seed does not deal with *The Falling Astronauts* in his survey of Atomic Culture and the Space Race (in: Rob Latham (ed.): *The Oxford Handbook of Science Fiction*. Oxford: Oxford UP, pp. 340–351), even though he briefly discusses Malzberg's *Beyond Apollo* (ibid., p. 349).

43 Malzberg: *Falling*, p. 182.

result of this attempt is disastrous and confirms the similarities between Busby and Martin: they are both insane. "Got to do it, Busby, [Martin says] wanted to do it myself but couldn't quite make it, turned out that I was one of their goddamned machines, they had their hooks in too deep. But I came close, you can go all the way. Don't listen. Don't listen to any more. Just do it."[44] This is not, of course, what Oakes and the director wanted Martin to tell Busby, but it is surely what Martin thinks. The ravings of a madman, but in their own deranged way also an act of rebellion.

The Falling Astronauts is characterized by an atmosphere of barely contained hysteria. It presents readers with grotesque, almost surreal scenes; it includes the narrator's dreams, or rather nightmares, such as the press conference in the third chapter, where a "mad-eyed reporter"[45] asks all the embarrassing questions "real" reporters never ask. The fact that we are not offered a real ending is consistent with the overall tone of the novel: the texts stops when "the final act [whatever that may be] is [...] exactly thirty-six hours and twenty-five minutes away... and counting".[46] The open ending is remarkably threatening and anguishing.

Malzberg's novel is about the US space program, but also about the Cold War, and he clearly sees a deep, intimate connection between the two, far deeper than Gunn and Wyndham. This is not merely a polemic move, but a choice that anamorphically mirrors historical realities, such as Wernher von Braun's campaign for an armed space station in the early 1950s, the role he played in the Redstone project, or on the other side of the balance of terror, the R-36ORB intercontinental missile built by the USSR and deployed from 1969 to 1983, a weapons system that made nuclear bombing from space a reality.

There is a further layer of meaning in this novel, an allegorical one, in which the Agency is an anamorphic image of the USA and its citizens are all astronauts; mad, alienated astronauts like Martin and Busby. This is a classic metonymical displacement: a part of the country (the Agency, that is, NASA) stands for the whole nation, something that the metaphor of the New Frontier launched by President Kennedy made quite clear to contemporary readers. What Malzberg suggests through his novel is that we are all astronauts, little cogs in a gigantic machine, and that this leads to madness and (possibly nuclear) death.

Surely this was not a message that could be accepted by the science fiction community, busy celebrating the daring feats of the Apollo missions: science fiction writer Bob Shaw declared that "Malzberg's *Beyond Apollo* is, to me, the epitome

44 Ibid., p. 190.

45 Ibid., p. 15.

46 Ibid., p. 191.

of everything that has gone wrong with s[cience] f[iction] in the last ten years or so",[47] a rather harsh judgement that could as well apply to *The Fallen Astronauts*. *Beyond Apollo* (1972) is, to a certain extent, a sequel to the first novel, though there is an unexplained gap, since there is no mention of what happened to Busby and his nuclear weapons. However, it seems that armageddon has not taken place. In the end, there was a mission to Mars that was a total failure (but there is no detailed description of it); then a Venus mission was attempted with a two-man crew in order to save money. Evans, the narrator of the novel, is the only survivor. The Captain did not come back.

Evans is detained in an institution, which may be a mental hospital or a military penitentiary; it is not clearly explained. A neurologist, Claude Forrest, is interrogating him, in order to find out what happened to the Captain, whether he and Evans reached Venus, if there is intelligent life there. Although Evans is always ready to be debriefed and answer Forrest's questions, he keeps changing his version of the facts: the Captain committed suicide (possibly because he had a nervous breakdown or for idealistic reasons); he was compelled to commit suicide by the telepathic inhabitants of Venus; he was killed by Evans; and so on. The different narratives told by Evans are of course mutually inconsistent, so that Forrest resorts to threats in order to force Evans to tell the true story of the mission. Despite this, Evans keeps coming up with a new version every day, only to be discarded the next.

Since the astronaut is detained in what could well be an asylum and is being given treatment – albeit an odd one – by a neurologist, we are induced to think that he is insane, which might explain his behavior and his unreliability as a narrator. However, the text also suggests that Evans may be pretending to be mad, because he knows something so terrible that it must not be revealed. Malzberg's *Beyond Apollo* is therefore a prime example of radical postmodernist ontological uncertainty in a narrative. Through his astronaut, who might be mad or feigning madness, Malzberg not only satirizes the mentality (or dream, or nightmare) of total control and rationality that characterizes the space program (note that *Beyond Apollo* refers to both the Apollo missions and once again the Greek solar god of reason), he also satirizes science fiction itself. In fact, Evans tells us right from the start, at the beginning of the second chapter (the first being only four lines long) that he plans to write a novel about the voyage and describes the captain as he will appear in it. Evans is both an unreliable astronaut, possibly insane, and an unreliable narrator at the same time, but also an unreliable novelist. He

47 Bob Shaw: Telling Like It Isn't. In: *Foundation* 7 & 8 (March 1975), pp. 67–70, here p. 67. The rest of Shaw's review of *Beyond Apollo* is simply scathing.

can therefore be viewed as Malzberg's avatar, spinning a series of aborted narratives of space travel, so that he not only attacks with searing sarcasm the archetypal hero of classic science fiction, but also shows himself as a science fiction author who is ruthlessly tearing his playhouse down, conjuring up and then discarding the classical narrative devices of the genre, from space travel to the hostile aliens.[48]

Such an interpretation is corroborated by the ending: the final chapter[49] is a letter from an editor of the press which is going to publish Evans' novel – whose title is, unsurprisingly, *Beyond Apollo*. This confirms that the deranged astronaut is a science fiction writer, unable or unwilling to tell the straight story Forrest (and us readers) would like to hear (or read).

The third novel in Malzberg's NASA trilogy shows how loose and heterogeneous this triptych is. In *Revelations*, a former astronaut, Walter Monaghan, contacts a TV program called *Revelations* to tell "the Full Story [*sic*] of the agency".[50] Monaghan seems to be an older version of Martin, the protagonist of *The Falling Astronauts*. The novel begins with his letter to the TV program: "[u]ntil my recent discharge [...] from the program [...] I [...] worked my way into one of those pointless liaison jobs which were created for ex-astronauts who got caught in the depression and had nowhere to go".[51]

Though the first chapter of the novel suggests a connection to the first novel of the trilogy, what follows is focused on the life of Hurwitz, one of the assistants of Marvin Martin, a TV talk show host who achieved celebrity thanks to *Revelations*. This is a TV show in which guests are aggressively, sadistically interrogated by Martin and must answer embarrassing questions about their private life. Hurwitz's task is to select the guests, looking for people who have something outrageous and possibly shameful to tell, and at first he dismisses Monaghan. Reading the novel, which delves deep into the workings of reality TV (at a time when the television program *Big Brother* did not yet exist), we almost forget Monaghan and his revelations about the corruption and misery of the space program and its astronauts. But when program ratings decline, Hurwitz is urged by Marvin Martin to find interesting guests, so he retrieves Monaghan's letter and interviews him.

48 This is what Malzberg also does in his most experimental novel, *Galaxies* (1975).

49 Barry N. Malzberg: *Beyond Apollo*. Grand Rapids: Anti-Oedipus 2015, pp. 138–139.

50 Barry N. Malzberg: *Revelations: A Paranoid Novel of Suspense*. New York: Warner 1972, p. 15.

51 Ibid., p. 12.

Hurwitz notices a jarring inconsistency in Monaghan's statements about the space program. He maintains that "we have never gone to the moon, [...] everything [...] was contrived by the government to appear as if we had accomplished what we hadn't through the cunning use of the media and photographic techniques".[52] Only a few days later, he claims that "twelve of the sixty-eight men who have actually flown to the moon are now incurably insane [...]. It is the very quality of the moon experience which has done this to them."[53] The two statements contradict each other: Monaghan thus resembles Evans, the unreliable astronaut in *Beyond Apollo*.

We (and Hurwitz) ultimately discover that Monaghan is an imposter, who then shoots Marvin Martin live on TV during the show, yet *Revelations* does qualify as a part of the trilogy, because it is revealed that there is a conspiracy behind Monaghan, who has had false memories of his life as an astronaut implanted in his brain: even though Monaghan has never been a spaceman, he honestly *believes* he was one.

Much could be said about the fact that the character of Monaghan is evidently inspired by the figures of other, real and purportedly deranged murderers, like Lee Harvey Oswald (there is a reference to the Dallas assassination in chapter 11); that the novel anticipates the conspiracy theories denying the reality of the Moon landing; that the astronaut has become a sort of freak to be shown in a TV program whose purposes "seem less informational than barbaric"[54] as Martin "has used the format only to reduce participants [...] to shattered masks who, shambling parodies of themselves, seem barely capable of human speech by the time that he is ready of them"[55] – so that the machinery of TV is as crushing and alienating as the space agency in *The Falling Astronauts*. However, what is more relevant to us is the fact that an ordinary man like Monaghan can be turned into an astronaut and it is he, the bogus spaceman, who uses the astronaut as a metaphor by applying it to Marvin Martin. Before pulling his gun on Martin, Monaghan accuses him of having never really listened to what the guests of his show answered: "You are listening to the sound of your own voice, that's all: like an astronaut, the tinny, tiny sound of your own voice reverberating back to you endlessly, the echoes collapsing in and out of your skull."[56]

52 Malzberg: *Revelations*, p. 56.
53 Ibid., pp. 56–57.
54 Ibid., p. 124.
55 Ibid.
56 Ibid., p. 135.

If it is true that Malzberg's iconoclastic attack at the US Space Program and its heroes was inspired by J. G. Ballard's dead astronauts, beginning with those in "The Cage of Sand", it is also true that Ballard summed up and somewhat closed the hysterical, grotesque, at times raving epic of the insane spacemen. He did it in 1985, when the heroic age of the Apollo Program was already a glorious and slightly blurry past (and a year before the disaster of the space shuttle Challenger), with his short story "The Man Who Walked on the Moon". Malzberg had surely read Ballard and drawn inspiration from his oneiric, mesmerizing stories from the 1960s; in turn it is likely that Ballard read *Revelations*, inasmuch as both the narrating "I" of his story, a failed journalist and translator living in Ipanema, and the weird character he meets, Commander Scranton, an "impoverished American who claimed to have been an astronaut",[57] evidently derive from Monaghan, the bogus astronaut in Malzberg's novel.

Like Monaghan, Scranton only believes he has walked on the Moon. He may have the physique of the spaceman, with "his long jawed face and stoical pilot's eyes [which] seemed vaguely familiar from the magazine photographs",[58] but is actually "a failed crop-duster from Florida who had lost his pilot's license and whose knowledge of the Apollo flights had been mugged up from newspapers and television programs".[59] The story tells how the narrator befriends Scranton and ultimately replaces him after his death, going to live in his room "above the projection booth of the Luxor Cinema, [his] thoughts drowned by the soundtracks of science-fiction films",[60] and spending his days in the bars along Copacabana Beach, telling his story to the tourists for the price of a drink.

By the end of the story, the anonymous narrating "I" believes that Scranton really was an astronaut, as he "had travelled in space. He had known the loneliness of separation from all other human beings, he had gazed at the empty perspectives that I myself had seen."[61] Loneliness, alienation, despair: although this is not necessarily what real astronauts have experienced and experience in real flights, this is what the figure of the astronaut can embody. The spaceman therefore functions as a metaphor, with all his or her political, social, existential, psychological, even psychiatric implications. A figure which, in Ballard's story, does not herald a bright or frightening future (be it near or remote), as in the other science fiction

57 J. G. Ballard: *The Complete Short Stories*. London: Flamingo 2001, p. 1107.

58 Ibid.

59 Ibid., p. 1108.

60 Ibid., p. 1105.

61 Ibid., p. 1114.

narratives we have dealt with, because Scranton and his substitute actually *were* astronauts. “Already I was aware of a previous career,” muses the narrator, “which my wife and the pressures of everyday life had hidden from me. There were the years of training for a great voyage, and a coastline like that of Cape Canaveral, receding below me.”[62] The epic of space is over and all that is left are memories of the space age. Unsurprisingly, this was the title of a visionary novelette Ballard published in 1982, returning to the abandoned and haunted Cape Canaveral that the British author had already conjured up in the 1960s.

And yet the image, we might say the myth, of the astronaut abides. Ballard was well aware of this, so much so that when he imagined a new zodiac for modern (or postmodern) times in his 1978 short story “Zodiac 2000,” among the new, paradoxical signs that should allow us to make sense of our daily life, such as the sign of the Clones or that of the Cruise Missile, he also proposed the sign of the Astronaut, flying “away across the free skies of inner space”.[63] This is a last, but not at all least, meaning of the mad astronaut: an explorer of the measureless abysses of the human mind, be it individual or collective.

62 Ballard: *The Complete Short Stories*, p. 1115.

63 Ibid., p. 988.

Ansgar Oswald

The Space Traveler

Ambassador, Cult Figure, and Cultural Icon

2015 was an important year in the history of space travel: the year had a number of major anniversaries, including the fiftieth anniversary of the first spacewalk by Alexei Leonov[1] and forty years of international space exploration carried out by the Apollo-Soyuz Test Project since 1975.[2] The opening, on September 18, 2015, of the London Science Museum exhibition "Cosmonauts: Birth of the Space Age", attended by Alexei Leonov, the doyen of astronauts and one of the last great living witnesses from the early pioneering times of space travel, showed that space travel is now an established element of our cultural identity.[3] The London exhibition ended on April 12, 2016 and thus on the fifty-fifth anniversary of the first manned space flight, undertaken by Yuri Gagarin – a particularly appropriate way to commemorate that historical milestone and a cultural event of great significance.

Thanks to the internet, the world can be connected with a few mouse-clicks. It also connects us to space travel, bringing it into our everyday life. Nothing is too far away now. Space travelers themselves are now agents in social media networks

1 Robin McKie: Alexei Leonov, the First Man to Walk in Space: In: *The Guardian*, May 9, 2015. https://www.theguardian.com/science/2015/may/09/alexei-leonov-first-man-to-walk-in-space-soviet-cosmonaut (accessed: August 5, 2017).

2 National Aeronautics and Space Administration: Apollo-Soyuz Test Project. https://imagine.gsfc.nasa.gov/science/toolbox/missions/astp.html (accessed: August 5, 2017) and Mike Wall: Apollo-Soyuz Spawned First Handshake in Space by US-Soviet Crews 40 Years Ago. In: *Space.com*, July 17, 2015. https://www.space.com/29979-apollo-soyuz-test-project-40th-anniversary.html (accessed: August 5, 2017)

3 See http://www.sciencemuseum.org.uk/visitmuseum/Plan_your_visit/exhibitions/cosmonauts (accessed: August 1, 2017).

Fig. 1
Advert campaign *Red Bull Stratos*, using Felix Baumgartner's "Space Jump" from October 2012 as a motive, combined with the slogans "How high you want to fly today" and "Red Bull gives you wiiings".

such as Facebook, Twitter, and YouTube. For example, the current German ESA astronaut Alexander Gerst received around 260,000 likes on Facebook in August 2017 alone.[4] Gerst has become a prominent public figure in social media. Since the famous leap of the Austrian stuntman and BASE jumper Felix Baumgartner in October 2012, from almost 39,000 meters in the stratosphere, which was sponsored by the company Red Bull, he has also become part of everyday consumer consciousness. Baumgartner did set a certain benchmark; the promotional poster emblazoned with the advertising slogan "How high do you want to fly today? Red Bull gives you wiiings" (Fig. 1) could be seen everywhere.[5]

But sometimes simply wearing a spacesuit is enough for a (handsome) man to ensnare (equally flawless) women (Fig. 2). It is not the man who catches the eye, but rather his unusual attire; the human being is thus an arbitrary presence, only an adornment. Without doing anything special with the models, but relying

4 See https://de-de.facebook.com/ESAAlexGerst/ (accessed: August 1, 2017).

5 In the original German: "Wie hoch wollen Sie heute hinaus? Red Bull verleiht Flüüügel." See here Fig. 1 and for example the fragments of a similar advertisement poster in a piece by German artist Jens Lorenzen: *The Wall I, Element plus 14*, 2015. See http://www.jens-lorenzen.com/ (accessed: March 20, 2019).

Fig. 2
Axe advert campaign from 2013.

on a clear advertising message, a famous brand can thus effectively use men to sell personal care products. The technology of space exploration is per se something 'cool'. The space suit with a suitably handsome face inside it can compete effortlessly with muscular young men posing shirtless for a cosmetic product.[6] Advertising scenes with space imagery are rather rare in advertising and even rarer are spacemen themselves. However, this is a telling comment on our image-driven world where the spaceman appears to be something very special. When the spaceman does feature, such as the astronaut Buzz Aldrin – a seasoned space

6 See http://brandchannel.com/2013/04/03/axe-saves-face-with-skincare-line-as-brand-gets-ready-to-head-to-space/ (accessed: August 1, 2017).

Fig. 3: The 23 aspiring astronauts, chosen during the Axe marketing campaign in 2013, with veteran astronat Buzz Aldrin.

traveler, seen posing in the middle of a group of people chosen by the Axe Space Academy for a trip into space in Fig. 3[7] – then he can compete on equal terms with German national soccer team coach, Joachim "Jogi" Löw, who featured in advertising campaigns for Nivea. Both are successful representatives of their own world, whose innate superiority ensures that the psychology behind the advertising campaigns is successful.[8]

Furthermore, space exploration can give the impression of being a high performance sport. Given the levels of physical fitness, the tough training programs, and the work expected of an astronaut, this is not as strange a supposition as it may seem. Space expeditions are grueling affairs, challenging a person mentally and physically. By the time the forty-third and forty-fourth space missions on board the International Space Station finished in mid-September 2015, Gennady Ivanovich Padalka, who had already been commander of the orbital station on

7 See http://www.digitalspy.com/fun/news/a450318/buzz-aldrin-launches-lynx-space-academy-video/#~piTUIBr9wfqNqo (accessed: August 1, 2017).

8 See for example the press statement at https://www.beiersdorf.de/presse/news/local/de/all-news/2016/06/2016-06-07-vertragsverlaengerung-jogi (accessed: August 1, 2017).

four occasions, had set a new record for time spent in space, at a total of nearly 900 days. Earlier that year, ESA astronaut Samantha Cristoforetti broke the record for a European astronaut with the longest stay on the International Space Station: 199 uninterrupted days in space. Viewed in this light, space travel can be regarded as a kind of Olympic sport.

The German broadcasting station *Deutsche Welle's* complaint that the cultural development of space is still in its infancy, because so far only Canadian astronaut Chris Hadfield has dared to play guitar in the space station (he publicly released a zero-gravity music video tribute to David Bowie's 1969 song *Space Oddity*), is a sign of false expectations and a general lack of observation.[9] The cultural development of the universe has in fact been happening right from the start of space travel, now more than ever, but perhaps in a different way than was expected. Although it was not the famous German TV chef Tim Mälzer cooking on board the space station, the ESA astronaut Samantha Cristoforetti still had a potential audience of millions on YouTube when preparing "one of her bonus food recipes".[10] A few months after Alexander Gerst's return from space in November 2014, the *Süddeutsche Zeitung* summed up his career with the following headline: "From shy scientist to national hero: the astronaut Alexander Gerst is the best advertisement space travel could ask for."[11] The enthusiasm of the *Süddeutsche Zeitung* is reminiscent of the febrile atmosphere during the pioneering phase of space travel.

Right from the beginning, space travel was a matter of prestige with the space traveler as the protagonist: initially as an explorer, then as a conqueror, a national hero, and symbol of cultural superiority with claims to moral and physical leadership. The space traveler was thus following in the footsteps of earlier adventurers, such as João Vaz Corte-Real, allegedly one of the first men to discover America in the Renaissance, Christopher Columbus, and Amerigo Vespucci.[12]

9 Marie Todeskino: Auf kultureller Mission im Weltall. In: *Deutsche Welle*, August 24, 2013, http://www.dw.com/de/auf-kultureller-mission-im-weltall/a-17024364 (accessed: August 1, 2017).

10 *Cooking in Space: Mackerel, Quinoa and Leek Cream Tortilla* (US 2015, ESA/NASA). http://www.esa.int/spaceinvideos/Videos/2015/06/Cooking_in_space_mackerel_quinoa_and_leek_cream_tortilla (accessed: August 1, 2017).

11 Josef Kelnberger: Botschafter aus dem All. In: *Süddeutsche Zeitung*, May 11, 2015: http://www.sueddeutsche.de/panorama/raumfahrt-botschafter-aus-dem-all-1.2475039?reduced=true (accessed: May 15, 2015).

12 Ulli Kulke: Der Mönch, der Kolumbus den Weg wies. In: *Die Welt*, January 29, 2013. https://www.welt.de/geschichte/article113201148/Der-Moench-der-Kolumbus-den-Weg-wies.html (accessed: August 4, 2017). See also Siegfried Schoppe: *Heinrich der Seefahrer, Kolumbus und Magellan: Planung, Versuch und Irrtum bei der Entdeckung der Neuen Welt durch Portugal*

On April 12, 1961, Yuri Gagarin, a Soviet air force colonel, flew into outer space. After his return to Earth he was celebrated as a hero, living proof of the superiority of a whole country's social system. The Soviet space traveler, the cosmonaut, was from then on regarded as a role model for the ideal socialist human being. It was a Soviet citizen who had turned the dream of a journey into outer space, first mentioned in literature by the ancient Greek satirist Lucian of Samosata (120– after 180 AD), into reality.[13] However, something else had happened too, which took humankind beyond the temporary and fragile nature of everyday life and which changed the world forever.

The measure of all things

Like Nicolaus Copernicus' observations during the Renaissance, the first space flight profoundly changed all previous perceptions of our home planet. For the first time, a human being had stepped away from his earthly perspective and no longer looked out on the world, so to speak, from the windows of his home on Earth. He had now seen the Earth from the outside as his earthly home, as if viewing it from beyond his front garden. Gagarin was in the protective shell of his spaceship, weightless and detached from the Earth. He described his impression of what he observed while in orbit at a press conference in Moscow on April 15, 1961, only three days after his return from space: "I orbited the Earth in the spaceship. And during this weightless travel around our planet I saw from all

und Spanien vor 500 Jahren. Norderstedt: BoD 2012, pp. 96–77. In 1492, when Columbus made his first landfall on his journey westward, he was convinced he had reached India. Until the end of his life he was convinced that he had reached Asia: Robert H. Fuson (ed.): *Das Logbuch des Christoph Kolumbus: Die authentischen Aufzeichnungen des großen Entdeckers*. Bergisch-Gladbach: Lübbe 1989, p. 56. It was only after the voyages of discovery of Amerigo Vespucci for the Spanish and Portuguese that the cosmographer Matthias Ringmann called him the discoverer of the New World in his work *Cosmographiae Introductio* (1507). This led to the German cartographer Martin Waldseemüller drawing a new world map, which was the first to show "America" as a country separate from Asia. Vaz Corte-Real, as well as Columbus and Cabot and other later explorers, was searching for a shorter route from Europe to Asia. There is some evidence that in the race between the Portuguese kings and the kingdom of Castille and Aragon (the House of Trastámara) for supremacy, the written history of the period and the story of Columbus' role were first and foremost influenced by later historical developments, as the House of Trastámara (later of Habsburg) established its dominance in the New World. The history of the discovery of America is thus to be read with some caution, not least because of the differing accounts in the sources.

13 See Lucian of Samosata: Ἰκαρομένιππος or The Skyman. In: *Six Dialogues of Lucian*, transl. from the Greek and with an Introduction by Sidney T. Irwin. London: Methuen 1894, pp. 1–28.

sides how wonderful and unique our Earth is and from here I address an urgent message to the world: mankind, let us preserve and increase this beauty rather than destroy it."[14]

Gagarin's simple observation marks a new dimension in the experience of space and yet in principle upholds the visual experiences that had shaped life since the time of the Renaissance. It recalls the first recorded modern description of a landscape, preserved in the family letters of Francesco Petrarca (Petrarch) from 1336. In these letters, the humanist and poet enthusiastically describes the visual experience of seeing the depth of the landscape below him during an ascent of Mont Ventoux in Provence, which seemed to open up before him, thus articulating the discovery of spatial infinity. This consciousness of space led to works of art and architecture that powerfully depicted perspective in a new way.[15]

The idea of infinity as a way of thinking at the time, according to the philosopher and linguist Hanna-Barbara Gerl, was the prerequisite "to understand the world in terms of knowledge and its consequent actions as an object which was at the disposal of mankind".[16] In essence, it was the rediscovery of an idea of human beings in relation to their surroundings that can already be identified in the theory of Roman architect, Marcus Vitruvius Pollio, from the first century BCE. His work, *De architectura libri decem*, describes the perfect proportion between the human being and architecture. It is the only surviving manual of architectural theory from classical antiquity and even today still has a valid theoretical basis in architecture.[17] It was only by recourse to ancient texts that humankind created a value structure that has enabled humans to anchor themselves as the measure of all things in the spatial perspective and to therefore justify their role as the sovereign creator of the cosmos.

14 My translation. Yuri Alekseyevich Gagarin on his press conference in Moscow on April 15, 1961: The quote is from a leaflet stored in the RSC Energija Museum. The original Russian is: "Облетев Землю на корабле-спутнике, я увидел, как прекрасна наша планета. Люди, будем хранить и приумножать эту красоту, а не разрушать её!": https://ru-ru.facebook.com/rianru/photos/a.10152367356929271.1073742828.325794294270/10152367357094271/ (accessed: August 5, 2017).

15 Hanna-Barbara Gerl: *Einführung in die Philosophie der Renaissance*. Darmstadt: WBG 1989, p. 33.

16 Ibid., p. 34: "[…] die Welt in Wissen und daraus folgenden Handeln als Gegen-Stand menschlicher Verfügung zu begreifen".

17 Marcus Vitruvius Pollio: *De architectura libri decem: Zehn Bücher über die Architektur*, transl. from the Latin by Curt Fensterbusch. Darmstadt: WBG 1981. It is for example quoted by Andres Lepik in: *Das Architekturmodell in Italien 1335–1550*. Worms: Wernersche Verlagsgesellschaft 1994, pp. 120–126, here p. 121.

The connection between the ancient desire to fly into space and the search for the guiding idea of modern space travel is therefore only understandable from the viewpoint of Renaissance humanism, which began at the turn of the fourteenth century. Let us go into further detail.

Until this time, the idea of a journey into space was seen as immoral. For a scholar in the eleventh century such as Manegold of Lautenbach, it was clear "that God had not destined human beings to explore the movement of the stars and the concourse of the planets".[18] However, the deepening rift over the interpretation of Creation, between religious interpretation on the one hand and scientific observation on the other, subsequently led to demands for a rational explanation of the cosmos. These demands were a result of altered human perceptions caused by the rebirth of social, intellectual, and economic life in European cities at the end of thirteenth century.

By the fifteenth century, Italian humanist Giannozzo Manetti had declared the human being to be the sovereign of the cosmos and thus anchored humans philosophically as the epitome of Creation's divine proportions, and thus as a measure of all things from a spatial perspective. The image of the human, as defined by him, in the Renaissance ideas of "dignity and sublimity" (see the title of his treatise from 1452 *De dignitate et excellentia hominis*)[19] indicates the direction of his thought. His contemporary, Giovanni Pico della Mirandola, supports this theory when he interprets human beings as microcosms which unite all the qualities of the Universe in their bodies, with their rational souls and inner spirits, and consequently above everything else as agents who are entirely responsible for their actions. Mirandola thus regarded the essence of human beings, namely their position in the world and their free will, as a significant trait of their dignity.[20]

Individual conscience was thus the final arbiter of human action. Subjective perception was based on observation and close examination as a path towards reality

18 Manegold von Lautenbach: Liber contra Wolfelmum. In: Wilfried Hartmann (ed.): *Quellen zur deutschen Geistesgeschichte*, vol. 8. Weimar: Böhlau 1972, reprint: Munich: Monumenta Germaniae Historica 1991, p. 89; quoted in Kurt Flasch: *Einführung in die Philosophie des Mittelalters*. Darmstadt: WBG 1987, pp. 77–78: "[...] daß Gott den Menschen nicht dazu bestimmt hat, den Lauf der Sterne und das Zusammentreffen der Planeten zu erforschen".

19 See the critical edition by Elizabeth Riley Leonard (ed.): *Ianotii Manetti de dignitate et excellentia hominis*. Antenore: Padova 1975.

20 Giovanni Pico della Mirandola: De hominis dignitate. In: Herbert-Werner Rüssel (ed.): *Über die Würde des Menschen (dt.) nebst einigen Briefen und der Lebensbeschreibung Pico della Mirandolas*. Amsterdam: Pantheon 1940, p. 49 et seq. Here I am following Gerl: *Einführung*, pp. 65–68.

and thus towards knowledge, with the eye, the primary sense organ, considered the instrument for correct judgment. Perspective had already been demonstrated clearly in the paintings of Giotto di Bondone and Duccio di Buoninsegna in the early fourteenth century, and was described as a theoretical concept for the first time by the Italian author on art and architecture, Leon Battista Alberti, in 1435. It was then elevated to become one of the seven already existing liberal arts through scientific discussion by the Italian mathematician and Franciscan friar Luca Pacioli, in his *De Divina proportione* of about 1497 (printed in Venice, 1509).[21]

The acquisition of pragmatic skills was regarded as a necessary accompaniment to the theory of the human being as being capable of self-determination. Geometry, mathematics and the natural sciences henceforth determined the rules and methods of the optical exploration of outer space and the technical progress for potentially mastering it. The human being was always imagined right at the center of all this, the starting point and main reference. The rational and practical analysis of space began to be evident in architecture and art. The polymath Leon Battista Alberti, for example, developed spatial awareness from the disciplines of architecture, painting, and sculpture – endeavors guided by the human eye – into a new view of the world. The function of the human being in the cosmos was redefined and the standard values for the analysis of space were laid down. The discovery of spatial infinity and the definition of the human as a self-determined rational being in early Italian Renaissance humanism thus formed the spiritual and cultural basis for the technical feats that have led to the space travel of today.

The Renaissance saw the birth of the idea of human progress: the human being leads the way. If we take the phrase of the nobleman Jaques in William Shakespeare's play *As You Like It*: "All the world's a stage",[22] then space travelers are perhaps the most bizarre characters, because they play multiple roles that are sometimes contradictory.

21 Gerl: *Einführung*, pp. 128-130; Hannah Baader: Das fünfte Element oder Malerei als achte Kunst: Das Portrait des Mathematikers Fra Luca Pacioli. In: Valeska von Rosen / Klaus Krüger / Rudolf Preimesberger (eds): *Der stumme Diskurs der Bilder: Reflexionsformen des Ästhetischen in der Kunst der Frühen Neuzeit*. Berlin: Deutscher Kunstverlag 2003, pp. 177–203.

22 William Shakespeare: *Mr. William Shakespeare's Comedies, Histories & Tragedies: Published According to the True Originall Copies*. 1st Folio ed. London: Isaac Jaggard and Ed Blount 1623.

The explorer, the national hero, the ambassador, the advertising medium

Space exploration cannot be separated from the political and social developments in the world, but is rather a mirror image of them, only in a different dimension. It is a product of military development in the arms race between two competing political systems, whose secular spheres of influence emerged from the new world order after the end of World War II. Accordingly, Soviet-trained cosmonauts, like previous explorers, are pioneers of a new era, actors in this power struggle, and also messengers of the future. The same applies to their non-Soviet counterparts, astronauts.

The view of the world that Gagarin described, in his capacity as a messenger of the future, is both an unspoken message about the triumph of technological progress and also a moral message to us concerning the Earth, namely that we should keep a balance between reshaping it and protecting it.[23] His message was repeated with increasing frequency by other space travelers later, who also appealed for humanity to change its ways. Their special insight was that the Earth is not only beautiful, but also a fragile whole, which we should preserve as a place worth living in for us and for future generations. The cosmic perception of space was quickly followed by the awareness that in the infinite darkness of space, only our Earth is unique – a view, confirmed by all space travelers, including astronaut Scott Kelly with his gallery of spectacular photos from 2015 and 2016 on social media.[24]

The cosmonaut as a Soviet ideal human being

The social significance of role the space traveler becomes comprehensible through the figure of the cosmonaut. When Gagarin set off into space in the spaceship Vostok on April 12, 1961, he did so in order to demonstrate the superiority of the socialist worldview. The sheer courage needed to carry out such a venture was a success in itself and public enthusiasm was palpable in the frenzied reaction to Gagarin's successful mission. After the first successful launch of a Soviet

23 Gagarin made this statement as a figurehead of technical progress and yet was fully aware of the need to preserve the world: http://www.azquotes.com/author/5270-Yuri_Gagarin (accessed: August 5, 2017)

24 Jason Davis: In Praise of Scott Kelly, Astronaut and Human Being. In: *The Guardian*, March 4, 2016. https://www.theguardian.com/commentisfree/2016/mar/04/in-praise-of-scott-kelly-astronaut-nasa (accessed: August 3, 2017). Scott Kelly: On His Year in Space: "Maybe You Do Go Bananas". In: *The Guardian*, March 5, 2016. https://www.theguardian.com/science/2016/mar/04/nasa-astronaut-scott-kelly-year-in-space-interview (03.08.2017).

Sputnik in 1957, it was already clear for the writer Stefan Heym in his 1959 publication, *Das kosmische Zeitalter* (The Cosmic Era): "The days are over when the imagination of writers rushed ahead of life into the realm of utopia. Physicists and engineers have seized the initiative and make the dreams of utopia become reality. Their artificial planet has conquered Earth's gravity field, has kissed the moon while passing it and orbits the sun, red flagged."[25] Astronautics was now part of the "new, larger industrial revolution",[26] which would create a golden age with new people in a new society as its economic foundation. The socialist world had its new hero who personified the superiority of its own system. In 1953, after Stalin's death, the revolutionary phase of communism in the Soviet Union was buried forever and with Nikita Khrushchev an entirely new one had begun, which resulted in radical attempts to modernize society. The structure of this modern society was based on the idea of a move towards the second phase of a communist society that would be the realization of a principle described by Karl Marx, in which all people would live free from all economic, political, social, and religious constraints, with space travel being the highest expression of this freedom. Following Lenin, the education of a new human being was an integral part of communist politics and the cosmonaut was the eagerly anticipated model human being.[27]

Moreover, the astronaut's perception of the Earth as a whole entity, held together by the forces of nature, which know no boundaries, was reflected in the global claims of the Soviet Union, which it used to compete with the USA, the leading power of its capitalist opponents. Based in this world, but at the same time displaced from it, the cosmonaut provided the atheist socialist world with a figure who crossed all cultural, ethnic, and national boundaries in the multi-ethnic Soviet Union. It also provided a tangible character for the abstract idea of the Soviet human as an ideal of the collective human development towards a higher stage of existence – in other words, a figure around whom everyone could easily unite.

25 My translation. Stefan Heym: *Das kosmische Zeitalter.* Berlin: Tribüne 1959, pp. 9–10. The quote in the original German is: "Die Zeiten sind vorbei, wo die Phantasie der Schriftsteller dem Leben vorauseilte, ins Reich der Utopie. Die Physiker und Ingenieure haben die Initiative an sich gerissen und machen die Träume der Utopisten zur Wirklichkeit. Ihr künstlicher Planet hat das Schwerefeld Erde überwunden, den Mond im Vorbeiflug geküßt und umkreist die Sonne, rot bewimpelt."

26 Ibid., p. 21.

27 Ansgar Oswald: Kosmische Architekturikonen in der UDSSR: Architektur und Design als Mittel gesellschaftlicher Inszenierung und politischer Propaganda. In: Philipp Meuser (ed.): *Architektur für die russische Raumfahrt.* Berlin: DOM 2013, pp. 37–91, here p. 63.

The cosmonaut was a star, a celebrity, and at the same time ideally suited to take the leitmotif of socialism to its next stage of development. In photography, painting, sculpture, and graphic design, the cosmonaut was a dominant image in social culture and in everyday life. The cosmonaut influenced architecture and urban design, in which the modern methods of construction and design based on rational functionalism shaped "new housing for a new Society",[28] and created an urban landscape that not only provided a suitable living environment, but also had a striking appearance that looked to the infinity of space.[29]

At the heart of all this were community buildings designed to catch the eye – cultural sites, administrative buildings, sports facilities, and public buildings such as television towers that resembled sculptures and sometimes looked like flying saucers or rockets (Fig. 4); these buildings took their place in everyday life as messengers from outer space.[30] At the same time the architecture of Soviet modernism was, especially in the Caucasian Soviet republics, rooted in the local region by using abstracted traditional design patterns. Regional politics and the Socialist International thus found a common language of the optimistic belief in progress, which was in itself typical of the 1960s and 1970s. This optimism continued to determine architecture until the end of the 1980s and the belief in progress inspired design ideas featuring the iconic figure of the astronaut that were immortalized in the socialist world on a cultural and visual level through the ubiquity of art: from postage stamps to monuments.[31]

The cosmonaut elevated scientific ideals into the sphere of the sacred with sometimes striking allusions to ancient motifs. Next to the ideological trinity of Karl Marx, Friedrich Engels, and Vladimir Lenin came the trinity of the visionary masterminds of Soviet spaceflight, whose achievements were scientifically measurable: the Soviet rocket scientist and pioneer of the astronautic theory Konstantin Tsiolkovsky, the technical trailblazer and rocket designer Sergei Korolev, and the space pioneer Yuri Gagarin. Even in the architecture of the street, cosmonauts were omnipresent, represented as savior-like figures who, thanks to their ascent to the heavens, were leading the people to a higher stage

28 Hans Scharoun 1946, quoted in Annegret Burg: Der Spreebogen: Ort, Geschichte und Vorgaben des Wettbewerbs. In: Felix Zwoch (ed.): *Hauptstadt Berlin: Parlamentsviertel im Spreebogen (Bauwelt).* Berlin: Birkhäuser 1993, pp. 20–35, here p. 33: "Wir bauen eine neue Gesellschaft, aber diese Gesellschaft darf nicht in die Gehäuse der alten kriechen. Wir müssen ihr neue Gehäuse schaffen."

29 Annegret Burg / Maria Antonietta Grippa: *Stadtbild Berlin: Identität und Wandel.* Berlin: Wasmuth 1991, pp. 57–58.

30 Oswald: Kosmische Architekturikonen, pp. 55–84.

31 Ibid.

Fig. 4
Terxiev Tsarucov & Semashko architects: TV Tower, Tashkent, 1978–1985.

of development. As Tsiolkovsky once wrote: "The Earth is the cradle of humanity, but mankind cannot stay in the cradle forever."[32]

The philosophical interpretation of the future had found its concrete power in scientific rational design, as the relief at the Museum of Cosmonautics shows. There is no sculpture of Lenin on the Lenin Prospect in Moscow, but instead a majestic, futuristic one of Yuri Gagarin. It is made of titanium and stands on a

32 Dave Dooling: *Konstantin E. Tsiolkovsky: The Father of Astronautics and Rocket Dynamics*. http://www.nmspacemuseum.org/halloffame/detail.php?id=27 (accessed: August 4, 2017). In the original Russian: "Земля – колыбель человечества, но нельзя вечно оставаться в колыбели."

Fig. 5: Pavel Bondarenko / Yakov Belopolsky / F. M. Gazhevsky / A. F. Sudakov: The Yuri Gagarin Monument at the Lenin Prospect in Moscow, 1980. Titanium, 42.5 meters high.

38-meter high column, also clad with titanium (Fig. 5). A monument conceived for eternity that, over the course of time, continues to demonstrate that the cosmonaut is a role model and that space travel is a technical feat that will both survive all earthly social conditions and act as neutralizing force on them.

Once the epitome of a new age, in 1975 the role of the cosmonaut changed to become a pioneer of peace and a harbinger of international understanding. With the launch of the joint Soviet-American Soyuz-Apollo project in July 1975, the race for domination in space ended. The former opponents now became partners for the first time, even before signing the CSCE Helsinki Final Act the same year. It was the beginning of space travel as an international project of civilization, which continued, on the Soviet side, with the Intercosmos program of international space travel. This program reached far beyond the Soviet sphere of influence and thus laid the foundation for today's cooperation. However, the ascent of the human being goes beyond all socio-political and scientific aspects and is essentially a journey towards self-knowledge.

The cosmonaut as an artist

Cosmonauts may be the measure of all things, but they also have earthly claims to a reasonable level of comfort, because a "human being cannot fly into space sitting on a toilet"[33] as Sergei Korolev, the legendary chief designer of the OKB-1 design office for rockets and spaceships (today known as RKK Energija), once responded to complaints. He instructed the architect Galina Balashova to remedy the situation and she created a design for the interior of the three-seater spaceships "in which the cosmonauts can live."[34] Balashova not only gave the spaceships and the orbital stations a clearly defined and coherently designed unity, but also the landing capsules, which, in their functional and aesthetic harmony, created earthly living rooms inside objects designed for the conquest of space. In 1975, when the US astronauts from the Soyuz-Apollo program entered the spaceship Soyuz 19 for the first time, they remarked: "We haven't yet achieved such aesthetic harmony in our own space technology." The creation of working and living areas, making the spaceship and the orbital station like flying houses in space, clearly marks the cultural conquest of space.[35]

This conquest was also achieved through the artistic work by space travelers themselves. With the mechanical eye of the camera lens, space travelers can capture the whole Earth set in the darkness of the universe through their unique view of the infinite perspective of space. Through careful observation they can experience the Earth in its radiant beauty and vitality as the origin and source of all forms of life, but at the same time they can see precisely, from this cosmic viewpoint, all its fragility and the threat the humans pose to it. As eyewitnesses to what is happening, they are both credible witnesses and at the same time ambassadors who can cut across all human, cultural, religious and national boundaries.[36]

33 My translation. Maryna Demydovets: Erste Architektin der Raumschiffe, Auftrag mit Seltenheitswert: Galina Balaschowa gestaltete Räume für das Leben in einer anderen Welt. In: Philipp Meuser, *Architektur für die russische Raumfahrt*. Berlin: DOM 2013, pp. 132–159, here pp.132–134: "Ein Mensch kann nicht auf einer Toilette sitzend ins All fliegen."

34 My translation. Ibid., p. 134: "[...] einen Entwurf von einem Raumschiff [...], in dem die Kosmonauten wohnen können".

35 My translation. Ibid., p. 139: "[...] eine derartige ästhetische Harmonie in der Weltraumtechnik haben wir nicht erreicht".

36 See for example the "Dear Moon" project by the Japanese entrepreneur, billionaire, and art collector Yusaku Maezawa, who plans to go to the moon in 2023 with the private US space agency SpaceX, taking a group of artists with him, who will then create art works, reflecting and representing their view of the Earth. See https://dearmoon.earth/ (accessed: September 27, 2018).

These personal photographic records of humanity's deep-seated fascination for our earthly home are works of art. At the same time, space travel has opened up a sense of perspective urgently required if we are to fulfil the global mission set out in Agenda 21 of the 1992 UN Conference in Rio de Janeiro: "Think globally – act locally".[37] According to this mission, instead of thinking on a simplistic global level, the regional diversity of nature and the cultures of our planet should be strengthened and preserved for our children. Could it be that astronauts will play a role in this universal mission as ethical teachers and as role models of modern citizens of the world? Will they one day officially assume the role of UN ambassadors for the largest cultural challenge facing humanity?
Progress as a symbolic term for a better future is not a socialist concept. With its accompanying and universally applicable humanist moral values and its perception of the Earth from the perspective of spatial infinity, it is in fact one that stands for the cosmopolitanism that evolved during the humanism of the Renaissance and with which the Enlightenment of the eighteenth century entered today's modern era. The space traveler personifies the fulfilment of the greatest human dream and yet at the same time space flight has led human beings back to the question of their own origins. Whatever human beings might choose to call themselves as travelers in the universe, they still belong to the Earth and are committed to it. With this visionary self-knowledge, they have the best chance of fulfilling humanity's dream of its future.

37 Ernst Ulrich von Weizsäcker: *Erdpolitik. Ökologische Realpolitik an der Schwelle zum Jahrhundert der Umwelt*. Darmstadt: WBG 1992, pp. 119–123. "Think globally – act locally!" is the guiding principle of the local Agenda 21 of one major objective of the United Nations Conference on Environment and Development (UNCED) in Rio de Janeiro in 1992: Eick von Ruschkowski: Lokale Agenda 21 in Deutschland – eine Bilanz. In: Bundeszentrale für politische Bildung, *Aus Politik und Zeitgeschichte*, B 31-32/2002. https://www.bpb.de/apuz/26785/lokale-agenda-21-in-deutschland-eine-bilanz?p=all (accessed: May 12, 2019).

Colleen Boyle

Through the Eyes of the Astronaut

Mediator of the Human Imagination

> The process of understanding nature as well as the happiness that man feels in understanding – that is, the conscious realization of new knowledge – seems [...] to be based on a correspondence, a 'matching' of inner images pre-existent in the human psyche with external objects and their behavior.
> Wolfgang Pauli[1]

Photographic images made by the National Aeronautics and Space Administration (NASA) are observations driven by scientific investigation but also unwitting portals to the place that we call "space". Although the majority of photographic images produced by NASA are highly automated – belonging more specifically to the category of remote sensing – those made by human astronauts provide a unique perceptual link to outer space. From the pioneering photographs of Earth made by the Mercury astronauts to images of astronauts aboard the International Space Station, it is the images produced of and by astronauts that ultimately allow us to imagine a world of which we have no direct experience. In this manner, we all become astronauts.

1 Wolfgang Pauli quoted in Harry Robins: *The Scientific Image: From Cave to Computer*. New York: Abrams 1992, p. 147.

The astronaut-angel and the transcendental I/eye

Existentialist Mikel Dufrenne claims that the "advent of representation occurs with the upsurge of space and time"[2] and therefore coming to terms with the form and function of imagination will be a topic of discourse until such a time when human consciousness can observe itself from a position that remains outside the manifold of perception. The possibility of this ever occurring seems absurd. To be outside the manifold of perception would surely be a place so disorienting as to induce a form of blind madness, or, conversely, a brief moment of absolute clarity, in which all is instantly seen. If there is any being that has come close to such an experience it is the astronaut, one of a handful of humans who travels physically beyond the known limits of what has been perceived. The astronaut takes our imagination with them and allows us a brief moment of looking back upon ourselves through their space-borne eyes.

I shall begin my discourse, however, not with astronauts, but with their analogous partner: the angel. Piero della Francesca's painting of 1474, *Madonna di Senigallia* (Urbino, Galleria Nazionale delle Marche, 1474; Fig. 1) depicts the Virgin and Child with accompanying angels on either side. My mother – someone with quite an active imagination – once told me that she thought the angel on the left was wearing an astronaut's helmet. Although I agreed that the curve of his hair into his collar did in fact resemble the shape of an astronaut's helmet, I stopped short of agreeing that it looked as if he *was* wearing one. In retrospect, I had missed picking up on a key way in which our imagination works with images, however, my mother's fruitful vision did lead me to consider how astronauts and angels operate within the parameters of their extraordinary occupations.

According to Christian tradition,[3] an angel is a messenger of God, an intermediary capable of moving between two distinct worlds: the unseen realm of Heaven and the terrestrial world of humankind. In Piero della Francesca's painting, the angel to the left stands in a doorway, quite literally upon the threshold between two spaces. The world from whence he may have come is shown as light cast through a window, illuminating the chamber directly behind him. This ethereal, light-filled world will never be directly accessed, never seen with our own eyes, but the angel carries the truth of its presence, of its reality.

The astronaut too is caught haphazardly between a known world and an unknown void, between the seen and the unseen. Prior to the early astronaut

2 Mikel Dufrenne: Imagination. In: Sunhil Manghani / Arthur Piper / Jon Simons (eds): *Images: A Reader*. London: Sage 2006, p. 138.

3 Angels of this description are also known in the Jewish and Islamic faiths.

Fig. 1: Piero della Francesca: *Madonna di Senigallia*, 1474. Oil on panel, 67 x 53.5 cm, Galleria Nazionale delle Marche, Urbino.

missions, NASA sent automated eyes in the form of remote sensors, catching but a glimpse of the greater ocean upon which humankind, like the earliest of Earthly explorers, was about to embark.[4] Machines sent back data, claiming the reality of these new starlit locations via the veracity of the photographic image. The exterior world of our solar system and beyond was not constructed by "direct sensory examination but through a mental survey of its 'clear and distinct'

4 The correlation between early explorers of the Earth and space exploration is further taken up in Valerie Neal: *Where Next Columbus? The Future of Space Exploration*. New York: Oxford UP 1994.

Fig. 2
Gordon Cooper: Charles (Pete) Conrad aboard Gemini V, 1965.

representation",[5] piece by piece, frame by frame, and self-assuredly predicated on that transcendental I/eye of Western modes of representation that have kept us at an objective distance from reality since Plato's cave.

Few humans living today will ever directly experience space travel. No matter how many images of space we might encounter or how well our inner schema of space might be developed, a gap will still remain in our experience and understanding. Something will always remain unseen and there will always be a gap between reality and its representation, but perhaps the astronaut – like the angel – can provide a bridge via which we can traverse the chasm with our imaginations.

When astronaut Gordon Cooper took a photograph of his crewmate Charles Conrad on their Gemini 5 mission in 1965 (Fig. 2), he showed us a man caught between two worlds: the known, and the unknown. He achieved this, not by following any prescriptive NASA directive or mission photography schedule, but through an awareness of the effects of light on his subject that belied previous

5 Jonathan Crary: *Techniques of the Observer: On Vision and Modernity in the Nineteenth Century.* Massachusetts: MIT Press 1990, p. 46.

photographic experience and an artistic sensibility.[6] The resulting portrait sees Conrad appear before the bright cabin window as a man reckoning with the reality of the world, caught within the interior of a space capsule and riddled with doubt. Here, in Cooper's portrait of Conrad, the subject turns his helmeted head from the window to ask us: *Can you believe what I'm seeing?* Unlike the gaze of Piero della Francesca's angel, which confidently delivers an answer, Conrad turns to us with very human doubt. I would like to propose that it is in fact this doubt, this need to understand, that invites the Earth-bound viewer to imaginatively go with the astronaut to an unknown territory littered with premade images and with many more yet to come. They are our conduit into space; threshold riders to the stars.

> And I think of your eyes in the dark
> And I see the star
> And I look to the light
> And I might wonder right where you are[7]

The intermediary role of imagination

Human imagination is difficult to define and has been subject to much discussion since antiquity. One philosopher who studied the imagination in great depth was Scotsman David Hume. For Hume, not only did imagination allow us to see things in our 'mind's eye', it played a key mediatory role in how we come to understand the world and its objects. He thought it did so by joining ideas together, not randomly, but by linking one idea to another in a natural order. Exactly how these strings of ideas were brought together was left somewhat vague by Hume, but he did describe three different qualities ideas may contain that enable them to be connected: "resemblance, contiguity in time and space, and causal connection".[8] He described the attraction between ideas as akin to some kind of force, like gravity or magnetism, and that its "effects are everywhere conspicuous; but as to its causes, they are mostly unknown,

6 In fact, Cooper's handling of the medium was so good that Les Gaver, former director of photography at NASA public affairs, referred to it as "the best … almost magazine-quality". See Ron Shick Julia Van Haaften: *The View from Space: American Astronaut Photography 1962–1972.* New York: Potter 1988, p. 12.

7 Pete Shelley: Homosapien (*Homosapien*, 1981, Island Records).

8 Mary Warnock: *Imagination*. Berkeley: U of California P 1976, p. 17.

and must be resolved into original qualities of human nature", which he then claimed he would not pretend to explain.[9]

Despite stopping short of a full explanation of its machinations, Hume leaves the distinct impression that imagination is an *active and constructive* function that allows us contact with an external reality and the concept of a contiguity of existence. He also interrogated how imagination might operate over space and time, claiming that the degree of intensity of a mental image was contingent upon the proximity of an object spatially or temporally. The closer in time, the more vivid the mental image would be. Likewise, something just outside the house is easier to imagine than something far away. However, more interestingly – at least in the case of astronauts and angels – Hume also allows for imagination at a distance and describes how the mind can become "excited by the necessity to overcome obstacles in thinking"[10] such as gaps in visibility, space and time. Importantly, he points out that in order for the "affection" of the imagination to be roused it cannot work with nothing. The target of the imagination's affection must "conceal some part of its object by throwing it into a kind of shade", while at the same time showing enough to "pre-possess us in favour of the object" and leaving some work for the imagination to complete, which then "rouzes [*sic*] the spirits and gives an additional force to the passion".[11] The imagination loves to reach, but it must have something to reach for. The more distant and obscured an object is the further the imagination has to stretch. In order that the imagination "go the distance", so to speak, it must relate one idea to another, finally linking back to its present situation. In this sense, the imagination is also diffused:

> Now when any very distant object is present'd to the imagination, we naturally reflect upon the interpos'd distance, and by that means conceiving something great and magnificent receive the usual satisfaction. But as the fancy passes easily from one idea to another relat'd to it, and transports to the second all the passions excit'd by the first, the admiration which is direct'd to the distance naturally diffuses itself over the distant object.[12]

This diffusion is, however, not a weakening or negative action that a general understanding of 'diffuse' might imply. It is more a sense of extension in that

9 Warnock: *Imagination*, p. 17. This explanation was to come later with Emmanuel Kant's concept of the *schema*.

10 Ibid., p. 39.

11 Hume quoted in ibid., p. 39.

12 Hume quoted in ibid., p. 40.

the mental excitement experienced in overcoming the distance is now applied, via extension, to the object imagined. Both time and distance seem to represent a pleasant challenge for the imagination and, according to Hume: "In collecting our force in order to overcome the opposition, we invigorate the soul and give it an elevation with which it would not otherwise have been aquaint'd"[13]. If this is the case, it seems reasonable to claim that the ultimate unknown object – outer space – has the capacity to extend the reach of the imagination and elevate the soul to sublime heights. Furthermore, the astronaut can set off the chain of perceptual links that finally reach our unknown destination and then return to our present place. The astronaut, like an angel, appears to us in a known form (Hume's 'resemblance'), allowing the imagination to find a firm foothold as it joyfully reaches further, into the unknown.
Immanuel Kant elaborated on this idea with his concept of *synthesis* whereby perceptions are placed together in a format where one representation in the mind is connected to other representations in order to form knowledge:

> Space and time contain a manifold of pure *a priori* intuition, but at the same time are conditions of the receptivity of our mind–conditions under which alone it can receive representations of objects, and which therefore must also always affect the concept of these objects. But if this manifold is to be known, the spontaneity of our thought requires that it be gone through in a certain way, taken up, and connected. This act I name synthesis.[14]

However, this hypothesis is predicated on the idea that you *already have* something to match *to*. Dufrenne may claim that representation has been around since the advent of space-time, but the *expansion* of space and time was required to create any schematic basis to act as the starting point for complex image-making, particularly when it comes to the problem of imaging unseen aspects of our reality. It may be simple to make representations well within the bounds of the manifold of perception, but something is needed to bridge the gap if the bonds of representation are to be broken, ultimately allowing the perceiving subject to move from the known to the unknown, from the seen to the unseen. True knowledge of outer space, therefore, could potentially be difficult to develop when humanity has nothing to rely upon but secondhand images. What if, however, we could place our imagination in the service of the angel/astronaut?

13 Hume quoted in Warnock: *Imagination*, p. 40.
14 Immanuel Kant: *Critique of Pure Reason*, 1781 (A77), 2nd ed. 1787 (B102).

Rhetorical wreck

Homosuperior in my interior
But from the skin out
I'm Homosapien too
And you're Homosapien too[15]

Not everyone would agree that an astronaut is an effective conduit for the imagination. Astronauts are often accused of being "dull" and not at all good at relaying their extraordinary experiences of space flight. But to be fair, profound experiences often have a way of avoiding description. How do you describe zero gravity to someone who has not felt it, or, how do you describe looking at the whole planet from a great distance to someone who has not seen it? Words such as "beautiful", "magnificent", and "spectacular" fall short of their cosmic targets again and again. It is little wonder that by the time NASA officials and the press have filtered, edited, and rehashed anything that an astronaut might have to say that the words seem hopelessly inadequate and overly factual to the point of being emotionless. According to astronaut Walter Cunningham, in the "glory years of space what the country kept forgetting was that we were people",[16] not perfect, not all-knowing angelic creatures without fault, but all too fallible human beings.

Astronaut Andy Thomas was the target of such criticism when he toured Australia in 1998. Australian journalist, David Brearley, wrote:

> It's a sorry fact that several hundred learned men and women in space have failed to produce one memorable quote, excepting Armstrong's neatly scripted one-liner on arrival. He fluffed it, incidentally, and he hasn't said diddly since. [17]

It would appear that as well as being accomplished pilots and scientists, the public (according to at least one disgruntled journalist) would much prefer an astronaut who is equally well versed in the finer arts. If an astronaut is everything

15 Pete Shelley: *Homosapien*.

16 Walter Cunningham, quoted in Ronald Weber: *Seeing Earth: Literary Responses to Space Exploration*. Athens, OH: Ohio UP 1985, p. 47.

17 David Brearley: One Giant Yawn for Mankind. In: *The Weekend Australian*, October 31, 1998, p. 22. Neil Armstrong had meant to say, "That's one small step for *a* man, one giant leap for Mankind."

the NASA publicity machine of the 1960s described – that is, the all-American hero, the pinnacle of mankind – then it would seem only reasonable that they feel just as comfortable discussing chiaroscuro and existentialism as advanced aerodynamics and telemetry. This is, of course, a lot to ask, but it did not stop Brearley from suggesting to Andy Thomas: "Given that we've already sent no end of boffins into space, is there not a case for bumping a scientist off the next shuttle and sending a poet up instead?"[18] Thomas's reply was: "Not at all, I think we express ourselves very well".[19] And, for ordinary people, they probably do. Someone akin to the idea of a "Renaissance Man" had been on the mind of Norman Mailer when, in 1970, he suggested it would not be until men who "spoke like Shakespeare" were sent into space that humankind would be bestowed with any adequate description of that unseen territory. In the meantime, Mailer was disappointed at having to make do with astronauts whom he felt were "philosophically naïve, jargon-ridden, and resolutely divorced from any language with grandeur to match the proportions of [their] endeavor".[20] When the prevailing and highly stereotypical image of astronaut as "geek", "boffin" or just plain "dull" is combined with NASA's administrative skills, it is a wonder they get heard at all. Long-standing prejudices mean that astronauts are not associated with the words necessary to describe their strange experience, experiences that previously belonged to artists, poets and writers – imaginatively, at least.

It would seem that the astronaut is doomed to fail to deliver the words we require, for ironically, we refuse to let them escape the rhetoric we have built around them. Just as Brearley had baited Thomas, the literary community has long set the space program up for failure when it comes to words. Ronald Weber writes an amusing account of one such occasion in his book, *Seeing Earth,* whereby prior to the Apollo 11 landing an article in *Esquire* magazine speculated as to what would be said by the first astronaut to step on the Moon. In the *Esquire* article, journalist William Honan claimed it was already:

> '[...] perfectly clear – it would be folly to deny it any longer – that while the space program is poised on the brink of a truly epoch-making triumph of engineering, it is also headed for a rhetorical wreck.' The immediate source of the wreckage was the lack of imagination and perception on the part of astronauts who had failed to tell us what

18 Ibid., p. 22.

19 Ibid.

20 Norman Mailer in Weber: *Seeing Earth*, p. 60.

space was really like. All we had gotten from them was that it was "beautiful". They had used the word, the writer observed, 'like a Boy Scout jackknife, for every imaginable task'.[21]

This rhetorical wreck is humorously taken up in *Between Time and Timbuktu,* a 1972 television play based on the work of Kurt Vonnegut, where a poet, Stony Stevens, wins a competition to go into space. Television commentators express hope that he will provide better descriptions of space than "earlier astronauts like 'Bud Williams', who portrayed Mars as looking exactly like his driveway back in Dallas".[22] However, after his adventure, Stony simply leaves a note in his abandoned capsule that reads: "Everything was beautiful and nothing hurt".[23] Stony was unable to elaborate on what he saw because he had no adequate schema, either linguistic or visual, upon which to build. We are not sufficiently equipped, whether we be astronauts, poets or plumbers, to describe space with the rhetoric to which we may aspire because it lies beyond our general experience. In the case of the experience of space travel, a poet might well be lost for words and upon their return we may not be able to *see* what they are *saying*, at all. It may not be until the experience of the perceiving subject, schematic or otherwise, has been greatly expanded upon that the human imagination will find enough leverage to reach the stars and finally put some semiotic substance behind the empty shells of clichés such as "beautiful", "spectacular", or "indescribable".

The discussion of an astronaut's capacity, or perceived lack thereof, to describe their experiences in space, is important to pursue because they provide a necessary adjunct to the photographic images via which we connect with outer space. Astronauts are, in effect, the human equivalent of a caption or annotation. It is through the astronaut that we experience the narrative of a journey we have not taken part in, through their eyes that we come to perceive outer space. The astronaut is the animator of the image, however, to expect them to do so with all the rhetorical flair of Shakespeare is unfair. What the astronaut is capable of doing is gradually expanding our perceptual horizons, whether that be through their more successful attempts at photography or through their excited descriptions of space travel – even if it does involve the use of the word

21 Weber: *Seeing Earth*, p. 59.

22 Ibid., p. 86.

23 Ibid.

"beautiful". For if we look and listen well enough, we just might find out what they are so excited about.

> To say that only a poet can adequately express the emotions of space flight does injustice to many non-poets who have talked about it. It also seems to suggest that the man in the street will only listen to a poet. Sadly, in our society, the man in the street very seldom listens to a poet. [24]

But we did listen to Chris Hadfield.

The astronaut image-maker

> Alone in a 1-person spaceship (my suit), just holding on with my 1 hand, with the bottomless black universe on my left and the World pouring by in Technicolor on my right. I highly recommend it.[25]

Canadian Chris Hadfield outlines his long journey to becoming one of the world's most well-known astronauts in his book, *An Astronaut's Guide to Life on Earth.* He describes his career path, selection, training, and flight experiences with the clear objectivity of a person used to following procedure and yet having the room to think laterally should the occasion arise. He appears humble and yet aware of the sacrifices and struggles he (and his family) incurred in order to be one of 500 or so humans who have travelled into outer space. Hadfield endured long waiting periods between missions (1995 to 2001 and then 2001 to 2012), all in all achieving three flights in a 35-year career. It was during those prolonged periods that Hadfield learned to make the most of every opportunity that was presented to him. This left him in good stead to deal with some extraordinary situations as highlighted on his book jacket: breaking into a Space Station with a Swiss army knife; disposing of a live snake whilst piloting a plane; and being temporarily blinded while clinging to the side of a spacecraft. Nonetheless, the

24 Dr. Andrew Thomas, correspondence with the author dated November 20, 1998.

25 Chris Hadfield quoted in Alex Kantrowitz: Five Highlights from Commander Chris Hadfield's Reddit AMA From Space. https://www.forbes.com/sites/alexkantrowitz/2013/02/18/five-highlights-from-commander-chris-hadfields-reddit-ama-from-space/#ebcde8510061 (accessed: August 7, 2017).

text still reads with the color of calm detachment with which most astronauts are painted, and I was left thinking that the word "guide" in the title should have been changed to "manual". Hadfield even played down his extraordinary impact on music and visual culture from the unique vantage point of the International Space Station.

NASA has learned over the years that astronauts and images are some of the most powerful public relations tools they have and that good public opinion results in funding. The original Mercury crew fought battles with engineers about windows, the right to controls, secreted cameras on board flights, and suffered censorship and manipulation at the hands of administrators.[26] NASA tightly controlled their images on covers of high-impact media such as *Life* magazine. Public interest in these sanitized images began to decline in the 1970s and the Space Shuttle of the 1980s lacked the wonder of the unknown or an alien destination, only piquing public interest and making the front page when things went horrifically wrong.

NASA had to take a new and liberal approach in the twenty-first century and it was astronauts like Hadfield who forged the way using social media from the International Space Station (ISS) to once again take on that angelic mantle and act as mediator between Earth and space. By opening himself up to individuals back on "Spaceship Earth",[27] Hadfield allowed our imaginations to overcome the obstacle, or as Hume put it, the "opposition" of distance and thereby "invigorate the soul and give it an elevation with which it would not otherwise have been aquaint'd". At the time of writing, Hadfield has over 2,390,000 followers on Twitter and Forbes has called him "the most social media savvy astronaut ever to leave Earth".[28]

Music has always played a big role in Hadfield's life and so he made good use of the guitar that is permanently aboard the ISS. With his son Evan's encouragement, he gained David Bowie's permission to make a video (Fig. 3) of a slightly altered version of the iconic 1969 song, *Space Oddity.* Evan told him that it "would corner the market on wonder"[29] and indeed, after finishing his

26 See my previous work: The Artist and the Astronaut. In: *Meanjin: Fine Writing and Provocative Ideas* 59:3 (2000), pp. 201–210.

27 "Spaceship Earth" was a term predominantly popularized by Buckminster Fuller via his 1968 publication *Operating Manual for Spaceship Earth.* However, the term has been intermittently in use since the nineteenth century.

28 Kantrowitz: Five Highlights from Commander Chris Hadfield's Reddit AMA from Space.

29 Chris Hadfield: *An Astronauts Guide to Life on Earth*. New York: Little Brown 2013, p. 230.

Fig. 3
Chris Hadfield performs David Bowie's *Space Oddity* aboard the International Space Station just before he returned to Earth in 2013.

final mission and arriving back on Earth, the first question from the press was, "Did you know that *Space Oddity* has had seven million hits?"[30] It has now had over 41 million hits, however, as Hadfield replied to the press, the purpose of the video was not to get hits but "make the rare and beautiful experience of space flight more accessible".[31] Hadfield's re-interpretation of the words and music of one of the world's greatest artists combined with spectacular images of outer space and the humble environment of the ISS make for compelling viewing.[32] He shows us his world in the stars, one that remains distant and physically inaccessible to most and yet now – revived by the rhetoric of Bowie's pop and the honesty of Hadfield's invitation – one we know just a little bit better. Our collective and individual schema of the place called outer space just got a little more complex. Perhaps Hadfield is Mailer's "Renaissance Man", even if he did hack open a space capsule with a Swiss army knife.

30 Ibid., p. 261.

31 Ibid.

32 Chris Hadfield: Space Oddity. https://www.youtube.com/watch?v=KaOC9danxNo (August 7, 2017).

Fig. 4: Apollo 15 (AS15-82-11217a). End of a roll of film.

Fig. 5: Apollo 8 (AS08-16-2628). Double exposed Earth.

Lost in the edit

> I don't wanna classify you
> Like an animal in the zoo
> But it seems good to me to know
> That you're Homosapien too[33]

One of the great tragedies of photography is that it divides time and space into frames. Of course, all representation must do this in order to distinguish itself from reality. In order to be an object of contemplation, the image must be framed for a viewer, for a contemplating consciousness. The image is re-presented within the frame – projected, if you will, from another space and time – to be yet again projected into the ambiguous space of perception, or as Louis Marin states: "[...] the frame will furnish one of the privileged spaces of producing 'knowing,' 'believing' and 'feeling'".[34] The frame asks to be addressed and draws us into its space purposefully as it crops out a slice of reality to represent, but as it does so it simultaneously implies the presence of something left behind. This absence implied by presence is the inherent rhetoric of the frame, a visual device

33 Pete Shelley: *Homosapien.*

34 Louis Marin: The Frame of Representation and Some of Its Figures. In: Paul Duro (ed.): *The Rhetoric of the Frame: Essays on the Boundaries of the Artwork*. New York: Cambridge UP 1996, pp. 82–83.

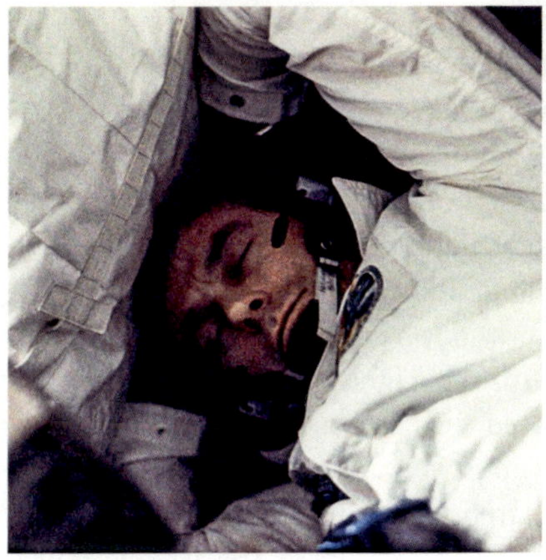

Fig. 6: (AS17-162-24049).
Sleeping aboard Apollo 17.

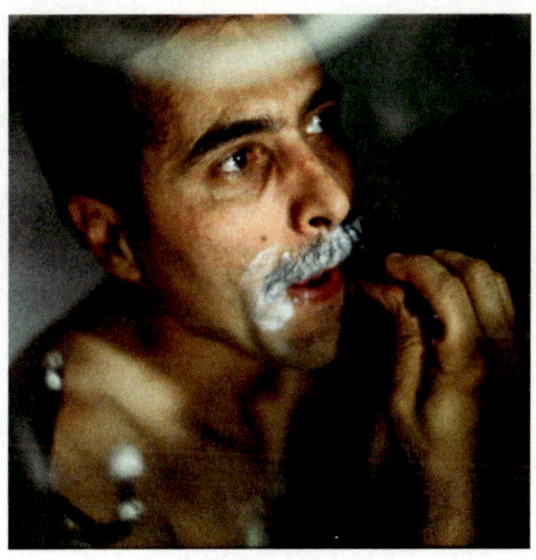

Fig. 7: (AS17-163-24170).
Shaving aboard Apollo 17.

that discloses one of the paradoxes of seeing. In order to represent the world, the world must be contained – framed – and there must always be that which remains behind and unseen. Moreover, there are an infinite number of frames to be taken from that cloudy continuum.

In 2015, NASA made the decision to upload over 8,400 Apollo mission images to the Internet site Flickr. The fact that NASA was sharing images with the world was nothing new. NASA had always made their images available in the public domain. However, if you had wanted to see every frame shot on one roll of film (or "magazine") in its correct order, then that was harder to find. It was even harder to find them in high resolution without contacting the NASA Public Affairs Office or the repository for all images of the Moon, the Lunar and Planetary Institute, based in Houston.[35] So, as much as NASA's images were for the world to enjoy, this was the first time they were made so readily accessible. Furthermore, for the first time, the general public could see all the frames that NASA had edited out of their public releases. Here were the out-of-focus photos, the over-exposed, the under-exposed, or the ends of the film (Fig. 4). Here were ones shot through grubby windows, with camera shake or lens flare, and even double exposures (Fig. 5). These overlooked photographs may not have been considered as useful at the time, but their public outing in the twenty-first century is a sharp reminder of the difficulties of conducting photography in the tough

35 In the late 1990s, I was employed as an image researcher at the Melbourne Planetarium for some years and found hunting for high-resolution images quite frustrating.

environment of zero-gravity. By the time of the Space Shuttle, photography in outer space had become formulaic and standardized, producing homogenized images that belied their individual astronaut-photographers.

These previously neglected frames also demonstrate that astronauts spent some of the tedious time of their trip to the Moon photographing one another. Some of those portraits had made it through the NASA public relations machine, but many were left behind. Pictures of astronauts sleeping (Fig. 6), shaving (Fig. 7), or just having fun, showed activities that may not have complied with the manufactured image of the heroic astronaut with the "right stuff", but perhaps gave the astronauts a sense of normalcy when faced with a task that truly transcended anything known. Thus, these images open up part of the astronaut psyche to the viewer revealing them as nothing more than humans in extraordinary circumstances, full of fears, doubts, and frailties. The humanity of the astronaut provides us with the leverage we require to put ourselves in their space boots and our imaginations are gifted a solid model upon which to build an understanding of something we have not experienced for ourselves.

Transcending the manifold

> Once a photograph of the Earth, taken from the outside, is available – once the sheer isolation of the Earth becomes plain – a new idea as powerful as any in history will be let loose.
> Fred Hoyle, 1948[36]

The obviously named "Earthrise" image (Fig. 8), taken by Apollo 8 astronaut William Anders in 1968, belongs to a long history of aerial photography and within that history there is a particular narrative, a context in which the image sits. As I have outlined in previous work, this image did not miraculously appear. On the contrary, from French artist Nadar photographing Paris from a balloon to Stuart Brand and the Whole Earth Catalog,[37] its trajectory was set a long time

36 Fred Hoyle quoted in Oran W. Nicks (ed.): *This Island Earth*. Washington D. C: National Aeronautics and Space Administration, Scientific and Technical Information Division, Office of Technology Utilization 1970, p. 3.

37 The *Whole Earth Catalog* was a counterculture magazine/almanac/do-it-yourself-book published by Stanford-educated Stewart Brand between 1966 and 1972. Brand had called for the release of a rumored NASA satellite image of the "whole Earth", which he believed would unite humans in a shared destiny.

Fig. 8
Apollo 8 (AS08-14-2383).
William Anders: Earthrise.

ago.[38] Nonetheless, what the Flickr upload of frames from the Apollo 8 film magazines reveals is the very moment when Anders' imagination reconnected with a schema and alerted him to the presence of an image that was to profoundly affect humanity.

The Apollo 8 mission audio transcripts easily alert one to the fact that this was a reconnaissance mission with photography of the Moon at its core. The astronauts had a considerable amount of training before they left, but despite this, the transcripts show a distinct sense of disorientation and isolation. Phrases such as: "The Earth should be right over there. Is the Earth over there?" and then "Oh, here it is. There's the Earth over there …"[39] indicate that these men were out of their visual depth and struggling to re-adjust their sense of place. However, as the previous sentences suggest, they knew what to look *for*. Thus, when they saw the Earth rise above the surface of the Moon they were quick to pick it up. And, what they saw was not the Earth and the Moon as real objects in real space, but a *picture to be taken:* "Oh my God! Look at that picture over there! There's the Earth coming up. Wow, is that pretty".[40] When you look at the film magazines on Flickr, you can see the very moment of recognition in the B&W frame AS08-13-2329 (AS08-14-2383 being the subsequent color version shot by Anders: Fig. 8).

38 See Colleen Boyle: Eyes of the Machine. In: Daniel Rubenstein / Johnny Golding (eds): *On the Verge of Photography: Imaging Beyond Representation*. Birmingham: ARTicle 2013, pp. 211–236.

39 Apollo 8 Mission Transcripts, day one. https://www.jsc.nasa.gov/history/mission_trans/AS08_CM.PDF (accessed: August 7, 2017).

40 William Anders: *Apollo Flight Journal, Apollo 8, Day 4: Lunar Orbit 4*. https://history.nasa.gov/afj/ap08fj/16day4_orbit4.html (accessed: March 12, 2019).

Fig. 9
Apollo 8
(AS08-12-2185).
The first
appearance
of Earth on
an Apollo 8
film magazine.

Browsing Flickr, you can also see that another camera, set to take stereo pairs (one frame per 20 seconds), had been picking up similar shots (see AS08-12-2185 (Fig. 9) to AS08-12-2188). The point, here, is that a disoriented astronaut on his very first mission matched his internal visual schema – founded purely on images and no first-hand experience – with pure perceptual input and recognized it immediately *as a picture to be made*: "Earthrise".

Because of this sublime image, Hoyle's term "sheer isolation" was now something that could be quite plainly understood and indeed, an idea as powerful as any in history was let loose. All it took was a journey of heroic proportions with three very fragile men: the unwitting explorers who enabled us *all* to become astronauts and discover planet Earth as if for the very first time.

Ad astra: to the stars

There may never be another moment like the capture of the "Earthrise" photograph. The Earth-bound human imagination may never again feel the joy of stretching so far as to see our home planet from the flipped perspective of the Moon. Our internal schemata, the perceptual building-blocks via which we know outer space is not quite as bereft as it once was, thanks to the photographs and descriptions made by astronauts. That sense of doubt that images of space initially carried with them has all but dissipated as we have become more comfortable with taking an imaginative leap off the planet.

Furthermore, if the early images taken by astronauts seem incomplete or flawed then we surely must forgive them, because it is these 'mistakes' that allow for the development or modification of visual schemata. Early astronaut acquired photography was full of brilliant mistakes, but the smooth NASA machine has taken care of that, making contemporary photography in space as easy as wielding your camera here on Earth – all in the name of a good picture. Error allows for breaking free of a cycle of schematic cloning where homogeneity and stagnation ensues.

The rough, inexpert, almost vernacular, images of the early NASA astronauts bring us closer to the complexities of the astronaut-photographer and their remarkable journey, and thus, one step closer to the reality of outer space. However, if we continue to look at space in the same standard way, we will miss out: we shall not see the as yet unseen. Our collective schema of space will remain neglected and we will never find ourselves in the enviable position of Anders when a picture, the likes of which the world had never seen, was revealed to him. The angel-astronaut, traveler between worlds, will be rendered mute and a rescue mission desperately needed if the image of space is to avoid a rhetorical wreck.

The world needs the likes of Chris Hadfield to think differently about how the astronaut-angel might communicate the unique experience of space travel and thus provoke our imaginations to once again reach into the unknown. Besides, when we allow NASA to do the editing, we miss out on pictures of astronauts like this (Fig. 10):

Fig. 10
Portrait of
Gemini 4 astronaut
James McDivitt,
1965.

Alexander Hauk / Sophia Hauk

Wall Calendar Journalism

How an Astronaut is Giving Journalism New Impetus: The Protestonaut as an Appeal for a Better World

The project

Media reports about the necklace worn for the leaders' debate, royal weddings, B-list celebrities' alcohol problems or football players' beards: four examples of the increased dumbing down of the press.[1] Banalities and gossip get in the way of topics that are actually important, topics that concern each and every one of us. The Protestonaut (Latin: *protestari* – publicly testify,[2] Greek: *-naut* – sailor) is an innovative journalistic format that aims to draw attention to important points and challenges with photos and short texts. The leitmotif is an astronaut who appears in all the photos and whom the creators have christened "the Protestonaut". The figures, data and facts used are all based on scientific studies. *The Protestonaut Calendar*, published annually since 2014, is a kind of a "keynote speech in print". The intention is to provide food for thought and stimulate discussion. The Protestonaut has appeared in several exhibitions and has been nominated for various journalistic competitions. In addition, a book debut on the impact of austerity policy in Greece emerged from the project in 2017.[3]

1 Lydia Nordengrün: "Boulevardisierung" des Qualitätsjournalismus. In: *MedienMittweida*, January 8, 2014. http://medien-mittweida.de/boulevardisierung-des-qualitaetsjournalismus (accessed: July 28, 2017).

2 Protest. In: *Wikipedia*. https://de.wikipedia.org/wiki/Protest (accessed: July 27, 2017).

3 Alexander Hauk / Sophia Hauk: *Griechenland in Zeiten der Kürzungspolitik*. Mindelheim: Högel 2017.

Idea and origin

The Protestonaut was not a mere flash of inspiration, it grew organically from the creators' thoughts and ideas, a process lasting several months. As a photographer, Sophia Hauk has a background in advertising, Alexander Hauk in politics and journalism. In early 2014, the desire grew to create a joint project, to which they could both contribute their skills and interests. A calendar appeared to be the appropriate format, because they were able to gauge the workload. From the start, the creators wanted to produce a high-quality product. Due to Alexander Hauk's interest in politics and economics, it was also clear that the focus should be on political issues. He wanted to turn the calendar into a product of journalism: a blend of a classic calendar and journalism, a crossover innovation. It also fit well with the discussion that was just beginning to take shape about the credibility of the media and concepts such as "Lügenpresse" (media of lies), later "Lückenpresse" (media of omission),[4] and the term "fake news", which in Germany is connected principally to the US president.[5] Was it possible that mainstream media was not objectively reporting on events in Germany and the world? Or even that they were deliberately lying? Well aware that they would be unable to provide a definitive answer to this question, the calendar creators started work mid-2014, selecting topics and shoot locations, and researching all they could find about the chosen topics.

A vital question remained unanswered at the beginning: What should the common element be, the proverbial thread running through calendar? Examples of themes used by other calendars include a specific region, such as the Allgäu; structures, such as bridges; objects, such as cars; or animals, such as cows. The search for a suitable character began.

Character

The calendar's creators did not want appear in the calendar scenes themselves. But what kind of figure could they use? It should be serious and neutral, a

4 Ulrich Teusch / Christian Rabhansl: "Lückenpresse": was in den Medien fehlt. In: *Deutschlandfunk Kultur*, September 24, 2016. http://www.deutschlandfunkkultur.de/selbstkritischer-journalismus-lueckenpresse-was-in-den.1270.de.html?dram:article_id=366690 (accessed: July 26, 2017).

5 Marc Pietzke: Donald Trumps Pressekonferenz: "Ihr seid Fake News!". In: *Spiegel Online*, January 11, 2017. http://www.spiegel.de/politik/ausland/donald-trump-gibt-pressekonferenz-ihr-seid-fake-news-a-1129595.html (accessed: June 26, 2017).

recognizable figure. A well-known person, such as a politician, was out of the question for reasons of objectivity. An actor could not be used, simply because of the amount of time required. The use of a superhero like Superwoman or Batman was not possible because of the image rights.
As the project was getting off the ground, there were numerous reports in the German media about the astronaut Alexander Gerst, his "Blue Dot" mission, and his space flight to the international space station ISS in May 2014.[6] These reports helped to find the figure they were looking for: astronauts are explorers and have to rise to numerous challenges.[7] In space, they have an exceptional view of the Earth as they float above the blue planet and its problems. Anyone could be inside that Protestonaut suit: a shop assistant, a bank clerk, a local politician, a student, a manager, a job-seeker, a teacher, an investor – or the viewers of the calendar themselves – an every(wo)man, as it were.

The name

The name of the character should be short, meaningful and neither already assigned nor protected. In addition, the name should be internationally understandable with no negative associations. It took a lengthy period to choose a name. In the end the portmanteau "Protestonaut" was decided upon, which has its roots in both Latin and Greek. The Latin *protestari* is commonly translated as "publicly testify";[8] the Greek suffix *-naut* means sailor or captain.[9] Thus, the name perfectly describes the Protestonaut, a figure that publicly draws attention to political and economic conditions, focusing on a selection of different topics, like a seafarer who sails to different islands. The word "Protestonaut" is copyright-protected and has been registered with the German Patent and Trademark Office.

6 Alexander Gerst's Mission "Blue Dot – Shaping the future". In: *DLR* (Deutsches Zentrum für Luft und Raumfahrt). http://www.dlr.de/dlr/desktopdefault.aspx/tabid-10768/ (accessed: July 27, 2017).

7 Ulrich Weih: Der steinige Weg von Alexander Gerst ins All. In: *T Online*, May 28, 2014. http://www.t-online.de/nachrichten/esa-space-channel/id_69345362/astronaut-alexander-gerst-weg-zu-den-sternen-ist-steinig-.html (accessed: July 27, 2017).

8 Protest. In: *Wikipedia*. https://de.wikipedia.org/wiki/Protest (accessed: July 27, 2017).

9 Raumfahrer. In: *Wikipedia*. https://de.wikipedia.org/wiki/Raumfahrer (accessed: June 21, 2017).

Costume

Before the first photoshoot could start, a suitable costume had to be found. In shops and online there were only astronaut costumes for carnival. These would have been very cheap, but they would have seemed like a foreign component in the photographs. Better spacesuits were available for rent from Babelsberg film studio, but this was rejected for cost reasons. Even with optimal planning and coordination, the costume for the twelve motifs and the title page would have to have been rented so often that a purchase seemed more sensible. Finally, a seller on eBay from the USA offering a well-made replica of a spacesuit was found. The replica spacesuit consisted of a helmet, suit, oxygen equipment, gloves, and shoes. It is predominantly made from white denim and, of course, is not functional.

Method

The creative process of the Protestonaut is comparable with the work of a journalist.[10] The start of the annual calendar project is marked by extensive research. In the search for the topics, many questions arise: Which topics are relevant? Which have received too little attention in the past? What facts have been overlooked in the media? The search for subjects is accompanied by the search for relevant studies and literature.

The viability of the topics also plays an important role. Not every subject can be photographed at reasonable cost. Not every eye-catching topic can be backed up with enough informative and objective data. In fact, there are often many different results to be found on a certain topic, usually depending on who commissioned the study. It is not surprising that, for example, stakeholders representing employers and employees come to different conclusions regarding the effects of a minimum wage.[11]

The special attraction of the work on the *Protestonaut Calendar* is the comparison of study results and figures from journals. The calendar creators have gained

10 Markus Behmer / Bernd Blöbaum: Wer Journalisten sind und wie sie arbeiten. In: *bpb*, June 6, 2011. http://www.bpb.de/izpb/7527/wer-journalisten-sind-und-wie-sie-arbeiten?p=all< (accessed: July 27, 2017).

11 Mindestlohn: keine negativen Beschäftigungseffekte. In: *IG Metall Bayern*, June 24, 2014. https://www.igmetall-bayern.de/nachrichten/ansicht/datum/2014/06/24/titel/mindestlohn-keine-negativen-beschaeftigungseffekte//?type=98&cHash=a4d40f67083b025e523af799a4f69f71 (accessed: June 22, 2017).

Fig. 1: Sophia Hauk: *Climate Change*, 2015.

the impression over the last couple of years that the concept of objectivity is remarkably flexible, even in scientific studies, and is often strongly dependent on the wording of the question. Although the selection of themes, motifs, and information sources is an assessment in itself, the creators also try to find the most objective information possible. One example is the text accompanying the picture of climate change (Fig. 1):

> According to estimates, global temperatures will increase by up to 4.5 °C by 2050. In Germany, more extremely hot days and more frequent flooding are to be expected, particularly in the foothills of the Alps and the east. Worldwide, more and more people will have to migrate.[12]

The text was based on several sources, including the Federal Environment Agency and CO2ONLINE GGMBH websites as well as the book *Zwei Grad mehr in*

12 Alexander Hauk / Sophia Lukasch: *Der Protestonaut-Kalender 2015*. Mindelheim: Högel 2014.

Fig. 2: Sophia Hauk: *Equity*, 2015.

Deutschland: Wie der Klimawandel unseren Alltag verändern wird (Two Degrees More in Germany: How Climate Change Will Affect our Everyday Life) by Friedrich-Wilhelm Gerstengarbe and Harald Welzer.[13]

Implementation

Once the topics have been chosen, the search for suitable shooting locations begins. Sometimes a license is required. In some places, for example in theatres, museums or zoos, photography is allowed for private use but not for publication. These licenses are often expensive. In some cases, the individual motifs involve substantial travel and hotel bookings. The next steps are editing the pictures and honing the texts. After several drafts, the final texts are translated into English, and one year into Greek as well. Then the motifs and texts are sent to designer Alexander Weiß, who typesets the calendar.

13 Friedrich-Wilhelm Gerstengarbe / Harald Welzer (eds): *Zwei Grad mehr in Deutschland: Wie der Klimawandel unseren Alltag verändern wird*. Frankfurt am Main: Fischer 2013.

Fig. 3: Sophia Hauk: *Peace*, 2015.

Motifs

For the first two years, various unrelated topics were included in the calendar, but in 2017, for the first time the calendar had an overall concept – the effects of austerity policy. The 2018 calendar also has an overall concept based on children's rights. On each photo, one can see a child with the astronaut. The topics covered were: child poverty, the right to places in day-care centres, the right to leisure time, healthy diets, refugees, bullying, inclusion, child labour, the right to education, social media, violence against children, and the right to seeing both parents on a regular basis, even if they have separated. In 2019, the makers of the calendar decided to focus on a variety of topics once again, such as the extinction of insects, the waste of food, and air pollution.

The motifs for the 2015 calendar) were predominantly shot in Hamburg and Berlin. Other shots were taken in Frankfurt (Fig. 2), Görlitz, Kiel and Mindelheim. The topics were: climate protection (January), free trade agreements (February), freedom of the press (March), agriculture (April), education (May), poverty (June), demographic change (July), modern working hours (August), data protection (September), justice (October), defense (November: Fig. 3), and

Fig. 4: Sophia Hauk: *Digital Change*, 2016.

mobility (December). The cover picture shows the Protestonaut in front of a field of windmills.[14]

The motifs for the 2016 calendar (Figs. 4–7) were shot in Berlin, Hamburg, Füssen and Mindelheim. Topics were digital change (January), retirement (February), addiction (March), "refugees welcome" (April), stopping the brain drain (May), tax fraud (June), drinking water (July), overfishing (August), gentrification (September), the pay gap (October), to be or not to be (November), and the protection of animals (December). The cover picture shows the Protestonaut at a dam in Kaprun, Austria.[15]

In 2016, for the first time, all the texts were translated into English in order to make the Protestonaut also available on an international scale. There was also an extra motif on youth unemployment. For this, the calendar creators developed a motif that was designed according to their specifications by the illustrator Carsten Mell. It shows an astronaut hovering in space above an Earth-like sphere composed of the words "Job wanted" in German, English, French,

14 Hauk / Lukasch: *Der Protestonaut-Kalender 2015.*

15 Ibid.

Fig. 5: Sophia Hauk: *Drinking Water*, 2016.

Spanish, Italian and Greek. This motif was also turned into a Protestonaut t-shirt, which aims to provide a positive impetus to assist companies in the search for specialists, help the unemployed to find employment and express solidarity with the unemployed internationally.

The 2017 calendar was a special edition, because the creators were on the road in Greece for several weeks. The creators were here supported by journalist Odysseas Athanasiadis and project manager Lea Aimee. As mentioned above, the calendar was devoted to the subject of austerity policy. The motifs covered nationalism (January), shop closure (February), solidarity (March), ruins (April), industrial production (May), healthcare (June), tourism (July), rural depopulation (August), schools and kindergartens (September), forced privatization (October), suicide (November), and self-organization (December). The cover picture of the calendar shows the Protestonaut in front of a shipwreck on the beach in the Greek town Gythio.[16] The wreck could be interpreted as symbolic of the impact of austerity on Greece.

16 Ibid.

Fig. 6: Sophia Hauk: *Overfishing*, 2016.

Ten years have passed since the outbreak of the global financial and banking crisis.[17] In the hope of correcting the resulting problems in global financial and economic systems, many countries have opted for a policy that goes under various names: described generously as "budgeting", neutrally as "reductions" or "austerity policy", and by many of the affected parties as "impoverishment policy". Countries who decide on austerity policies greatly reduce government spending, increase taxation, and focus increasingly on privatization rather than state ownership.[18] No other country in Europe has had as much experience with austerity policy as Greece. The Protestonaut went there to observe and document its effects and developments (Figs. 8 – 10). After all these years of deprivation,

17 David Böcking: Forscher fürchten Comeback von Giftpapieren. In: *Spiegel Online*, February 6, 2017. http://www.spiegel.de/wirtschaft/soziales/finanzmarkt-forscher-warnen-vor-comeback-von-verbriefungen-a-1133288.html (accessed: July 21, 2017).

18 Alexandra Endres: Die Austeritätspolitik verletzt Menschenrechte. In: *Zeit Online*, July 20, 2015. http://www.zeit.de/wirtschaft/2015-07/sparpolitik-griechenland-menschenrechte (accessed: July 21, 2017).

Fig. 7: Sophia Hauk: *Tax Fraud*, 2016.

one thing is clear: austerity policy has not saved Greece.[19] And it is no longer just about Greece. It is about the future of Europe. Austerity policy is, in our view, accelerating the separation of the European states.

The 2018 calendar also had an overall concept. All motifs drew attention to children's rights and child protection. For the first time, there were other people in the calendar apart from the Protestonaut, mostly children.

Internet and social media

The motifs were published in a DINA3 photo calendar. In addition, a website (www.Protestonaut.de) was created and social media accounts on Facebook (www.facebook.com/Protestonaut), Twitter (https://twitter.com/protestonaut), Instagram, YouTube and Pinterest were set up. Journalistic content (texts, photos, videos, interviews) created by Alexander and Sophia Hauk is regularly posted on these accounts.

19 Giorgos Chondros: Griechenland: Warum die linke Regierung nicht erfolgreich sein darf. In: *Telepolis*, April 3, 2017. https://www.heise.de/tp/features/Griechenland-Warum-die-linke-Regierung-nicht-erfolgreich-sein-darf-3673572.html (accessed: July 25, 2017).

Fig. 8: Sophia Hauk: *Nationalism*, 2017.

Fig. 9: Sophia Hauk: *Privatisation*, 2017.

Feedback and press comment

The *Protestonaut Calendar* now has a small fan base that is constantly growing. This is shown by positive correspondence, including letters from well-known politicians. Brigitte Zypries for example, parliamentary secretary of state at the Federal Ministry of Economics and Energy, wrote to the creators: "Thank you for the original contribution to Article 5 of the constitution!" The incumbent President of Germany and former Minister for Foreign Affairs sent an autograph with a dedication to the Protestonaut. The creators even received a motivating letter from the Office of the President. Since the calendar texts are by now also written in English, the calendar creators receive orders from many countries, as far away as Australia. Numerous media reports have certainly contributed to its popularity: "The world-famous Pirelli wall calendar has competition,"[20] writes the *Augsburger Allgemeine* newspaper. The *Hamburger Abendblatt* notes: "The Protestonaut both looks good and provides food for thought."[21] *Bild.de* writes: "Astronaut travels to the dark side of the world."[22] The conclusion of *Die Freiheitsliebe* is: "Art can be political, if it wants to be. But unfortunately, most of the time it is not. The Protestonaut is a refreshing counter-example." "Starting a discussion – this is the aim of politics graduate Alexander Hauk and photographer Sophia Lukasch with their 2015 *Protestonaut Calendar*. Not with scandalous pictures, but with facts. And they succeed," writes *UNICUM CAMPUS MAGAZIN*.[23]

The journalistic photo calendar has appeared in numerous exhibitions, including shows in Berlin, Hamburg and Heidelberg. In 2019 Sophia and Alexander Hauk were invited to take part at the exhibition for the Wilhelm-Dröscher-Preis in the event location CityCube in Berlin. The project has been entered into several competitions and was nominated for, among other things, the Alternative Media Prize.

20 Ein Astronaut regt zum Nachdenken an. In: *Augsburger Allgemeine*, October 20, 2014. http://www.augsburger-allgemeine.de/mindelheim/Ein-Astronaut-regt-zum-Nachdenken-an-id31729292.html (accessed: July 27, 2017).

21 Nico Binde: Was macht der Astronaut eigentlich in Hamburg? In: *Hamburger Abendblatt*, November 25, 2015. http://www.abendblatt.de/hamburg/article206719895/Was-macht-der-Astronaut-eigentlich-in-Hamburg.html (accessed: July 27, 2017).

22 Kritischer Kalender: Astronaut bereist Schattenseiten der Welt. In: *Bildplus*, November 17, 2015. http://www.bild.de/regional/berlin/kunst/protestonaut-kalender-zeigt-schattenseiten-auf-der-welt-43434816.bild.html (accessed: July 28, 2017).

23 Eine Diskussion anstoßen. In: *UNICUM*, 12/2014, p. 4.

Fig. 10: Sophia Hauk: *Tourism*, 2017.

Conclusion

In a time of digital change and rapid flux, the *Protestonaut Calendar* is a journalism project that encourages a moment of pause and consideration. The language of the calendar is factual and objective: figures, data and facts are researched, collected, and compared. This gives the calendar credibility at a time when the credibility of the media has been called into question.

The target group is interested in politics and art. The creators may have been concerned at the start that they might eventually run out of topics, but they are now sure that social developments will continue to provide plenty of topics in the future. Alexander and Sophia Hauk regularly receive suggestions from friends and acquaintances.

The Protestonaut would not have been possible without the consumers and the help of numerous friends, acquaintances and supporters. For this reason, special thanks go to them. The focus of this non-profit project is on quality. Thus the creators do not shy away from long distance travel to put the topics on paper as clearly as possible. Every year after publication, the project is faced with the challenge of recouping the costs.

The Creators

Alexander Hauk lives and works as a journalist and press officer in Berlin and Hamburg. Born in Mindelheim, he has been a member of the Bavarian Federation of Journalists for many years. In times of media flux, he has chosen to forge a new path and has published a print product together with his wife in the form of a calendar.

Whether she is photographing children, stars or fashion: the commercial photographer Sophia Hauk illuminates whatever is in front of her lens. Her clients include well-known companies, agencies, and editorial offices. She lives and works as a self-employed photographer in Hamburg and Berlin.

Jörg Hartmann

Female Space Travelers in Science Fiction Films 1898–2017

Introduction

We are all astronauts.[1]

When Buckminster Fuller compared the Earth to a spaceship in 1968, he implied that the crew of this spaceship included both men and women; the reality of the situation was, and still is, in spite of his metaphor, that it is mainly men who are astro-, cosmo-, or taikonauts. The dominance of male protagonists in the actual exploration of outer space seems at first glance very similar to their representation in popular media such as film;[2] it is mostly male engineers, scientists, captains, and fighter pilots who venture into the unknown in feature films. On closer inspection, however, it becomes clear that there is actually a popular tradition of female space explorers. In the medium of film, the use of this topos begins shortly after the establishment of the medium around 1900 and it continues until this day – with no end in sight.

Kristina Jaspers, curator of the exhibitions *Women in Space*, which was held in the Einstein Forum Potsdam in 2016, and *Things to Come. Science. Fiction. Film*, shown in the same year at the Deutsche Kinematik – Museum für Film und Fernsehen in Berlin, emphasized in the accompanying catalog that the

1 R. Buckminster Fuller: *Operating Manual for Spaceship Earth*. Mattituck, NY: Aeonian 1969, p. 15.

2 This article focusses on feature films, other media such as TV series are excluded, although there are remarkable counterexamples, such as the German/British TV series *Star Maidens* (DE/GB 1975, D: Freddie Francis).

Fig. 1
Luna (Jehanne d'Alcy) as film's first female space traveler in *La lune à un mètre* (*The Astronomer's Dream,* F 1898, D: Georges Méliès).

ever-changing depiction of women in film also has the function of indicating what kind of female role models each generation has. They "say something about how contemporary society sees them as well as what they expect from the future."[3] From this observation, the following questions arise: What changes have there been to the image of female astronauts over the course of history? How do these changes relate to social and technical developments? In framing the narrative of female space exploration, what role does the genre of science fiction play?[4] These three questions are addressed in this article through a chronologically structured analysis, which, in its final part, will summarise the answers.

Female space travelers in science Fiction films: 1898–1968

In 1898, three years after the first public film screening by the Lumière brothers, the stage magician Georges Méliès, who had already integrated the new medium

3 Kristina Jaspers: Fashion Icons und Role Models. In: K.J. et al. (eds): *Things to Come. Science. Fiction. Film.* Bielefeld / Berlin: Kerber 2016, pp. 44–50, here pp. 47–48 (my translation). In the original German: "[Sie] sagen sowohl etwas darüber aus, wie die jeweils zeitgenössische Gesellschaft sich sieht, als auch darüber, was sie von der Zukunft erwartet."

4 The corpus of this article is drawn from (fictional) feature films. Movies which are based on real events such as for example *Apollo 13* (US 1995, D: Ron Howard) or *Hidden Figures* (US 2016, D: Theodore Melfie) are not discussed here. Regarding the topic of this article see also most recently *Science Fiction Film & Television* 12:1 (2019): When the Astronaut Is a Woman, ed. by Lisa Purse / Lorrie Palmer. https://online.liverpooluniversitypress.co.uk/doi/10.3828/sfftv.2019.01 (accessed: April 8, 2019).

into his variety shows, presented the first female space traveler on screen. In *The Astronomer's Dream,*[5] a personification of a Moon woman, taking the form of a fairy queen, enters the attic of an astronomer after he has spotted her through his telescope (Fig. 1).

A similarly voyeuristic approach to viewing the heavens can be seen in many other space travel films up to 1910. The decisive factor for the development of this topos may have been the etymologically traditional gender assignment of the celestial bodies. In this regard, Ragnild Ljosland writes:

> The genders of the sun and moon can also be a tell-tale. The modern English poetic usage when personifying the sun and moon has taken up the French or Romance gender for *sol* (masculine) and *luna* (feminine), instead of retaining the Germanic grammatical genders where the sun is feminine and the moon masculine.[6]

The plot of early space travel narratives always follows a similar pattern: the unearthly beautiful, feminine object of male lust acts as a motivational element – the astronomer's discovery is followed by a yearning gaze, which in turn leads to his journey into space. The destinations of choice for these love-crazed astronomers are the heavenly bodies where the human-like aliens are found. Once there, the latter are successfully courted or kidnapped and, as long as the voyage does not end badly, they are brought back to Earth.[7] These early films of the "cin ema of attractions"[8] – which both through their visual appeal and their content meet the requirements of the genre – satirize the clumsy attempts of the unworldly astronomers to woo the aliens.[9] Their unworldliness is also reflected

5 *The Astronomer's Dream* (*La lune à un mètre*, F 1898, D: Georges Méliès). See also Jörg Hartmann: Träumen Astronomen vom Mann im Mond? Keplers "Somnium" (1634) und Méliès "La lune à un mètre" (1898) im geopoetischen Vergleich. In: *reflex: Tübinger Kunstgeschichte zum Bildwissen* 6 (2015), pp. 1–20.

6 Ragnhild Ljosland: Masculine and Feminine in Dialect. In: *The Orcadian* 27 (Sept. 2012), pp. 23–37, here p. 34.

7 See as examples: *Voyage Around a Star* (*Voyage autour d'une étoile*, F 1906, D: Gaston Velle); *Excursion to the Moon (Excursion dans la lune*, F 1908, D: Segundo de Chomón); *A Trip to Jupiter* (*Voyage sur Jupiter*, F 1909, D: Segundo de Chomón); *Marriage in the Moon* (*Matrimonio Interplanetario*, I 1910, D: Enrico Novelli); *The '?' Motorist* (GB 1907, D: Walter R. Booth).

8 Tom Gunning: The Cinema of Attractions: Early Film, Its Spectator and the Avant-Garde. In: Thomas Elsaesser (ed.): *Early Cinema: Space, Frame, Narrative.* London: BFI 1990, pp. 56–62.

9 For the tradition of the unworldly astronomer see Hans Blumenberg: *The Laughter of the Thracian Woman: A Protohistory of Theory.* New York: Bloomsbury Academic 2015.

by the idealized image of the woman they gaze on. As in medieval times, they are simply content to get access to the physical space that the female objects of their desire occupy. The reciprocation of romantic feelings by the woman only plays a role in a later film, namely the 1910 film *Marriage in the Moon*.[10]

Two space travel films by the British filmmaker Walter R. Booth were made at the dawn of the era of the feature film.[11] In *The '?' Motorist*, a man sits at the wheel of a car that turns into a spacecraft. The female passenger remains a passive spectator. In the extended remake of this film, *The Automatic Motorist*,[12] a pair of lovers once again travels to outer space by car. In this case, however, the man also becomes a passive passenger. Technology has taken over by placing a male-looking robotic chauffeur in the driving seat.

The first feature-length film devoted to space travel was produced in Denmark in 1918. In *A Trip to Mars*,[13] a former ship's captain and his all-male crew set out for planet Mars, where they find a human-like civilization. The captain of the spacecraft and the daughter of the wise Martian leader then fall in love. The future bride travels to Earth of her own volition, but only after her father gives his blessing. The humanoid Martian woman may still play the role of a coveted object, but it is her own independent decision to leave her home planet to spread a Martian message of peace through her love affair with the human captain. The pacifist attitude propagated in a *Trip to Mars* was aimed at the contemporary film audience, who saw the film when the First World War was still raging. The woman functions here as a bringer of peace.

Fritz Lang's film *Woman in the Moon*[14] of 1928 depicts the first human woman to travel into space. The script was written by a woman, Thea von Harbou, who was at the time married to him. The titular *Woman in the Moon* is the astronomy student Friede Velten. She is dressed like her male colleagues in trousers, shirt and tie – a cross-dresser in the style of Marlene Dietrich (Fig. 2). Friede is in no way inferior to her male counterparts, even when it comes to her courage. When her decision to go on the flight is questioned by her admirer Helius, she responds

10 *Marriage in the Moon* (*Matrimonio Interplanetario*, I 1910, D: Enrico Novelli).

11 David Bordwell: The Classical Hollywood Style, 1917–60. In: D. B. / Janet Staiger / Kristin Thompson (eds): *The Classical Hollywood Cinema: Film Style & Mode of Production to 1960*. New York: Columbia UP 1985, pp. 1–84.

12 *The Automatic Motorist* (GB 1911, D: Walter R. Booth).

13 *A Trip to Mars* (*Himmelskibet*, DK 1918, D: Holger Madsen).

14 *Woman in the Moon* (*Frau im Mond*, D 1928, D: Fritz Lang).

Fig. 2: Film history's first female and human astronaut: Friede (Gerda Maurus), clothed like the real-life female aviators of her era in *Frau im Mond* (D 1928, D: Fritz Lang).

confidently, speaking as as a representative for all women: "Helius, in these last moments, are you trying to embarrass the WOMAN in me?"[15]

The starship is named *Friede* after her, which also corresponds to the word 'peace' in German; it thus carries a double meaning when traveling to the Earth's satellite. The spacecraft has been interpreted as phallic in feminist science fiction studies, but it has also been considered a feminine object. According to Marleen Barr, "*Friede*, is a rounded maternal ship, pregnant with passengers."[16]

When a subsequent mishap means that it is no longer possible for all of the passengers to take the return trip, Friede decides to stay with Helius, her fiancé's rival for her affections. The female student thus becomes the *Woman in the Moon* in three separate ways. Due to the obvious meaning of his name, she forms with Helius an idealized pair of Sun and Moon. Their time spent waiting for a rescue

15 Original German wording of the intertitles: "Helius, wollen Sie im letzten Augenblick noch die F R A U in mir beschämen?" Fritz Lang: *Frau im Mond* (D 1928). DVD edition. Wiesbaden: Friedrich-Wilhelm-Murnau-Stifung 2001, 01:21:00.

16 Marleen S. Barr: *Lost in Space: Probing Feminist Science Fiction and Beyond*. Chapel Hill: U of North Carolina P 1993, p. 116.

mission from Earth, which is the ending of the film, offers Helius and Friede the promise of a lot of time together, free from the observation of others. The creation of an "extraordinary horizon"[17] on a cosmic scale becomes a reality for them. This human and planetary constellation gives Friede the opportunity to have an unconventional love affair, which would have been inconceivable under the repressive conditions on Earth, her decision has been made without being influenced by anyone else. In comparison with her female predecessors on film, who are often condemned to passivity and obedience, Friede proves to be an active and self-aware woman, freeing herself from conventions. However, in order to lead her ideal life she must endure hardship far away from human society on the barren Moon.

Fritz Lang and Thea von Harbou's *Woman in the Moon* was one of the last films of the silent film era. A contemporary press report used the title "How the Moon Was Brought Down to Earth",[18] as a way of conveying the great impact the film had made on the public – the metaphor that Georges Méliès had already used in 1898, however this time in reverse. The title not only shows how cinema could bring distant, coveted objects (here symbolized by Luna) closer to Earth, but also its ability to realize ideas which were far-fetched at the time, such as female astronauts. These ideas were extensions of existing developments in the real world of the viewing public. They contributed towards popularising the idea of space travel and its male and female protagonists. Marie Lathers points out the interaction between film and reality: "In the 1940s, engineers remembered Lang's film and created an image of the Moon Girl that was tattooed, so to speak, onto the rocket. From the early years in film, the image of woman, the art of cinema, and the work of rocket scientist were entangled in narratives about journeys into outer space."[19]

The developments in rocket technology after the First World War were based on military objectives. They had nothing to do with manned journeys into space, but rather with creating explosive projectiles that could accurately hit their

17 In German: "Sonderhorizont", see Niels Werber: *Liebe als Roman: Zur Koevolution intimer und literarischer Kommunikation*. Munich: Fink 2003, p. 25. "Sonderhorizont" in this context describes what sociologist Niklas Luhmann sees as a fundamental premise for intimate communication: to see the other person's world through his or her eyes, to adopt the other person's view on the world. See Niklas Luhmann: *Liebe als Passion: Zur Codierung von Intimität.* Frankfurt am Main: Suhrkamp 1994, p. 200.

18 Anatol von Hübbenet: Wie der Mond auf die Erde geholt wurde. In: *Westermanns Monatshefte* 73 (1929), pp. 593–599.

19 Marie Lathers: *Space Oddities: Women and Outer Space in Popular Film and Culture, 1960–2000.* New York: Continuum 2010, p. 3.

targets. Undefined fears of air raids and of a second world war were given a concrete form in *Things to Come*,[20] giving rise to fantasies of escaping from Earth. In the film a huge cannon has been built and stands there ready to make them reality. Towards the end of the film, which was based on a novel by H. G. Wells, a young man and a young woman are tasked with finding new habitats for humanity. Michael Pinsky describes the role of the female protagonist as that of a primal mother: “Morris Passworthy and Catherine Cabal […] are an ironic Adam and Eve, destined for nothing in particular as individuals, but are stepping-stones for wherever humanity might travel.”[21]

In the United States of the 1930s, narratives that had scientific speculation at their core developed into the genre of that became known as “science fiction”.[22] Unlike in Europe, where technical fantasies were mainly aimed at adults, series such as *Buck Rogers*[23] and *Flash Gordon*[24] were aimed at target audiences of children and adolescents. The roles given to women in these space operas were of little practical use to a future space program:

> From comic strips and graphic novels to television and film, science fiction served as a classroom for ideas about women in space. Female roles and popular figures in science fiction art and literature up to the space age typically lacked any strength of character, influence on board ship as part of the crew’s command structure, or qualities that would suggest they were anything more than a good and wholesome female companion for their space pioneering men.[25]

The first American film in which a female astronaut is a highly educated, innovative scientist, was *Rocketship X-M*[26] of 1950. Dr. Lisa Van Horn, inventor of the fictitious fuel X-M, and four men take off to the Moon. Thanks to her quick-witted, confrontational nature, Dr. Van Horn is able to counter the intense male chauvinism of her boss. His clumsy attempts at rapprochement take on a

20 *Things to Come* (GB 1936, D: William C. Menzies).

21 Michael Pinsky: *Future Present: Ethics and/as Science Fiction*. Madison, NJ / London: Fairleigh Dickinson UP / Associated UP 2003, p. 81.

22 Simon Spiegel: *Die Konstitution des Wunderbaren: Zu einer Poetik des Science-Fiction-Films*. Marburg: Schüren 2007.

23 *Buck Rogers* (US 1939, D: Ford Beebe / Saul A. Goodkind).

24 *Flash Gordon* (US 1936, D: Frederick Stephani / Ray Taylor).

25 Amy E. Foster: *Integrating Women into the Astronaut Corps: Politics and Logistics at NASA, 1972–2004*. Baltimore, MD: Johns Hopkins UP 2011, p. 23.

26 *Rocketship X-M* (US 1950, D: Kurt Neumann).

satirical character when viewed from a modern perspective.[27] Perhaps, according to Bonnie Noonan, the scriptwriter Dalton Trumbo was aiming to expose the perfidy of the power games men played against women in the field of science, by exaggerating the situation: "The film's radical message lies in its attempts to extrapolate a future, wherein a representation of a socially acceptable professional woman is possible."[28] Patronizing attitudes can also be seen in *Project Moon Base*,[29] which was shot three years later. Although the film depicts a future in which the US has a female president and the film's protagonist, the female Colonel Briteis, holds a high military rank, Briteis is often portrayed as incompetent and protected by her male colleagues as soon as things become dangerous.

In the 1950s, the real world was on the verge of the Space Age. After the development of the V2 rocket and the transfer of German scientists to the Soviet Union and the USA, travel into space became tangible. Having already been spread and popularized by the genre of science fiction, space travel increasingly became an idea that inspired the imagination of the masses. In these years of the space race[30] between the United States and the USSR, the Soviet side made the more rapid progress: Sputnik in 1957, Yuri Gagarin in 1961, and Valentina Tereshkova in 1963, the first woman in space.

Pride in technical as well as in social progress can be seen in the films that were made in the Eastern bloc. Equality between men and women also plays a major role in their utopias presented as the present day. The DEFA film *The Silent Star*[31] depicts a mixed gender crew of equal rank. In addition to their equal social roles, women-specific topics are also discussed, such as pregnancy. The character of the female doctor, Sumiko Ogimura, has experienced the effects of radiation at close quarters as an eleven-year-old girl after the dropping of the bomb on Hiroshima, which has made her infertile.[32] The subject of pregnancy also plays a role in the

27 In one episode of the satirical series *Mystery Science Theater 3000*, the crew of a fictitious satellite is amused by the story of the film. See "Rocketship X-M", *Mystery Science Theater 3000* (US 1990, D: Jim Mallon).

28 Bonnie Noonan: *Women Scientists in Fifties Science Fiction Films*. Jefferson: McFarland 2005, p. 62.

29 *Project Moon Base* (US 1953, D: Richard Talmadge).

30 William E. Burrows: *This New Ocean: The Story of the Space Age*. New York: Random House 1998.

31 *The Silent Star* (*Der schweigende Stern*, GDR/P 1960, D: Kurt Maetzig).

32 On science fiction film in the GDR see Karsten Kruschel: Leim für die Venus: Der Science-Fiction-Film in der DDR. In: Sascha Mamczak / Wolfgang Jeschke (eds): *Das Science Fiction Jahr 2007*. Munich: Heyne 2007, pp. 803–888.

1963 Czech film *Ikarie XB-1*.[33] A mixed-sex crew travels to a yet unknown planet in a journey lasting several months. A scientist expecting a child is also on board. It is born the same moment as they reach the planet, a sign of a new beginning.
In the 1960s, away from the silver screen, an American program was set up to match the Soviet Union's groundbreaking achievement of sending a woman into space. Named Mercury 13, the privately funded program was able to attract suitable candidates. However, the women, Jerrie Cobb for example, could not meet the official criteria of NASA, which stipulated that astronauts first needed military training as jet pilots – a career path that was only open to men at that time.[34] Twenty years were to pass before Sally Ride became the first American astronaut. The first female taikonaut followed with Chinese Liu Yang in 2012. In 2019, no woman has yet set foot on the Moon.
By 1965, women were also on the navigation bridge on West German television, but their opportunities to do anything important or out of the ordinary were minimal. In the TV series *Raumpatrouille* (Space Patrol),[35] the security officer Tamara Jagellovsk simply follows the on-board regulations to the letter. It is to the credit of the US series *Star Trek*,[36] which was first aired in 1966 and is still being produced to this day, that women have been depicted on film as spacecraft crewmembers of equal rank with the men on board. *Star Trek* also went "where no one has gone before"[37] in other areas and broke social taboos surrounding ethnic groups. For example the famous kiss, which is often cited as the first kiss in American film between a woman of color, Lieutenant Uhura, and a Caucasian protagonist, Captain Kirk. The scene was shown in the 1968 episode, "Plato's Stepchildren".[38]

33 *Ikarie XB-1* (CSSR 1963, D: Jindrich Polack).

34 Rudi Williams: Women Aviators Finally Fill Cockpits of Military Aircraft. Washington: American Forces Press Service. March 19, 2003. http://archive.defense.gov/news/newsarticle.aspx?id=29276 (accessed: January 15, 2019).

35 Theo Mezger / Michael Braun: *Raumpatrouille: Die phantastischen Abenteuer des Raumschiffes Orion* (D 1966, Norddeutscher Rundfunk).

36 *Star Trek: The Original Series* (US 1966, Creator: Gene Roddenberry).

37 With "to boldly go where no man has gone before", the mission of the Starship Enterprise is stated in the intro sequence. In 1987, this line was changed to the more gender-neutral "where no one has gone before".

38 Concerning the roles of women in *Star Trek*, see Patricia Vettel-Becker: Space and the Single Girl. In: *Frontiers: A Journal of Women Studies* 35:2 (2014), pp. 143–178.

1968–1989

In the films discussed so far, the ancient dream of going to the Moon was anticipated in popular media such as literature and film. However, from the mid-1960s onwards, actual technical developments had caught up with the once futuristic visions of science fiction films – and thus largely stripped them of their thrill for cinema visitors. In search for new narratives, Hollywood explored the journey into the microscopic world as an undertaking essentially similar to the conquest of the macrocosmic universe.

In the 1966 film *The Fantastic Voyage*,[39] a crew reduced to the size of microbes in a submarine shrunken to microscopic size hurries to save the life of a seriously injured scientist by traveling inside his body.[40] The surgical assistant is played by Raquel Welch (Fig. 3). In the 1960s and 1970s, she was considered one of the great sex symbols of European and American cinema – a role she remains limited to in *The Fantastic Voyage*, as Alberto Brodesco notes:

> While the men's comments on their adventure are technical or philosophical, Welch's comments are emotional: "I never met anything like this", or "Listen: the heart!", or "Doctor, just think of it: we are the first ones to actually see it happen". Raquel Welch personifies the to-be-looked-at-ness of woman, just an object for the scopophilia of the male gaze: the presence of the woman is important only for the reactions she provokes on men (on screen and in the audience).[41]

The year 1968 saw the release of three important examples in the development of the space explorer theme in the science fiction film: *Planet of the Apes*,[42] *Barbarella*[43] and *2001: A Space Odyssey*.[44] In *Planet of the Apes*, time and space travel are intertwined: a team of three men and one woman fly into space – to find themselves on a planet that turns out to be the Earth of the future. The female astronaut, Stewart, is shown dead only seven minutes after the film begins.

39 *The Fantastic Voyage* (US 1966, D: Richard Fleischer).

40 "Following this 'cultural Ur-text' the topic of the voyage of shrunken people sent to explore the inner space of the body has become a trope that many feature films, television series and animated TV series have adopted, for aims that go from the spectacular to the comic to the didactic." Alberto Brodesco: I've Got You Under My Skin: Narratives of the Inner Body in Cinema and Television. In: *Nuncius* 26:1 (2011), pp. 201–221, here p. 202.

41 Ibid., p. 206.

42 *Barbarella* (*Barbarella: Queen of the Galaxy,* F 1968, D: Roger Vadim).

43 *Planet of the Apes* (US 1968, D: Franklin J. Schaffner).

44 *2001: A Space Odyssey* (GB/US 1968, D: Stanley Kubrick).

In a dialogue between the male astronauts about their deceased colleague, their understanding of her role becomes clear: "Did I tell you about Stewart? Now there was a lovely girl. The most precious cargo we'd brought along, she was ... to be the new Eve. With our hot and eager help, of course."[45] The female protagonist, labelled as "precious cargo", is thought of merely in terms of her beauty or, more specifically, her value as a guarantor of human reproduction.

In *Barbarella* the eponymous heroine, an astronaut from the forty-first century, sets out to find and stop the male villain Duran Duran. In the film's initial scene, Barbarella performs a striptease in zero gravity, which sets the tone for the next ninety minutes. In her essay "Bringing Barbarella Down to Earth",[46] Lisa Parks links the character with contemporary society, in which women were excluded from participating in the space program.

> While scientists and politicians positioned feminine sexuality as a threat to the scientific rational and nationalist imperatives of the American space program, Barbarella represented a dangerous alternative: a female astronaut who was sexy, single and political – a highly volatile combination.[47]

On her mission, Barbarella also has various erotic adventures and not just heterosexual ones (Fig. 4), but also bisexual and even sadomasochistic ones. As film scholars like Mazin Saffou point out, *Barbarella* can be seen as portraying the incarnation of male erotic fantasies of female sexuality.[48] At the same time, the fact that she consciously initiates and enjoys her erotic encounters can lead to an opposite interpretation of the film, namely as a deliberately overstated commentary of the emerging hedonist counterculture on the repressed sexual morality of the time. While women often had to follow long-established role models, Barbarella is a heroine who lives as a sexually liberated woman according to her own rules.

Although the women in *2001: A Space Odyssey* are only shown as a mother and daughter who remain on Earth, or as Russian scientists in supporting roles, the

45 Franklin J. Schaffner: *Planet of the Apes*. DVD edition. Los Angeles: Foxmovies 2012, 01:02:13.

46 Lisa Parks: Bringing Barbarella Down to Earth. In: Hilary Radner (ed.): *Swinging Single: Representing Sexuality in the 1960s*. Minneapolis: U of Minnesota P 1999, pp. 253–257.

47 Ibid., pp. 253–254.

48 Mazin Saffou: Cartesian Dualism and the Orgasmotron: Interiority and Eroticism in Barbarella. In: Philippe Mather (ed.): *Rediscovering French Science-Fiction in Literature, Film and Comics*. Newcastle upon Tyne: Cambridge Scholars 2016, pp. 161–173.

Fig. 3
Cora Peterson (Raquel Welsh) in a form fitting dress in *The Fantastic Voyage* (US 1966, D: Richard Fleischer).

film is considered "the greatest science fiction film ever made, and certainly one of the most philosophical".[49] The birth of a new version humanity and accordingly a new relationship between the principles of masculinity and femininity plays an integral role in the film. The clash of the sperm-shaped spacecraft and the egg-like Jupiter can thus be seen as an act of fertilization on a metaphorical level. From this encounter the "star child" emerges, which floats back to Earth at the end of the film. Film and gender scholar Barry Keith Grant observes that it cannot be determined whether the star child[50] is male or female.[51] However,

49 Jerold J. Abrams: Nietzsche's Overman as Posthuman Star Child in 2001: A Space Odyssey. In: J. J. A. (ed.): *The Philosophy of Stanley Kubrick*. Lexington: Kentucky UP 2007, pp. 247–267, here p. 247.

50 Cf. Annette Burfoot: The Fetal Voyager: Women in Modern Medical Visual Discourse. In: Ann B. Shteir / Bernard V. Lightman (eds): *Figuring it Out: Science, Gender, and Visual Culture*. Hanover, NH: Dartmouth College Press 2006, pp. 337–358.

51 Barry Keith Grant: Of Men and Monoliths: Science Fiction, Gender and 2001: A Space Odyssey. In: Robert Phillip Kolker (ed.): *Stanley Kubrick's 2001: A Space Odyssey. New Essays*. Oxford: Oxford UP 2006, pp. 69–87.

Fig. 4
Barbarella (Jane Fonda) helps an angel to regain his will to fly in *Barbarella: Queen of the Galaxy* (F 1968, D: Roger Vadim).

it should be added to Grant's observation that the doll created by Liz Moore is based on the physiognomy of the male lead actor.[52]

In *Solaris*,[53] often referred to as the Russian counterpart to *2001*, the cycle of life is also an important part of its narrative. However, whereas *2001* traveled to outer space, *Solaris* embarks on a journey inside its protagonist's mental space. In Tarkovsky's film, a psychologist orbits a planet in a space station, when suddenly a woman appears who looks like his former lover, who had in fact killed herself years earlier, because she did not feel loved by him. Is this female 'astronaut' just an illusion? The psychologist realizes that this 'woman' is a materialization of his own thoughts, created by the planet that the space station is orbiting. The planet

52 Making the Starchild in "2001": A Tribute to Liz Moore. In: *2001 Italia*. http://www.2001italia.it/2013/05/making-starchild-in-2001-tribute-to-liz.html (accessed: August 24, 2017). In the sequel *2010: The Year We Make Contact* the board computer SAL 9000 represents a border case: although a machine through and through, it speaks with a female voice to the astronauts.

53 *Solyaris* (*Solaris*, SU 1971, D: Andrei Tarkovsky).

Fig. 5: A sentient ocean planet creates this 'female' cosmonaut (Natalja Bondartschuk) as a simulacrum in *Solyaris* (*Solaris*, SU 1971, D: Andrei Tarkovsky).

is covered by a plasma ocean, which has its own self-consciousness. Despite several attempts by the psychologist to get rid of the female figure, he fails to do so. Over time he begins to understand the female 'astronaut' as more than just a materialized projection of his fantasies. She is an independent being, who wants to learn more about him as well as about herself as a product of his intellectual world. By becoming involved with her, the psychologist comes to terms with his grief and feelings of guilt. As an emissary of something that traditionally is associated as feminine, the flowing ocean, she helps the scientist seeking a rational explanation to find emotional access to his world of experience (Fig. 5).

The first Moon landing took place in 1969, but shortly afterwards, in 1972, NASA's Moon landing program was canceled. The huge effort to get to the Moon seemed to be out of all proportion to the barren desert found out there. Public demands that more attention be paid to the problems on Earth became louder.[54] Some science fiction films reacted to this demystification of the universe by re-focusing on problems of the human world. The plot of the dystopian film *Silent Running*[55] concerns a future where the flora of the Earth has been

54 Hans Blumenberg: Mondbezwingung und Umweltschutz. In: H. B.: *Die Vollzähligkeit der Sterne.* Frankfurt am Main: Suhrkamp 1997, pp. 439–441.
55 *Silent Running* (US 1972, D: Douglas Trumbull).

destroyed and plants are only kept alive under large domes near Jupiter.[56] In the same way as *Solaris*, the boundaries between the inner and outer world of the body are deliberately blurred and *Silent Running* deals with a journey from our earthly home to cosmic remoteness. There is no female astronaut among the crew, but the male astronaut, depicted as a kind of neo-romantic sensitive monk,[57] combines masculine qualities – aggression that leads to manslaughter – with more feminine qualities, gentleness, and concern for nature in the domestic 'nest'.[58] With reference to Buckminster Fuller's metaphor of the "spaceship Earth", Sabine Höhler writes about the high-tech spaceship as a refuge for nature:

> It is certainly no coincidence that the film is set entirely on a spaceship, which had become a major symbol of both the fears and the hopes associated with the Earth's transformation into an endangerded planet. At the height of the Space Age, the spaceship merged notions about the fragility of life with the triumphs of science and technology.[59]

1977 was the year that marked the beginning of the *Star Wars* saga[60] with its many prequels and sequels. To date it is the most financially successful series in the history of spaceship films. However, its influence on the re-orientation of the role of female characters is relatively low. In the narrative, which follows the classical scheme of a fairy tale, the female protagonist plays the archetypal role of a princess. Only in the later films in this saga, such as *Rogue One: A Star Wars Story*[61] (2016) does the narrative emancipate itself from this tradition.

56 "The designs for the geodesic domes which would become such an iconic element of *Silent Running* were inspired in part by the 'Climatron' from the Missouri Botanical Gardens [...]. Opened to the public in 1960 the Climatron is billed as 'the first geodesic dome to be used as a conservatory, incorporating the principles of R. Buckminster Fuller, inventor of the geodesic system'." Mark Kermode: *Silent Running*. London / New York: Palgrave Macmillan on behalf of the British Film Institute 2014, p. 29.

57 See also Matthew H. Hersch's contribution, "Redemptive Space: Duty, Death, and the Astronaut-Soldier, 1949–1969" in this volume.

58 A picture showing Freeman Lowel (Bruce Dern) as a male astronaut taking care of Mother Earth can be seen in Hersch's article (Fig. 6) in this book.

59 Sabine Höhler: *Spaceship Earth in the Environmental Age: 1960–1990*. London: Pickering & Chatto 2015, p. 101.

60 *Star Wars* (US 1977, D: George Lucas).

61 *Rogue One: A Star Wars Story* (US 2016, D: Edwards Gareth).

In the history of film, *Star Wars* refers back to the tradition of space opera[62] of the Golden Era.[63] The fact that the genre could become 'nostalgic' and thus look back on itself is an indication of the establishment of certain narrative conventions within the science fiction genre. A film that uses these patterns, but reverses them, is *Dark Star.*[64] The astronauts who are travelling in this film's wrecked spaceship are not the clean-shaven heroes of the films of the 1950s and 1960s. With their long hair and unkempt beards, they look more like a rock band. They are mothered by the onboard computer, which, appropriately enough, is called "Mother" and speaks to the astronauts with a female voice. Mother is indeed more compassionate than HAL in *2001*, but its role is limited to informing and instructing. They can also do nothing about the out-of-control bomb on board. The bomb, in turn, speaks with a male voice. It seems that the role of the female can be replaced by a machine, but the role of the men, who make the real decisions on board, cannot.

By using the idea of placing the danger to the mission *inside* the space ship, *Dark Star* is a forerunner to Ridley Scott's *Alien.*[65] With regard to the subject of this article – female space travelers in science fiction films – this film is one of the most often studied. As with *Dark Star,* it shows a crew that is on its way home in a vessel more a floating death trap than a spaceship.[66] The crew does not consist of scientists, but is a motley group of blue-collar workers who are just doing their job. When a foreign life form, the hostile alien, appears on board, their journey home becomes a struggle for survival. *Alien* is not only the first spaceship movie in which a woman plays the central role, but also one where the role of women is radically re-interpreted. In contrast to all the films previously discussed, the main character, Ellen Ripley, plays the role of a truly combative woman. As an astronaut, she acts as a leader and fighter, a mother figure and a woman capable of acting rationally. In the fight against the alien, it is appropriate that she has the role

62 David Pringle: What Is This Thing Called Space Opera? In: Gary Westfahl (ed.): *Space and Beyond: The Frontier Theme in Science Fiction.* Westport, CT: Greenwood 2000, pp. 35–47.

63 "The phrase Golden Age valorises a particular sort of writing: 'Hard SF', linear narratives, heroes solving problems or countering threats in a space-opera or technological-adventure idiom." Adam Roberts: *The History of Science Fiction.* Basingstoke: Palgrave Macmillan 2007, p. 195.

64 *Dark Star* (US 1974, D: John Carpenter).

65 *Alien* (GB 1979, D: Ridley Scott).

66 Andreas Böhn: Von Aliens, seltsamen Müttern und pervertierten Geburten: Fremdkörper im Science-Fiction-Film. In: Christian Franz Hoffstadt (ed.): *Der Fremdkörper.* Bochum: Projektverlag 2008, pp. 33–44.

Fig. 6: In space no one can hear you scream? Ellen Ripley (Sigourney Weaver) in *Alien* (GB/US 1979, D: Ridley Scott).

of the 'last (wo)man standing', which has so far been reserved for men (Fig. 6). To this day, Ellen Ripley is the cinematic icon of female empowerment. Scholarly literature about this film and its prequels and sequels fills entire bookshelves.[67] The interpretations of her are manifold and include, for example, psychoanalytic approaches and those that see in her the incarnations of male fears concerning an increasingly stronger role of women in contemporary society of the late 1970s.
In the 1980s, science fiction films become more and more 'meta-referential' with regard to the history of their own genre. References to other movies or sequels such as the *Star Wars, Star Trek,* and the *Alien* franchises, become more and more common. This development is accompanied by the (re-)combination of several motifs related to the subject of women in space. The real political background against which these films play out is no longer the space race, nor the sense of disillusionment after the cessation of the lunar landing program and

67 Cf. Amy Taubin: The 'Alien' Trilogy: From Feminism to AIDS. In: Pam Cook / Philip Dodd (eds): *Women and Film: A Sight and Sound Reader.* London: Scarlet 1993, pp. 93–100; Elizabeth Graham: *Meanings of Ripley: The "Alien" Quadrilogy and Gender.* Newcastle upon Tyne: Cambridge Scholars 2010.

the refocusing of attention back to the Earth, nor the second wave of feminism,[68] but rather the increasingly escalating conflict between the political blocs of the East and the West.

A film that addresses this topic is *2010: The Year We Make Contact*.[69] In this sequel to *2001,* Russian and American space explorers are together on board a Russian spacecraft. Cosmonaut Tanja Kirbuk is the head of the mission, whose task it is to find out why an earlier journey to Jupiter failed. She, as an officer of the Soviet Air Force, is subject to her commanders on Earth, but, after careful consideration, she chooses to ignore them at decisive moments. She decides to follow the proposal of the male US astronaut and concludes that the situation on board the spacecraft requires the need for cooperation with the Americans. She thus proves to be less stubborn than the male military leaders located on Earth.

In *Aliens*,[70] the sequel to *Alien*, Ellen Ripley returns. Awakened from her cryo-preservation, she and a group of marines return to the planet where she once found the alien and which has been colonised by humans in the meantime. Once there, however, they find only one survivor, the ten-year-old girl Newt. Ripley discovers that her own daughter has died during her cyrogenic sleep, so she adopts Newt as a substitute daughter and becomes a kind of surrogate mother. The marines are gradually killed in the fight against the aliens on the planet, so that the climax of the film is a showdown of Ripley versus the Alien. The alien turns out to be a queen and thus she too is a female being. By fighting her Ripley is willing to sacrifice herself for Newt. She defends her at all costs against the alien, who in turn only wants to protect her own species. Two women in typically female roles?

Right from the beginning, the character of Ripley is given a very feminine role in *Aliens*, a marked contrast to the script of the first *Alien* film. The narrative can therefore focus on a subject that is inseparable from femininity: motherhood. Two archetypes are placed against each other in the film: Ripley as the 'good mother' and the Alien Queen, who as 'bad mother' personifies all

68 "While the first-wave feminism of the 19th and early 20th centuries focused on women's legal rights, such as the right to vote, the second-wave feminism of the 'women's movement' peaked in the 1960s and '70s and touched on every area of women's experience – including family, sexuality, and work." Elinor Burkett: Women's Movement: Political and Social Movement. In: *Encyclopedia Britannica*, February 13, 2019. https://www.britannica.com/topic/womens-movement (accessed: March 24, 2019).

69 *2010: The Year We Make Contact* (US 1984, D: Peter Hyams).

70 *Aliens* (US 1986, D: James Cameron).

Fig. 7
Ellen Ripley as mother and fighter. "This time it's war." Sigourney Weaver as Ellen Ripley on the movie-poster for *Aliens* (US 1986, D: James Cameron).

the stereotypical male fears regarding the female body such as childbirth and untamed sexuality (Fig. 7).[71] In *Alien* and its sequels, the image of a heroine, represented by the character of Ellen Ripley, is constantly being reworked and redefined. The film critics Georg Seeßlen and Fernand Jung regard the 'role model' that Ripley embodies as the real science fiction part of the *Alien* saga.[72]

71 For a full discussion on the 'monstrous feminine' in the *Alien* films see Barbara Creed: Horror and the Archaic Mother: *Alien*. In: B. C.: *The Monstrous-Feminine: Film, Feminism, Psychoanalysis*. London / New York: Routledge 1993, pp. 16–31.

72 Georg Seeßlen / Fernand Jung: *Science Fiction. Geschichte und Mythologie des Science-Fiction-Films*. Marburg: Schüren 2003, p. 363.

Fig. 8: Compared to men, women are better at multi-tasking. Lindsey Brigman (Mary Elizabeth Mastrantonio) in *The Abyss* (US 1989, D: James Cameron).

Aliens director James Cameron often creates strong female roles in his films.[73] In *The Abyss*,[74] which he also directed, Cameron again puts a woman in the spotlight. The motif of a woman in a spaceship is evident here in the similar plot framework based on a submarine journey. Most of the action of the film takes place underwater, when the crew of a civilian oilrig is forced to search for a vanished nuclear submarine by the U. S. military. The female protagonist not only has to manage this emergency, she is also exposed to several other conflicts. She has to cope with the increasingly paranoid military on board and is confronted with her former husband. Finally, she meets the aliens who live at the bottom of the sea. In contrast to the male soldiers on board the submarine, she seeks not to kill but to understand these lifeforms and their peaceful message for humanity. *The Abyss* has a more complex narrative than most of the films before it. It also has a female character that is more clearly defined and less schematic. In addition to her social skills, she also has irreplaceable technical expertise; she is the one who designed the drilling platform – an unusual role even for the science fiction genre, where female scientists usually have less practical occupations (Fig. 8).

73 A preference for independent-minded women is also evident in Cameron's private life. He was married to director Kathryn Bigelow, producer Gale Ann Hurd, and actress Linda Hamilton. Cf. Christopher Heard: *Dreaming Aloud: The Life and Films of James Cameron*. Rev. ed. Toronto: Doubleday Canada 1998.

74 *The Abyss* (US 1989, D: James Cameron).

1989–2017

When looking at the history of the science fiction film genre and the role of women, it is particularly noticeable that no women have been involved in writing screenplays or as directors, with the exception of the *Woman in the Moon*, where the screenplay was written by Thea von Harbou and based on her novel. Only the 1997 film *Contact*[75] can be considered another exception to the rule. The original screenplay was written by Carl Sagan and Ann Druyan, whom he later married. The film is also interesting on other levels for the subject of women in space. For example, the real-life American astronomer Dr. Jill Cornell Tarter, director of the Search for Extraterrestrial Intelligence (SETI) research centers, was the inspiration for the film's main character, radio astronomer Ellie Arroway.

Ellie is portrayed as a highly talented but disillusioned natural scientist. After losing her faith in a Christian God due to the early death of her parents, she devotes herself to research into the universe as an astrophysicist, using only rational calculations. However, her search for extraterrestrial life also takes on the character of a personal and even spiritual experience (Fig. 9). Before she manages to make contact with extraterrestrials, as a woman she must assert herself in a male-dominated scientific world, coming up against several personal and institutional obstacles such as her male boss, a religious fanatic, and a male lover who sabotages her application to become an astronaut. In contrast to the ambitious but morally upright Ellie, the men appear to be ruthless when it comes to realizing their goals as scientists, religious zealots or lovers. However, there are also male figures that support Ellie. Her interest in science was encouraged early on by her father. She also receives crucial financial support from an eccentric male billionaire.

She eventually travels to the planet from where an extraterrestrial signal has been received and there she meets an alien. It takes the form of her deceased father and gives her some insights intended to console her, such as the fact that humankind is not alone in the cosmos. Ellie receives no scientifically credible knowledge from the alien, merely an affirmation of her own convictions. This conversation helps Ellie to compensate for her deep-seated feelings of loss, which were the catalyst for her obsessive research. Her mourning process can also be understood more generally as a way of coping with the so-called "contingency shock"[76] which, according to some philosophers, has marked the entire epoch of

75 *Contact* (US 1997, D: Robert Zemeckis).

76 Günther Stern [Günther Anders]: Pathologie de la Liberté: Essai sur la non-identification. In: *Recherches Philosophiques* 6 (1936), pp. 22–54.

Fig. 9: The truth will not be televised. Dr. Eleanor Arroway (Jodie Foster) in *Contact* (US 1997, D: Robert Zemeckis).

modernity.[77] According to the alien, the answer to the estrangement that accompanies this "breakdown of the traditional order of things"[78] simply lies in closer social engagement. In a fatherly tone, it speaks to Ellie: "You feel so lost, so cut off, so alone, only you're not. See, in all our searching, the only thing we've found that makes the emptiness bearable is each other."[79]

The film leaves its viewers unclear whether Ellie's journey actually took place or whether the alleged encounter was a hallucination. When Ellie gives a report to the Senate on her adventures, her experiences are questioned. It is implied that she has the victim of a hoax staged by the billionaire and has suffered a nervous breakdown while she was in the spacecraft. With the insinuation that she is not able to distinguish between the truth and a vision, Ellie is put into the role of the

77 Michael Makropoulos: *Modernität und Kontingenz*. Munich: Fink 1997.

78 Hans Blumenberg: Ordnungsschwund und Selbstbehauptung: Über Weltverstehen und Weltverhalten im Werden der technischen Epoche. In: Helmut Kuhn / Franz Wiedmann (eds): *Das Problem der Ordnung*. Frankfurt am Main: Klostermann 1962, pp. 37–57.

79 Robert Zemeckis: *Contact* (US 1997). DVD edition. Burbank: Warner Home Video 1998, 02:00:23.

hysterical woman – a stereotype that has existed since ancient times.[80] Despite being placed under great pressure, Ellie remains true to her convictions. Towards the end of the film, she is depicted passing on her astronomical knowledge to interested pupils, but without any missionary zeal.

Ellie's characterization as a woman who acts calmly and is always true to her deepest convictions, adds another facet to the image of women in space films. Unlike Ellen Ripley, the heroine of the *Alien* series, Ellie has no need to employ physical force or violence to survive in an action-packed scenario. *Contact* is, thanks to the careful working out of its narrative, a quiet, intelligent drama, with an emotionally and intellectually complex female figure at its center. Ellie is a female character on the big screen whose visionary thinking enables her, right from the start, to outshine her one-dimensional, overly rational contemporaries. In the course of the story, she is also capable of recognizing that the world has an inexplicable, transcendent side. By being able to reconcile factual research with emotional, aesthetic, and religious thinking, she succeeds in achieving a holistic vision of the world – and yet she remains completely down to earth.

A few years went by before cinemagoers got another opportunity to see a female character placed in the center of the action. In the meantime, *Event Horizon*[81] mixed, in a very similar manner to *Alien*, the genres of science fiction and horror. *Event Horizon* shows a mission that encounters a spaceship that was thought to be lost in deep space. The conversational tone of the crew on the mothership is very direct, and, despite the numerous barbed comments, it is largely friendly. The female astronaut on board is accustomed to the rough manners and male chauvinism of her colleagues. When a black colleague offers her a coffee with the words, "Don't you want something hot and black inside you?",[82] she is able to treat this as comradely joking around. Her ability to know when to turn a deaf ear[83] marks her as an intelligent woman who is adept at communicating on different levels (Fig. 10).

As the plot develops and weird events begin to happen on board, the spaceship begins to look more and more like a haunted house transposed into outer space. Each crewmember is haunted by his or her past, and, very reminiscent of the

80 Cf. Gabriele Sobiech: *Grenzüberschreitungen: Körperstrategien von Frauen in modernen Gesellschaften*. Opladen: Westdeutscher Verlag 1994.

81 *Event Horizon* (GB/US 1997, D: Paul W. S. Anderson).

82 Paul W. S. Anderson: *Event Horizon* (GB/US 1997). DVD edition. Los Angeles: Paramount 2009, 0:11:54.

83 Friedemann Schulz von Thun: *Störungen und Klärungen: Allgemeine Psychologie der Kommunikation*. 53rd ed. Reinbek: Rowohlt 2016.

Fig. 10: How to cope with macho behavior at work? Lieutenant Starck (Joely Richardson) in *Event Horizon* (GB/US 1997, D: Paul W.S. Anderson).

film *Solaris*; the wife of a scientist on board the ship appears before him, even though she had committed suicide years before. While the male crewmembers have to deal with their personal feelings of guilt which have built up as a result of their love lives or of their war experiences, the female astronaut on board is haunted by delusions in which she can see her son. Back on Earth, he lives apart from her with his father and yet when she sees him apparently injured, she feels a strong urge to protect her child. Once again the subject of parenthood is associated with the female character.

A film that can be seen as a variant of the spaceship film is *Dark City*.[84] The beginning resembles a classic *film noir* and explores the theme of experiments on humans. It is only when the setting of the film turns out to be a kind of a laboratory floating in outer space that *Dark City* reveals itself to be a space movie. The role of the female character remains, in keeping with the repertoire of characters in *film noir*, limited to that of the love interest of the male protagnonist. Their adversaries, aliens in search of what constitutes the human soul, are all male. They are all pale and bald, because they use the bodies of dead humans as vessels to live in. The film does not provide any answers to the obvious question of why they only choose to use male bodies. Is this a squandered opportunity

84 *Dark City* (US/AUS 1998, D: Alex Proyas).

Fig. 11: That 'male gaze'. Mr. Hand (Richard O'Brien) in *Dark City* (US/AUS 1998, D: Alex Proyas).

that results in a hole in the plot? Or is it a deliberate concession to the theory of the "male gaze",[85] as a male viewer would likely have found the sight of bald pale women a real turn-off? (Fig. 11).

The 2000s was a decade also heralded by a film that at first glance has nothing to do with the topic of space exploration: Tarsem Singh's *The Cell*.[86] In this detective thriller with science fiction elements, space exploration appears, as in *The Fantastic Voyage*, to be a journey into inner space (Fig. 12). This time, however, the journey is not about going inside a body, but into the mind of a man. To get information about a crime scene, a female child psychologist immerses herself in the imaginary world of a serial killer by means of an experimental virtual reality treatment originally devised for coma patients. Although she loses herself in his thoughts and has to be saved by a (male) colleague, she still embodies a mixture of male and female characteristics; her empirical search for evidence is a particularly masculine principle,[87] while her mastery of social empathy is a quality with particularly feminine connotations. As a brilliant psychologist, she can literally put herself into the mindset of another person.

85 Laura Mulvey: Visual Pleasure and Narrative Cinema. In: *Screen* 16:3 (1975), pp. 6–18.

86 *The Cell* (US 2000, D: Tarsem Singh).

87 Philippa Gates: *Detecting Women: Gender and the Hollywood Detective Film*. Albany: Suny Press 2011.

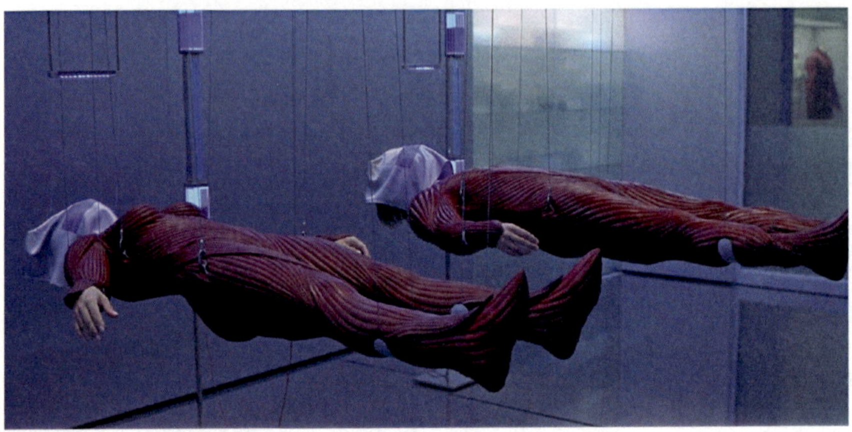

Fig. 12: Floating in inner space. Catherine Deane (Jennifer Lopez) in *The Cell* (US 2000, D: Tarsem Singh).

Another film that can be labeled as a variant of outer space exploration because of its similar plot structure, is *The Core*.[88] In this disaster movie, a female astronaut is hired to penetrate the core of the Earth. She is portrayed as a brilliant former astronaut, who was allowed to study at the Space Academy as young as thirteen. As a pilot of a space shuttle, she was able to calculate the coordinates for a safe landing in her head when the craft was about to crash. Nevertheless, she is often treated like a child by her male boss. Moreover, he explains to her that her intelligence intimidates him. A potential love affair between them, which had been hinted at, is thus quickly stopped. When the 'terranaut' proves her exceptional qualities in another emergency, she is even ashamed of them. The message that the film conveys is: being intelligent, highly talented, and professional may be helpful as a woman, but such a woman should not expect to be respected or loved by male authority figures.

The 2010s were the years in the history of the space film when large Hollywood productions with women in lead roles followed in rapid succession: *Prometheus* (2012),[89] *Gravity* (2013),[90] *Interstellar* (2014),[91] *The Martian* (2015),[92]

88 *The Core* (US 2003, D: John Rogers).
89 *Prometheus* (GB/US 2012, D: Ridley Scott).
90 *Gravity* (US/GB 2013, D: Alfonso Cuarón).
91 *Interstellar* (US/GB/CA 2014, D: Christopher Nolan).
92 *The Martian* (US 2015, D: Ridley Scott).

Arrival (2016)[93] and *Life*[94] as well as *Alien: Covenant* (2017).[95] *Gravity* takes place in the present day and shows outer space and the activities of astronauts in a very realistic way. The science fiction elements in this film are minimal. In fact, it is more of a psychological drama that happens to be set in space. The focus of the action is on biomedical engineer Dr. Ryan Stone. She is on her first space mission. Her commander is the space veteran Matt Kowalski, for whom this trip is the last of his career. When the space station is destroyed by an accident, the two find themselves shipwrecked in outer space. While trying to get to the next space station, the viewer learns more about the life of the protagonist; she chose to go in space, in a literal sense to lose the ground under her feet, because of the unexpected death of her daughter on Earth. The next ninety minutes show how the astronaut fights her way back to life (Fig. 13) – which means getting back to Earth – on both a literal and a metaphorical level, until she once again has solid ground beneath her feet and can begin a new chapter in her life.
The film received criticism from a feminist point of view, because even though Stone has the most screen time, she is nevertheless:

> [...] flung from crisis to crisis with barely a clue about what to do. Knowledge in *Gravity* resides almost exclusively with George Clooney's Commander Matt Kowalski, while Stone struggles with psychological demons that would have debarred her from going to space with NASA.[96]

That may be partially true, Kowalski even re-appears after he has sacrificed his life for her and gives her useful advice, but this turns out to a dream. In her struggle with adverse circumstances and the resolution of her grieving process, Stone shows she has an inner strength. The character of the female astronaut in *Gravity* thus makes it one of the most inspirational women-in-space movies.
In *Interstellar*, which is set in a not-too-distant future, Earth has become uninhabitable. NASA sends a team on a journey into space to find habitable planets that humanity could relocate to. Two of the three main characters in *Interstellar* are female. Both are distinguished by their above-average intelligence and play key roles in the development of the narrative: the daughter of the male

93 *Arrival* (US 2016, D: Denis Villeneuve).
94 *Life* (US 2017, D: Daniél Espinosa).
95 *Alien: Covenant* (US 2017, D: Ridley Scott).
96 Dean Conrad / Lynne Magowan: Damn Dirty Dames: Dissecting Differences in Planet of the Apes. In: Matthew Kapell (ed.): *The Fantastic Made Visible: Essays on the Adaptation of Science Fiction and Fantasy from Page to Screen*. Jefferson, NC: McFarland 2015, pp. 101–117, here p. 105.

Fig. 13: Don't panic. Dr. Ryan Stone (Sandra Bullock) presents a rare example of a strong female lead character in a Hollywood movie in *Gravity* (US/GB 2013, D: Alfonso Cuarón).

protagonist Cooper discovers the mathematical equation that secures the survival of humankind. Cooper, who has supported her fascination with natural sciences, takes part in the journey to the supposedly habitable planets. He is accompanied by two male astronauts as well as a female scientist, the adult daughter of the head of NASA. It would have been easy for the filmmakers to make the scientist the love interest in the narrative, however, she takes on more responsible roles. As protector of a future generation of human beings, she also fulfils the role of a cosmic mother, when she monitors the frozen fertilized human eggs onboard.

She is also the expert who determines the route of the flight and yet she does not rely solely on scientific facts. It turns out that on her preferred habitable planet, she discovers the man whom she fell in love with years ago. In the speech that follows, she tries to bring the mathematical phenomenon of gravity into a kind of universal equation with the power of love, which she invokes as something that transcends time and space. The arguments put into her mouth by the screenplay are a series of sentimental stereotypes. They diminish her role as a scientist, but strengthen the other side of her character as an emotional being, as a human.

The Martian is a film adapted from a novel by Andy Weir. Compared with the literary version, the role of the two astronauts in the film is much more significant. The crew, on a mission to Mars that has to be abandoned unexpectedly, is led by a female commander. She is characterized by both her inner strength and

Fig. 14: Empathy, intuition, and compassion as feminine traits: Dr. Louise Banks (Amy Adams) in *Arrival* (US 2016, D: Denis Villeneuve).

her executive power. With her moral integrity and decision-making, which she expounds in front of the team, she creates a natural authority. It is thanks to her decisions and her confidence in her team that in the end, the entire crew, including the male astronauts, can safely return to Earth. The second woman on board also has a greater role in the film compared with the novel. Her love affair with one of the astronauts and the resulting pregnancy is only dealt with in outline, in contrast to the book. More emphasis is put on her computer skills: as a programmer, she ensures that an unexpected but necessary swing-by maneuver by the spacecraft is carried out successfully. As commander and programmer, the two female astronauts carry out tasks onboard that until now have been assigned to men.

Arrival is *not* a classic outer space movie. Since the protagonist, however, repeatedly enters the spacecraft of a group of extra-terrestrials and thus explores unknown space, this film is included in the present text as a provisional conclusion of the film chronology. The main character in *Arrival*, the linguist Dr. Louise Banks, is instructed by the US military to decode the language of a group of extra-terrestrials that have landed on Earth (Fig. 14). This task is achieved not only by means of her scientific skills. Her success is also due to her 'feminine' traits. Unlike the military man who is pressing for a military confrontation, she chooses the path of empathy, intuition and compassion. Compared to the 'masculine' values of dominance and violence, the 'feminine' counterparts of compassion, patience and cooperation, prove, after more than 100 years of film history, to be superior.

Conclusion

This article has shown that the image of the female space explorer in science fiction films has been subject to many changes throughout its history: these changes in medial representation begin with the mystical caricatures of the "cinema of attractions" and are followed by the bold, self-aware vision of the future represented in the early European feature films. In the American outer space serials, female characters are often used only to confirm the heroic status of the men. The gamut of roles assigned to women also includes ones in films produced in both the Eastern and the Western blocs, which are set on generation-starships where the crews have utopian visions for future societies. In these settings, women hold leading positions that were up to this time denied to them in real life. The range of roles also includes some revolutionary gender experiments, in which men are sensitive botanists, while women level heavy weapons at enemy intruders onboard. Female roles also encompass the eroticism of cool self-determination and the ability to engage with others at times of crises in international communication. This chronological overview has thus ended with a series of films portraying women as highly educated, emotionally competent and autonomous.
The way the image of women was and is depicted on the cosmic stage depends on a multitude of factors. These factors are in constant flux and at the same time are related to each other:

- Political, technical, and scientific factors, which have determined the development of real space travel in the twentieth century on which fictional outer space narratives have been built.
- Media factors, such as the formation of the cinematic dispositif, have an important role in determining how these circumstances are reflected and extrapolated.
- Financial factors, which are essential for the cost-intensive production of large-scale feature films, also play a role.
- Ideological requirements, which productions from the Soviet Union often had to meet, for example. However, producers measure the success of a film less by its educational value and more by its box office takings.
- Social aspects, in particular the position of women in society and the way society has changed, for example in the context of the feminist movement.

In this continually changing and interwoven field of discourse, science fiction films have conceived female characters that are characterized by their status, their actions, or their treatment by others. This analysis has shown that the image of the female astronaut in science fiction films is in most cases not too different from the contemporary real life status of women. Radical approaches, such as a society in which men can become pregnant instead of women, are avoided, although they would be quite attractive for the speculative way of thinking that forms the basis of science fiction.

Images of female space travellers are often clichéd. In 1974, David Ketterer states that the focus of the narrative, especially in the sub-genre of the space travel film, is usually directed on other areas: "the 'weaknesses' of poor characterization and lack of human interest in much SF can be seen as a strength, at least in 'cosmic' fictions in which individual concerns – including gender – are unimportant."[97] However, space travel plays out in fields of discourse traditionally considered as 'male': from warlike elements – the rocket was developed as a weapon – to the virtually Prometheus-like domination of fire with the aim of conquering a territorial or scientific frontier. Fictional female characters could be made much more radical, especially in the genre of science fiction, in order to explore the full potential of the theme of alienation,[98] but space films tend to follow societal developments rather than revealing a new vision of the future. Far more radical ideas are to be found in science fiction literature, which has fewer financial hurdles to overcome before reaching the public.[99]

This conservative approach of films also extends to the casting of women in leading roles. A study from the year 2014 concludes that a single female character has played the leading role in only 12 % of the one hundred biggest box office successes in science fiction and fantasy films. So the percentage is clearly below that of other film genres – a legacy of the history of its development? Lisa Tuttle writes: "Since Genre SF developed in a patriarchal culture as something

97 David Ketterer in *New Worlds for Old: The Apocalyptic Imagination, Science Fiction and American Literature* (1974) quoted in Lisa Tuttle: Women in SF. In: *SFE: The Encyclopedia of Science Fiction*, August 31, 2018. http://www.sf-encyclopedia.com/entry/women_in_sf (accessed: March 24, 2019).

98 Simon Spiegel: Things Made Strange: On the Concept of "Estrangement" in Science Fiction Theory. In: *Science Fiction Studies* 35:3 (Nov. 2008), pp. 369–385.

99 "Writers such as Ursula K. Le Guin, Samuel R. Delany, James Tiptree, Jr. (Alice Bradley Sheldon), Joanna Russ, Suzy McKee Charnas, and Marge Piercy transformed SF into a rich field for exploring feminist perspectives on gender, sexuality, and patriarchy." Helen Merrick / Lisa Tuttle: Feminism. In: *SFE: The Encyclopedia of Science Fiction*, August 31, 2018. http://www.sf-encyclopedia.com/entry/feminism (accessed: March 24, 2019).

written chiefly by men for men (or boys), the lack of female protagonists is unsurprising."[100]

The article has shown that the number of women in leading roles increases around the year 2000. By this time, the great visions of the future of space travel have given way to a more pragmatic realism. This has also changed the genre. "Hard science fiction", which is fixated on technical accuracy, is found less and less often in cinemas, along with extreme action and erotic adventures in outer space. Other content is now in the foreground, which also appeals more strongly to women as target audiences. This reorientation of content and values is new to the space explorer genre. Furthermore, although the categorization of language and understanding of women is still rather traditional, these space films can be seen as an encouragement for women to strive for a career in the STEM fields (science, technology, engineering, mathematics).

At the same time there are more female characters playing major roles in space films: a trend that reached a temporary peak in 2016 as confirmed by a study of the San Diego State University's Center for the Study of Women in Television & Film: "Females comprised 29 % of protagonists featured in the 100 top domestic grossing films of 2016. This represents an increase of 7 percentage points from 2015 and is a recent historical high."[101] Space films like *Rogue One: A Star Wars Story*, *Hidden Figures*, and *Arrival*, which were released in theaters in 2016, all contributed considerably to this trend.

100 Jason T. Low: Where's the Diversity, Hollywood? Sci-Fi and Fantasy Blockbusters Overwhelmingly White, Male. July 29, 2014. https://blog.leeandlow.com/2014/07/29/wheres-the-diversity-hollywood-sci-fi-and-fantasy-blockbusters-overwhelmingly-white-male/ (accessed: March 24, 2019).

101 Martha M. Lauzen: It's a Man's (Celluloid) World: Portrayals of Female Characters in the Top 100 Films of 2016. In: *Women in TV-Film*, July 2017. http://womenintvfilm.sdsu.edu/wp-content/uploads/2017/02/2016-Its-a-Mans-Celluloid-World-Report.pdf (accessed: September 29, 2017).

Marc Blancher

"Let's discover Space!"

Tintin and Other French-Belgian Comic Characters as Astronauts

Preliminaries: when discovery and control symbolize modernity

"We choose to go to the Moon in this decade and do the other things, not because they are easy, but because they are hard", said United States President John F. Kennedy in his famous Moon speech at the Rice University Stadium in Houston, Texas on September 12, 1962.[1] This assertion, which became a reality seven years later, can be interpreted as a verbalization of one of the most important concepts of modernity: the awareness of limits and the simultaneous will to vanquish them. Since the Industrial Revolution during the second part of the eighteenth and most of the nineteenth century and its solidification of human control over nature and the control of time,[2] humanity gives the impression that the possibilities of exploration are boundless. However, the perception of Earth-space would quickly change and its limits quickly reached by using the already developed technology. That is why scientists as well as authors will attempt to transcend these limits to a previously unknown extent, according to the possibilities that the new political ('national' or 'post-French Revolution') and socio-economic (with the Industrial Revolution and the associated progress) opportunities the

1 See Sonja Smith: Celebrating the 50th Anniversary of JFK's Moon Speech. In: *Texas Monthly*, September 12, 2017. https://www.texasmonthly.com/the-culture/celebrating-the-50th-anniversary-of-jfks-Moon-speech/ (accessed: July 1, 2017).

2 Steam power changed the relationship between humankind and space because of the gain in time and the new possibilities of exploration it brought. We can already observe a new generation with the projected 500 mph Hyperloop train from Dubai to Abu Dhabi or the teleport of photons 300 miles into space by Chinese scientists. Humanity's interest is no longer focused on the Moon, but on Mars, which symbolizes the next step of the colonization of space.

'capitalist' world grants. While scientists are researching the 'real' world, authors are making proposals about new, unexplored worlds.

These new worlds can be earthly but virginal, such as parts of colonial Africa, the setting in Henry Rider Haggard's novels about the English-born professional big-game hunter Allan Quatermain[3] (1885), written in the tradition of English colonial adventure novels. Patrick Howarth characterizes this kind of new hero with the epithet 'homo newboltiensis', hereby referring to the conception of the 'ideal male' as fashioned in the poetry of Sir Henry John Newbolt.[4]

The underlying philosophy of colonization is to discover, to explore, to exercise control, to convert indigenous people and to discover new worlds that previously had been impossible to explore. In the literary world of France in the nineteenth century, the period in which the concept of scientific modernity was born, the most famous incarnation of this 'literature of the exploration (of limits)' is without a doubt Jules Verne, who situates some of his plots in the subterranean (*Voyage au centre de la Terre*, 1864[5]), the undersea (*Vingt mille lieues sous les mers*, 1869–1870[6]) or in space (*De la Terre à la Lune*, 1865 and *Autour de la lune*, 1870[7]). Jules Verne looks ahead in areas such as subway[8] and submarine technology and proposes vehicles which will be only developed a few decades later in reality, whether in civilian society or in the military.

However, the nineteenth century is not only the century of science; it is also the century in which comics were born.[9] If the first decades of the genre focuses

3 The first volume of Quatermain's adventures is entitled *King Solomon's Mines.* Haggard's work is based upon the real-life adventures of the British big-game hunter and explorer of Colonial Africa, Frederick Courtney Selous (1851–1917).

4 See Patrick Howarth: *Play Up and Play the Game: Heroes of Popular Fiction.* London: Eyre Methuen 1973, pp. 13–14, where this ideal is characterized by quoting the English writer O.F. Christie's book *Clifton School Days* from 1935: "To be in all things decent, orderly, self-mastering; in action to follow up the coolest common sense with the most unflinching endurance; in public affairs to be devoted as a matter of course, self-sacrificing without any appearance of enthusiasm: on all occasions – except the regular Saturnalia – to play the Horatian man of the world, the Gentleman after the high Roman fashion, making a fine art, almost a religion, of Stoicism."

5 Jules Verne: *Voyage au centre de la Terre.* Paris: Le Livre de Poche 2014.

6 Jules Verne: *Vingt mille lieues sous les mers.* Paris: Le Livre de Poche 2001.

7 Jules Verne: *De la Terre à la Lune.* Paris: Le Livre de Poche 2001; J. V.: *Autour de la lune.* Paris: Le Livre de Poche 2003.

8 Jules Verne: *Paris au XXe siècle.* Paris: Le Livre de Poche 2002.

9 For the 'birth' of comics in nineteenth century, see Groensteen, especially the part "Pour introduire les bandes dessinées de Töpffer", in which he explains the similarities and differences between caricature and comics (he also describes one of the trips Töpffer's Dr. Festus took "in a flying telescope"). Thierry Groensteen: *M. Töpffer invente la bande dessinée.* Bruxelles: Les Impressions Nouvelles 2014, pp. 54–64.

on humor (because of the close relationship between the first comics and caricature[10]), French-Belgian comics take an early interest in adventure and discovery stories. One of the first characters to find himself in unknown worlds is the young Belgian reporter Tintin: one of his first adventures is situated in the Belgian-African colony Congo where, in the course of the story, he becomes a hero in the eyes of the indigenous people.[11] Despite the colonial and racist depiction of these people by Hergé, whose documentation was primarily based on an exhibition he saw in Belgium, this young Belgian reporter's adventure is a perfect example of the modern representation of discovery. As Jan Baetens puts it: "The use of the texts pronounced by the characters of the adventures of Tintin show to which degree Hergé is anchored in the ideals of the nineteenth century."[12] The parallel development of nationalism and the Industrial Revolution in the nineteenth century determined that the technical advances in the most important industrial, military, and political nations in the first half of the twentieth century. The technological progress achieved by the Third Reich, which developed V-2-Rockets during World War II, marks the first step towards the future space programs of both the United States and the USSR, since both countries eventually made use of Nazi technology to compete with each other for the domination of space, a race that culminated in the 1960s. This competition between the two post-war world powers and the correlated dream of walking on the Moon became one of the most important symbols of power and captivated the imagination of most of the artists from the period, including comic authors and illustrators.[13] This chapter deals with the representation of space travelers in selected French-Belgian comics from the 1950s and 1960s. It focuses on three complementary approaches to theorizing the image of space travelers in French-Belgian comics as incarnations of modernity in the nineteenth and the twentieth centuries: firstly, astronauts as heroes of literature for young people (1949–1969); secondly, as an example of the power of science; and finally as a dominant human being with philosophical significance.

10 Christian Delporte: Brève histoire de la caricature. In: Marie-Mélodie Delgado (ed.): *La caricature… Et si c'était sérieux ? Décryptage de la violence satirique.* Paris: Nouveau Monde 2015, pp. 21–30.

11 Hergé: *Tintin au Congo.* Tournai: Casterman 1960, p. 62.

12 Jan Baetens: *Hergé écrivain.* Paris: Flammarion 2006, p. 36: "Le traitement des textes des personnages des aventures de Tintin montre à quel point l'art de Hergé reste ancré dans les idéaux du XIXe siècle" (my translation).

13 Regarding the relationship between the potential anticipatory character of art and the topic of space travelling see Elsa de Smet: Au Clair de la Terre. Mon œil extraterrestre. In: *Images Re-vues*, November 3, 2017: http://journals.openedition.org/imagesrevues/4097 (accessed: March 22, 2019).

Comics as literature for young people (1949–1969)

French-Belgian comics have a long tradition in France where, since 1964, comics have been called "le neuvième art" (the ninth art)[14] and they had their Golden Age in the period between 1949 and 1969. During this period up to the beginning of the 1970s, as the established tradition changed to album publishing, the most popular form of comic publishing was in magazines such as *Le Journal de Spirou* (first published on April 21, 1938), *Tintin : le Journal des jeunes de 7 à 77 ans* (1946–1993) and *Pilote* (1959–1989).[15] The first publications contained not only French comic short stories and serial comics, but also a handful of American comics.[16] Many French authors (René Goscinny, Morris) had lived and worked for many years in the States and were familiar with American themes, such as Wild West stories.[17]

On the French side, there was a strong political desire to encourage and to support autonomous French-language creations, among other reasons, in order to counteract the American influence on Europe. This influence had grown since the USA's entry into World War II, the victory over the Third Reich, the early days of the Cold War, reliance on U.S. economic and military help to fight Communism and, especially, the European Recovery Program (the Marshall Plan). On July 16, 1949, the French Parliament passed a bill to stop the so-called 'dangerous influence' of American comics, of some comics (French ones too), and children's publications generally on French young people (it was then common, especially among conservative circles – so-called "ligues de moralité"[18], that is "moral leagues" – to think that especially American comics encouraged young people to become petty criminals) and to protect the French economy against American mass media (comics and other publications). Until 2011, publications for young readers were not allowed to positively represent many so-called 'risky'

14 Who actually coined the expression, introduced in 1964, is disputed between Claude Beylie on one side and Maurice de Bévère (Morris) and Pierre Vankeer on the other. See Thierry Groensteen: neuvième art. In: *neuvième art 2.0*, September 2012: http://neuviemeart.citebd.org/spip.php?article451 (accessed: March 22, 2019).

15 Philippe Mellot: La presse BD en Belgique et en France 1945–1950. In: *Paris Match Hors-Série : la saga du journal Tintin*. Paris: Paris Match 2016, pp. 20–25.

16 See also Spirou (Magazine). In: *Wikipedia*. https://en.wikipedia.org/wiki/Spirou_(magazine) (accessed: July 1, 2017).

17 The most famous titles are *Blueberry* (Jean-Michel Charlier / Jean Giraud, 1963), *Lucky Luke* (1946), *Jerry Spring* (Jijé, 1954), and *Les Tuniques Bleues* (Louis Salvérius / Raoul Cauvin, 1968). Regarding western comics, see the work of Paul Herman: Paul Herman: *Épopée et mythes du western dans la bande dessinée*. Grenoble: Glénat 1982.

18 Thierry Crépin / Anne Crétois: La presse et la loi de 1949, entre censure et autocensure. In: *Le Temps des médias* 1:1 (2003), pp. 55–64, here p. 55.

behaviors for the 'moral' education of young French readers.[19] In 1949, the Board of Surveillance and Control was created, which to this day reviews all publications (also for adults), although censorship is not as strict as it was in the 1970s, either for children's or adults' publications.

However, this censorship helped to create a real market for French-Belgian comics, especially for children, which was mainly controlled via self-censorship. Under the guidance of the so-called 'Brussels School', many titles were published. Several dealt with aeronautics and/or with space travel. One of the most famous is without a doubt *Tintin*, but there were also other works that deal with these topics: the *Espadon* (Swordfish) in Edgar Pierre Jacobs' work is a fictitious military jet aircraft und submarine. This work was first published in the *Tintin* magazine.[20] The character of the young French engineer, Yoko Tsuno (created in 1970 by Roger Leloup), often donned an astronaut suit, for example as she travels underground in *Le Trio de l'étrange*,[21] like Jules Verne's Professor Lidenbrock and his companions in *Voyage au centre de la Terre*. In *Les 3 Soleils de Vinéa*[22] (Fig. 1), she travels in space to Saturn. In the album *Z comme Zorglub* ([André] Franquin Greg [Michel Régnier], 1959), a character called Zorglub launches many rockets to the Moon. Aviation was already a theme in French-Belgian comics with *Les Aventures de Buck Danny* (created

19 The original formulation of legislation on publications for youngsters from July 6, 1949 (*Loi n° 49-956 du 16 juillet 1949 sur les publications destinées à la jeunesse*): "Les publications visées à l'article premier ne doivent comporter aucune illustration, aucun récit, aucune chronique, aucune rubrique, aucune insertion présentant sous un jour favorable le banditisme, le vol, la paresse, la lâcheté, la haine, la débauche ou tous actes qualifiés crimes ou délits ou de nature à démoraliser l'enfance ou la jeunesse." In 2011, this legislation was changed into: "Les publications mentionnées à l'article 1er ne doivent comporter aucun contenu présentant un danger pour la jeunesse en raison de son caractère pornographique ou lorsqu'il est susceptible d'inciter à la discrimination ou à la haine contre une personne déterminée ou un groupe de personnes, aux atteintes à la dignité humaine, à l'usage, à la détention ou au trafic de stupéfiants ou de substances psychotropes, à la violence ou à tous actes qualifiés de crimes ou de délits ou de nature à nuire à l'épanouissement physique, mental ou moral de l'enfance ou la jeunesse." See Legifrance: Loi n° 49-956 du 16 juillet 1949 sur les publications destinées à la jeunesse – Article 2. https://www.legifrance.gouv.fr/affichTexteArticle.do;jsessionid=56EC049D74698EC09E69F719385C254A.tpdila20v_2?cidTexte=JORFTEXT000000878175&idArticle=LEGIARTI000024039824&dateTexte=19490719&categorieLien=cid#LEGIARTI000024039824 (accessed: July 1, 2017). Cf. Crépin / Crétois: La presse et la loi de 1949, entre censure et autocensure.

20 See Alain Lerman: *Histoire du journal Tintin*. Grenoble: Glénat 1979.

21 Roger Leloup: *Le Trio de l'étrange*. Marcinelle: Dupuis 1979.

22 Roger Leloup: *Les 3 Soleils de Vinéa*. Marcinelle: Dupuis 1976.

Fig. 1: Cover from Roger Leloup: *Les 3 Soleils de Vinéa*. Marcinelle: Dupuis 1976.

Fig. 2: Cover from Albert Weinberg: *3 Cosmonautes*. Paris: Le Lombard 1978.

by Jean-Michel Charlier and Victor Hubinon in 1947), *Dan Cooper*[23] (created by Albert Weinberg in 1954: Fig. 2) and *Les Aventures de Tanguy et Laverdure* (created by Jean-Michel Charlier and Albert Uderzo in 1959). They all present the adventures of American (Buck Danny, Sonny Tuckson and Jerry Tumbler), Canadian (Dan Cooper) and French (Tanguy et Laverdure) jet pilots. These series are either realistic or works with science fiction elements, but are all based on a detailed scientific and document research by their authors.[24]

23 Albert Weinberg: *3 Cosmonautes*. Paris: Le Lombard 1978, p. 62. The aeronautic specialist Albert Weinberg helped Hergé with storyboarding and writing *On a marché sur la Lune*. Benoît Mouchart: *À l'ombre de la ligne claire: Jacques Van Melkebeke entre Hergé et Jacobs*. Bruxelles: Les Impressions Nouvelles 2014, p. 149; Dominique Petitfaux: Dan Cooper: Entre aviation et science-fiction. In: *Paris Match Hors-Série: la saga du journal Tintin*. Paris: Paris Match 2016, pp. 44–49.

24 Also worthy of mention is the comic series *Valérian, agent spatio-temporal* (created by Pierre Christin / Jean-Claude Mézières in 1967), which was adapted for film in 2017 by Luc Besson, entitled *Valérian et la Cité des mille planètes*.

Space travelers as examples of the power of science

Hergé (the pen name of Georges Rémi) is considered one of the forerunners of the comic genre for a number of reasons. Firstly, he created the famous "ligne claire"[25] graphic style, but he also supported the official recognition of comic authors and invariably placed his characters in significant historic and social events that occurred during his lifetime: communism in Russia,[26] the colonization of Africa,[27] expeditions to Egypt,[28] the Sino-Japanese war,[29] and Prohibition in the USA.[30] During World War II, he also published a story about the scientific discovery of a meteorite and the following race between two expedition ships, which both wanted to reach the meteorite first. The team racing against Tintin's team is led by the fictitious Sao Rico banker and rich Jewish-American businessman, Mister Bohlwinkel. Hergé adopts graphic and textual characteristics from the anti-Jewish propaganda of the Third Reich for this character, such as the hooknose and the association with financial power.[31]

For Hergé, the post-war period was a time to address space themes. In addition to the double-album about the adventures of Tintin, in 1951 he published the two albums about the adventures of Jo, Zette and Jocko, *Le Stratonef H. 22*, first published in 1938–1939 in magazines, in which he already deals with aeronautics.[32] The two volumes of Tintin's journey to the Moon (*Objectif Lune* and *On a marché sur la Lune*[33]) were published fifteen years before the Apollo 11 Mission and even before the launch of the first satellite, the Russian Sputnik 1, on October 4, 1957. In his discussion of the album *Les 7 Boules de cristal*, Jean-Marie Apostolidès wrote that "Hergé realizes that [...] Tintin would become a mythic character if he could transcend the immediate past."[34]

25 Mouchart: *A l'ombre de la ligne claire*, p. 149.

26 Hergé: *Tintin au pays des Soviets*. Tournai: Casterman 1999.

27 Hergé: *Tintin au Congo*. Tournai: Casterman 1960.

28 Hergé: *Les Cigares du pharaon*. Tournai: Casterman 1955.

29 Hergé: *Le Lotus bleu*. Tournai: Casterman 1946, p. 62. See Nicolas Verstappen: Le Lotus bleu. In: *Beaux-Arts Hors-Série: les secrets des chefs–d'œuvre de la BD*. Paris: TTM Éditions / Beaux-Arts Magazine 2014, pp. 6–21.

30 Hergé: *Tintin en Amérique*. Tournai: Casterman 1945.

31 Hergé: *L'Étoile mystérieuse*. Tournai: Casterman 1946, p. 22.

32 Hergé: *Le Testament de M. Pump (Le Stratonef H. 22–1)*. Tournai: Casterman 1950, p. 60; Hergé: *Destination New-York (Le Stratonef H. 22–2)*. Tournai: Casterman 1950.

33 Hergé: *On a marché sur la Lune*. Tournai: Casterman 1954.

34 Jean-Marie Apostolidès: *Hergé*. Paris: Flammarion 2006, p. 61: "Hergé prend alors conscience [...] que Tintin accède au rang de personnage mythique, à la condition de sortir de l'histoire immédiate." See also Thierry Groenstein: *La bande dessinée, son histoire et ses maîtres*. Paris: Skira Flammarion 2009, p. 42.

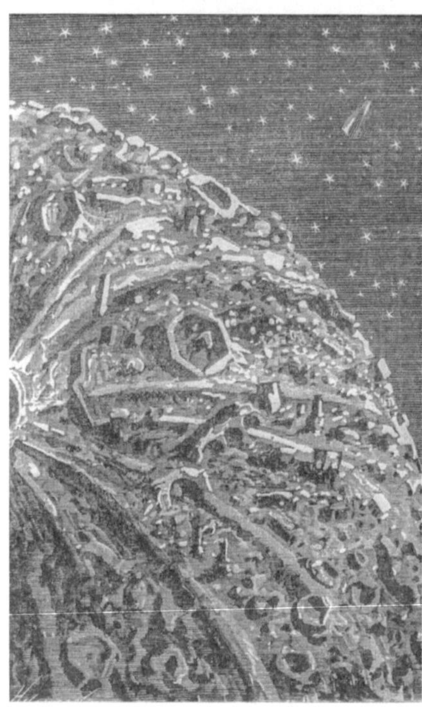

Fig. 3
Moon surface by
Émile-Antoine Bayard
from Jules Verne:
Autour de la lune.
Paris: J. Hetzel 1872, p. 128.

However, after World War II and under the conditions of the Cold War, typical superheroes were soon passé, making the success of more complex, often offbeat and flawed characters possible, such as those fostered by Marvel; Peter Parker alias Spiderman, for example, is actually an angst-ridden, shy teenager behind his mask. Following the example of the protagonists from this "Silver Age" of superheroes, the heroes of French-Belgian comics also changed appearances, for example the initially physically unimpressive anti-hero *Astérix*, developed from 1959 on by René Goscinny and Albert Uderzo. In the case of Tintin, Hergé does not explicitly impose similar constraints upon his character, but keeps him confined to a daily routine (*Les Bijoux de la Castafiore*[35]) or allows him and his friends to be left powerless after having defeated their adversaries, so that they have to be saved by alien forces (*Vol 747 pour Sydney*).[36]

35 Hergé: *Les Bijoux de la Castafiore*. Tournai: Casterman 1963.

36 Hergé: *Vol 714 pour Sydney*. Tournai: Casterman 1968. See Serge Tisseron: Tintin, notre héros. In: *Paris Match Hors-Série: la saga du journal Tintin*. Paris: Paris Match 2016, pp. 28–31.

Fig. 4: Moon surface by Hergé, from Hergé: *On a marché sur la Lune*. Tournai: Casterman 1954, p. 21, panel 1.

To draft both albums about Tintin's travel to the moon, Hergé consulted his scientist friend and author, Bernard Heuvelmans (1916–2001), who wrote *L'Homme parmi les étoiles* (1944) and documented the principles of space travel with the help of the books *L'Astronautique* (Alexandre Ananoff, 1950[37]) and *Notre amie la Lune* (Pierre Rousseau, 1943).[38] He was also inspired by movies such as *Le voyage dans la lune*[39] (F 1902, D: Georges Méliès), *Die Frau im Mond*[40] (D 1929, D: Fritz Lang) and *Destination Moon* (US 1950, D: Irving Pichel). In addition to Jules Verne's novel about travelling to the Moon from the nineteenth century, the science fiction novel *The First Men in the Moon* (H. G. Wells, 1900–1901), and Chesley Bonestell's paintings depicting the

37 The cover illustration of *Tintin* (May 11, 1950) refers explicitly to Ananoff's work by showing a copy of his book on the cover photo.

38 Dominique Maricq: *Les Trésors de Tintin: 22 fac-similés rares extraits des archives d'Hergé*. Bruxelles: Moulinsart 2013, pp. 63–68.

39 Two cover illustrations of *Tintin* (March 23, 1950 and March 30, 1950 editions) are an explicit allusion to Méliès' movie.

40 It is a film adaptation of the book of the same title by Thea von Harbou.

conquest of space,[41] Hergé was also inspired by the work of German V-2 rocket researchers, such as Wernher von Braun, Hermann Oberth, Martin Schilling, and Ernst Steinhoff.

Whether consciously or not, Hergé's work demonstrates a lot of similarities with Jules Verne's works *De la Terre à la Lune* (1865) and *Autour de la lune* (1870). In nineteenth-century French popular culture, Jules Verne's work is associated with illustrations by the draughtsman and illustrator Émile-Antoine Bayard. There also appear to be many graphic similarities between the illustrations of *De la Terre à la Lune* or *Autour de la lune* by Émile-Antoine Bayard (Fig. 3) and the scenes of *On a marché sur la Lune* by Hergé and his team (Fig. 4). Jean-Paul Tomasi and Michel Deligne assert that "There are [...] many similarities in the productions of both authors, and these are of a fundamental importance in order to understand Hergé's work."[42] In contrast, Hergé often said that he did not know Jules Verne's work, even that he had never read it. This assertion sounds implausible considering his age and the French culture of his generation. In fact, in July 1969, the French press agency AFP asked Hergé to comment the epic journey taken by the crew of the Apollo 11 mission, Neil Armstrong, Edwin Aldrin, and Michael Collins.[43] Hergé responded: "To make science fiction is disgusting... Jules Verne had more luck than me!"[44] This declaration by Tintin's author thus reveals a deep-rooted relationship between Hergé and Jules Verne's work.

The visual representation of space travel and of the Moon's surface by Hergé and Bob De Moor,[45] as well as the original red-and-white checkered design of the space rocket, directly inspired by a V-2 model by von Braun, is an explicit graphic and cultural reference to space travel and Moon exploration: the space rocket (Fig. 5) subsequently became an artefact of popular culture

41 Chesley Bonestell designed the landscapes of the above-mentioned movie *Destination Moon* from 1950.

42 Jean-Paul Tomasi / Michel Deligne: *Tintin chez Jules Verne*. Bruxelles: Lefrancq 1998, p. 7: "Il existe [...] de nombreuses ressemblances dans les productions des deux auteurs, et celles-ci sont d'une importance fondamentale pour la compréhension de l'œuvre de Hergé" (my translation).

43 In early 1969, Hergé gave both Moon albums as gifts to Frank Borman, the first astronaut who orbited the Moon with Apollo 8 in 1968.

44 "À vous dégoûter de faire de la science-fiction ... Jules Verne a eu plus de chance que moi!" Hergé, quoted in Pierre Juhel: Wolff, le complexe de Sbrodj. In: *Les personnages de Tintin dans l'Histoire: Les événements qui ont inspiré l'œuvre d'Hergé*, vol. 2. Paris: Sophia / Historia 2012, p. 53 (my translation).

45 Bob de Moor (1925–1992) was a Belgian comic author and also Hergé's right-hand man for landscape and technical drawings by the Studios Hergé (founded on April 6, 1950).

Fig. 5: Space-rocket by Hergé, from Hergé: Cover of *Objectif Lune*. Tournai: Casterman, 1954.

Fig. 6: Hergé: *Beginning of the Moon landing by Alan Bean und Pete Conrad during the Apollo 12 mission*, from Hergé's comic report on the Apollo 12 mission: La victoire d'Apollo XII. In: *Paris Match* 1073, November 29, 1969, pp. 30–33, here p. 31, panel 5.

and in France appears in many other artworks, such as in the music video *Mistral Gagnant* (1986) by the singer Renaud. The song by Renaud Séchand and Jean-Philippe Goude is a nostalgic anthem, in which the space rocket symbolizes both a dream world and childhood; according to a 2015 survey, it was still French people's favorite song. This is perhaps why the French magazine *Paris Match* commissioned Hergé to produce a cartoon report on the second Moon landing, from November 14–24, 1969 by the crew of Apollo 12, Alan Bean, Pete Conrad, and Richard Gordon (Fig. 6).

The philosophy of space travel

Tintin is a young reporter who is the epitome of the development in mass media (especially of the written press) since the nineteenth century and its increasing influence. His first sidekicks do not show any close relationship with science. This changes in 1943–1944, when the character of Tryphon Tournesol appears, first referred to only as "Monsieur Tournesol": He insists on offering his submarine prototype and joining the expedition in search of Red Rackham's treasure.[46] Up until 1950, he remains a fairly minor character, who is accidentally abducted after having committed a sacrilege in the eyes of the Incans when taking a sacred wristband with him,[47] and whose appearances are always related to his hearing difficulties and the comical scenes based on them.[48] However, in 1950, with the serialization of *Objectif lune* (by Hergé and Bob de Moor) in the magazine *Tintin*, the character takes on another dimension – he becomes an internationally accredited scientist working with the Syldavian government to lead a space travel project. This is also the first time that Tournesol is called "professor".[49] He becomes so angry when Captain Haddock says to him that he "acts like a fool" ("faire le zouave") that he shows Haddock and Tintin the space rocket he has designed. This other facet of Tournesol brings a little bit of fun to an album that is otherwise a serious and detailed didactic-realistic approach to space science. Many authors, such as Michel Daubert, consider Hergé's work and his space rocket to be one of the most seriously researched about space travel and rockets:

> Hergé's space rocket, with his checkered decoration taken from a German rocket designed by von Braun, is much more than the poetic pipe dreams by Cyrano, Jules Verne or Méliès, it is the first reliable vehicle of the conquest of space.[50]

The transcultural, philosophical, and scientific credibility of Professor Tournesol could be read in the translation of his name for English readers: "calculus", borrowed from the field of mathematics. *Objectif Lune* and *On a marché sur la Lune* are two albums whose action is based only upon modern scientists: on the one hand, Professor Tryphon Tournesol, who creates and develops the space rocket

46 Hergé: *Le Trésor de Rackham le Rouge*. Tournai: Casterman 1945, p. 5, panel 6.

47 Hergé: *Les 7 Boules de cristal*. Tournai: Casterman 1948, p. 40, panels 1–4.

48 Nicolas Verstappen: Tintin ou le rire universel. In: *Beaux-Arts Hors-Série: humour et BD*. Paris: TTM Éditions / Beaux-Arts Magazine 2011, pp. 126–131.

49 Hergé: *Objectif Lune*. Tournai: Casterman 1953, p. 7, panel 6. François Rivière: Moulinsart: Au cœur de la comédie. In: *Le rire de Tintin: Les secrets des grands maîtres de l'humour : Les meilleurs gags, les injures d'Haddock*. Paris: Beaux-Arts Magazine / L'Express 2014, p. 27. See also Tristan Savin: Le comique visuel, une suite de procédés bien rodés. In: *Le rire de Tintin: Les secrets des grands maîtres de l'humour: Les meilleurs gags, les injures d'Haddock*. Paris: Beaux-Arts Magazine / L'Express 2014, p. 74.

50 Michel Daubert: *Musée Hergé*. Paris: La Martinière 2013, p. 214: "La fusée d'Hergé, avec sa parure à carreaux reprise d'un missile allemand conçu par von Braun, est, bien plus sûrement que les élucubrations poétiques de Cyrano, Jules Verne ou Méliès, le premier véhicule fiable de la conquête spatiale" (my translation).

project, and on the other hand, engineer Frank Wolff,[51] who works for the country of Borduria and betrays the Syldavian project[52] because of his compulsive gambling. In the end, he commits suicide in order to save the rest of the team, which otherwise could not have survived because of a lack of oxygen.[53] Thus, the whole trip is only made possible thanks to human endeavor and virtues: the whole project was planned and conducted by the intelligent Professor Tournesol, but its eventual success is the result of the cooperation of a team (Tintin, Snowy, Captain Haddock, Professor Tournesol) as well as Wolff's self-sacrifice. Moreover, the perfect human and moral behavior of the entire crew, which cannot even be marred by the presence of Thomson and Thompson, works perfectly together with reliable space technology. Such a positive concept of modernity is already discernable in the chosen title of the second album, in the original French: *On a marché sur la Lune*. The pronoun *on* could be a linguistic use from spoken French language (indefinite *on* instead of the personal *nous* (["us"]), but it also could mean humankind in its entirety.

Even in the comical scenes, for example the zero gravity scene (one of the clumsy Thomson and Thompson twins accidently deactivates the artificial gravity[54]), the alcohol scene (Captain Haddock takes the liberty of going for a spacewalk under the influence of alcohol and has to be brought back inside by Tintin[55]) or the gliding on ice scene (while exploring caves on the Moon, Tintin and Captain Haddock discover ice[56]), the relaxed attitude of characters and their movements represent a form of superior human being, who, almost arrogantly, takes the liberty of 'dancing' and 'playing' on the Moon's surface.

This indifferent attitude, which appears repeatedly, seems to 'protect' the human crew members of the space rocket against the full impact of the scientific and

51 Hergé's character of engineer Frank Wolff was inspired by German-American astrophysicist Klaus Fuchs, who was a Russian spy. Pierre Juhel: Wolff, le complexe de Sbrodj. In: *Les personnages de Tintin dans l'Histoire: Les événements qui ont inspiré l'œuvre d'Hergé*, vol. 2. Paris: Sophia / Historia 2012, pp. 50–51.

52 Borduria and Syldavia are the names of two fictional Balkan countries in Hergé's work, on the west and the east side of the Iron Curtain.

53 Frank Wolff was the first character by Hergé who belongs neither to the 'goodies' nor to the 'baddies'. However, the publishing house Casterman made him correct the suicide letter he left on the space rocket and add the sentence "Maybe a wonder will enable me to survive too?" (French: "Quant à moi, peut-être un miracle me permettra-t-il d'en réchapper aussi?"). It was forbidden for literature for young people to encourage suicide. Hergé: *On a marché sur la Lune*. Tournai: Casterman 1954, p. 55, panel 3.

54 Hergé: *Objectif Lune*. Tournai: Casterman 1953, p. 5, panel 11.

55 Ibid., p. 8, panel 7.

56 Ibid., p. 36, panel 16.

Fig. 7
Cover from
Hergé:
On a marché sur
la Lune.
Tournai:
Casterman 1954.

Fig. 8: Hergé: *On a marché sur la Lune.*
Tournai: Castermann 1954, p. 30, panel 8.

symbolic dimension of the space travel they are undertaking; they are only promenading and joking. Furthermore, Hergé's space travelers do not receive any international attention via the media (this was a conscious decision by Hergé) and, although their space suits in general follow Alexandre Ananoff's model, Hergé decided not to use the helmet and instead gave his suits a transparent sphere of acrylic glass, so that readers could recognize the characters from all perspectives while wearing space suits. This is evident on the cover of *On a marché sur la*

Fig. 9
Paul Gavarni:
Le Flâneur, 1841.
Lithograph.

Lune, where the three main characters (Tintin, Captain Haddock, and Snowy) are seen from behind on the Moon's surface, with the rocket and the exploration vehicle in the background (Fig. 7).[57] The aforementioned arrogant and superior attitude climaxes in the Thomson and Thompson twins moon-walk scene: two Belgian policemen holding their canes and laughing and jumping hand in hand (Fig. 8).[58] This pictorial representation recalls the image of the dandy, the young wealthy man who shines on society, who exemplifies a form of *carpe diem* or of elegant time wasting, or the *flâneur* (the "stroller"), such as is represented in a lithograph from 1841 by Paul Gavarni (Fig. 9).[59] This *flâneur* was described by the German philosopher and cultural critic Walter Benjamin (1892–1940) as the essential figure of the modern city.[60] It was originally described by the poet Charles Baudelaire in *Le Peintre de la vie moderne* (original published in *Le Figaro* in 1863):

57 Hergé: *On a marché sur la Lune*. Tournai: Casterman 1954.

58 Ibid., p. 30, panel 8.

59 Illustration to: Auguste de Lacroix: Le Flâneur: In: Léon Curmer (ed.): *Les français peints par eux-mêmes: encyclopédie morale du dix-neuvième siècle*, vol. 3. Paris: Curmer 1841, pp. 65–72, here pp. 65–66. https://gallica.bnf.fr/ark:/12148/bpt6k1047978h/f142.image.r=les%20francais%20peints%20par%20eux-m%C3%AAmes%20tome%203 (accessed: July 1, 2017).

60 Walter Benjamin: *Charles Baudelaire: A Lyric Poet in the Era of High Capitalism*. London: Verso 1983, p. 54.

The crowd is his element, as the air is that of birds and water of fishes. His passion and his profession are to become one with the crowd. For the perfect *flâneur*, for the passionate spectator, it is an immense joy to set up house in the heart of the multitude, amid the ebb and flow of movement, in the midst of the fugitive and the infinite. To be away from home and yet to feel oneself everywhere at home; to see the world, to be at the center of the world, and yet to remain hidden from the world [...].[61]

When the journey becomes the destination

In the 1950s and the 1960s, the conquest of space became a symbol of political and military power, especially for the superpowers, the USSR and the USA, when they entered the "Space Race". For US-President Lyndon Johnson, "control of space means control of the world".[62] If Hergé did not share this political interpretation of the conquest of space, he nevertheless had already discovered its potential, mixing it with representations of universes that were then only dreamed about. In doing so, he made Tintin a modern hero who achieved things in fiction that were only made reality a few years later. The first real Moon landing by the Apollo 11 mission on July 20, 1969 not only changed the real world, but also the fictional world: in France, the real trip to the Moon inspired half-scientific, half-science fiction creations such as *Yoko Tsuno* (created in 1970) or specific episodes of comic series such as *The Smurfs* (*Les Schtroumpfs*), for example the album *The Astrosmurf* (*Le Cosmoschtroumpf*) published in 1970 (Fig. 10). However, this Smurf episode is not based on science, but in fact turns out to be a dream: One of the Smurfs has always dreamed of traveling to another planet and begins to build with only a few simple tools a wooden space rocket, which is unable to fly. In order to cheer up their disappointed and depressed comrade, the other village residents construct the complete illusion of a new planet and play the parts of aliens. However, the Smurf space traveler does not try to conquer the discovered planet and, instead, tries to become a member of this new world.

61 "La foule est son domaine, comme l'air est celui de l'oiseau, comme l'eau celui du poisson. Sa passion et sa profession, c'est d'épouser la foule. Pour le parfait flâneur, pour l'observateur passionné, c'est une immense jouissance que d'élire domicile dans le nombre, dans l'ondoyant, dans le mouvement, dans le fugitif et l'infini. Être hors de chez soi, et pourtant se sentir partout chez soi; voir le monde, être au centre du monde et rester caché au monde." Charles Baudelaire: Le Peintre de la vie moderne. In: C. B.: *Œuvres complètes*, ed. by Marcel A. Ruff. Paris: Seuil 1968, p. 552. The English translation is taken from: Charles Baudelaire: The Painter of Modern Life. In: *The Painter of Modern Life and other essays by Charles Baudelaire*, ed. & transl. from the French by Jonathan Mayne. London: Phaidon 1964, p. 9. First published in *Le Figaro* in 1863.

62 Bernard Marck: Conquête spatiale : L'Allemagne dominante. In: *Les personnages de Tintin dans l'Histoire: Les événements qui ont inspiré l'œuvre d'Hergé*, vol. 2. Paris: Sophia / Historia 2012, p. 59.

Fig.10
Cover from Peyo:
Le Cosmoschtroumpf / Le Schtroumpfeur de pluie. Marcinelle: Dupuis 1970.

The other (disguised) Smurfs have to use a trick in order to make him 'fly' home.[63] This representation of space travel, which works with an apparently dreamed-up world, does not conform to the one conceived of by Hergé. The emphasis will be rather set on the moral aspects in matters of the relationship between discovering its limits and harmony respectively within the social group, in this case the village.[64] In December 1978, he said himself, by impersonating Tintin during an interview, that in Tintin's Moon story "the journey was as important as the destination".[65] The question to this answer was: "You've already traveled the world and even to the Moon. But you didn't travel to the center of the Earth or simply to France?"[66]

63 Peyo: *Le Cosmoschtroumpf / Le Schtroumpfeur de pluie*. Marcinelle: Dupuis 1970, p. 38, panel 10.

64 Guillaume de Syon: Balloons on the Moon: Visions of Space Travel in Francophone Comic Strips. In: Alexander Geppert (ed.): *Imagining Outer Space*. London / New York: Palgrave Macmillan 2018, pp. 187-207, here p. 201.

65 "Ce qui comptait là, c'était le voyage en soi et non pas l'arrivée." Hergé, quoted in Pierre Boncenne: Tintin s'explique. In: *Lire* 40 (Dec 1978), p. 29 (my translation).

66 "Vous avez été dans le monde entier et même sur la Lune. Mais vous n'avez jamais été au centre de la Terre ou tout simplement en France ?" Ibid. (my translation).

Nils Daniel Peiler

Backlash of the Future

A Comparison of the Astronaut Image in Stanley Kubrick's *2001: A Space Odyssey* (1968) and Peter Hyams' *2010: The Year We Make Contact* (1984)

Although some of Stanley Kubrick's outstanding contributions to the history of film such as *Spartacus* (US 1960), *Lolita* (GB/US 1961) or *The Shining* (GB/US 1980) have been remade into new films and TV series, to this day *2001: A Space Odyssey* (GB/US 1968) remains the only Kubrick film ever sequeled. Peter Hyams' follow-up film *2010: The Year We Make Contact* (US 1984) is based on Arthur C. Clarke's second novel from his *Odyssey* tetralogy, *2010: Odyssey Two* (1982), being preceded by the novelization of Clarke's and Kubrick's screenplay for *2001: A Space Odyssey* (1968), and being followed by *2061: Odyssey Three* (1987) and *3001: The Final Odyssey* (1997). Clarke himself tells the detailed story of the production process of the film adaption of his novel from 1982 in his book *The Odyssey File* (1985), through the email conversations he had with director Peter Hyams communicating between Sri Lanka and California.

Both films not only carry the individual cinematic style of their director, but were also realized under different historic circumstances. Kubrick's project, that would later become *2001: A Space Odyssey*, was accepted by Robert H. O'Brien, the liberal president of Metro-Goldwyn-Mayer (MGM), the only studio that would agree to produce the experimental avant-garde science fiction film[1] in times of tight changes within the Hollywood Studio system: at the dawn of New Hollywood bursting onto the scene with films such as Mike Nichols' *The Graduate* (US 1967) or Arthur Penn's *Bonnie and Clyde* (US 1967), but after Kubrick's

1 "[E]very single company turned it down, and why MGM didn't, I have no idea [.]" Stanley Kubrick in an interview with Daniele Heymann on October 8, 1987 for French newspaper *Le Monde* (October 17, 1987). Typescript with handwritten annotations. The Stanley Kubrick Archives at the University of the Arts London, Folder SK/1/2/8/5 Daniele Heymann, p. 27.

box-office success with *Dr. Strangelove or: How I Learned to Stop Worrying and Love the Bomb* (US/GB 1964). In contrast, afterwards and until the mid-1980s, MGM was run by the entrepreneur Kirk Kerkorian under a more commercial focus and the company therefore decided to hire Hyams for a sequel to *2001*, whose success had already been proven and expected a less financial risk than a new project.

Hyams' film continues Kubrick's story with a search for the mysterious end of the spaceship Discovery's Jupiter mission, which can be done only in peaceful cooperation between American astronauts and Russian cosmonauts, while at the same time on Earth a war between the two superpowers looks likely. The mission is a success, Dave Bowman reappears, HAL is reactivated, and finally left behind to help the crew to return safely to Earth. The film concludes with a warning message from an extraterrestrial intelligence to humankind to live peacefully side by side and never to attempt to set foot on the moon Europa.

For his film, Peter Hyams asked for the personal approval of the *2001* writer-director team:

> The first two people I wanted to contact were Arthur C. Clarke and Stanley Kubrick. I had a long conversation with Stanley and told him what was going on. If it met with his approval, I would do the film; and if it didn't, I wouldn't. I certainly would not have thought of doing the film if I had not gotten the blessing of Kubrick. He's one of my idols; simply one of the greatest talents that's ever walked the earth. He more or less said, 'Sure. Go do it. I don't care.' And another time he said, 'Don't be afraid. Just go do your own movie.'[2]

Although Hyams thus filmed an officially approved sequel to the epoch-making film of 1968 for MGM, he had to struggle under some difficult constraints. Most of the sets and props from *2001: A Space Odyssey* had been destroyed and what had not been lost, e.g. original concept artworks, was not as easily accessible then as it is today in the Stanley Kubrick Archives at the University of the Arts in London. The director therefore had to rebuild the famous sets of the spaceship Discovery One – such as the pod hangar or many control panels – from the actual film images of *2001* themselves.

Only two actors from the original production were recast for *2010*, namely Keir Dullea, who has some brief reappearances as astronaut Dr. David Bowman, and voice actor Douglas Rain, again playing the supercomputer HAL 9000.

2 Vincent LoBrutto: *Stanley Kubrick: A Biography*. New York: Fine 1997, p. 456.

Fig. 1: Fictitious *Time* magazine cover with Arthur C. Clarke as american president and Stanley Kubrick as russian president in *2010: The Year We Make Contact* (US 1984, D: Peter Hyams).

Fig. 2: Cameo appearance of writer Arthur C. Clarke on the left, sitting on a bench feeding pigeons, to the right James McEachin and Roy Scheider, in *2010: The Year We Make Contact*.

Dr. Heywood R. Floyd, originally played by William Sylvester in *2001*, was recast with Roy Scheider for *2010* and HAL's engineer Mister Langley now became Dr. Chandra, played by Bob Balaban. To link *2010* to its predecessor, Hyams made use of iconic imagery and music from Kubrick's film: the monolith and the "star child" are seen once more and Richard Strauss' soaring tone-poem *Thus Spoke Zarathustra* and György Ligeti's atonal work for choir *Lux Aeterna* are heard again. *2010* also once more uses the thrilling sound effect that could be heard when Dave Bowman prepares to leave his pod for re-entering the Discovery spaceship through the emergency exit. Hyams opens his film with several

Fig. 3: Apple IIc computer used by Dr. Heywood Floyd in *2010: The Year We Make Contact.*

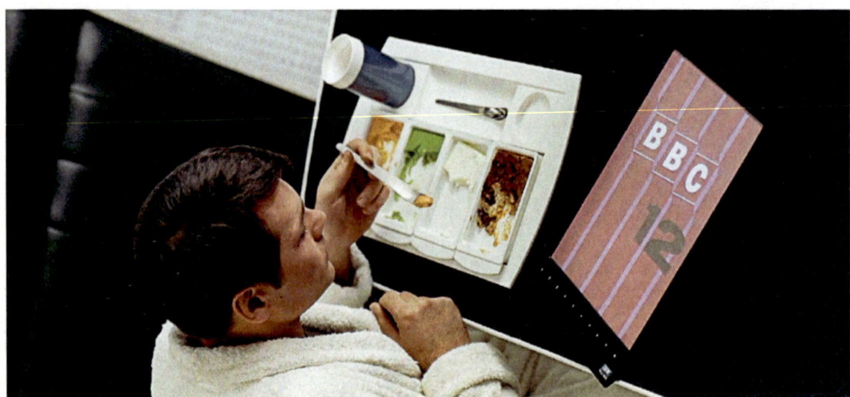

Fig. 4: Display with IBM logo showing the fictitious BBC 12 channel evening news show "The World Tonight" in *2001: A Space Odyssey* (GB/US 1968, D: Stanley Kubrick).

still images from *2001* with added text summaries to literally continue where Kubrick had left off years before. The science fiction film contains stock images of astronauts Dave Bowman and Frank Poole (played by Gary Lockwood in *2001*) that are embedded as set props in Dave's mother's hospital room as a framed picture on her nightstand or as photographs on a *New York Times* cover. *2010* also includes some in-jokes by showing stylized portraits of Arthur C. Clarke as the American President and Stanley Kubrick as the Russian President on a fictitious *Time Magazine* illustration (Fig. 1). Clarke can also be seen in a cameo appearance right at the beginning of the early scene in front of the White House, sitting on a bench feeding pigeons, while Victor Milson (played by James McEachin) and Dr. Heywood Floyd discuss the best political tactics to take men back into space (Fig. 2).

While Hyams tried to link his sequel closely to Kubrick's film as seen above, *2001* and *2010* differ greatly in general approach, tone and cinematic style. The former leaves the viewer with a lack of well-rounded narrative and many open questions remain unsolved. It is marked by a slow style and long scenes, outstanding montage, little dialogue, and an experimental approach to establish hitherto unknown mixed forms in mainstream cinema. The latter resolves the open questions but with simplistic answers, contains mainly fast edited Hollywood stock situations, and uses dialogue to tell the story instead of creating a more abstract audiovisual experience. Furthermore, while *2001*'s set design has a prognostic quality that demonstrates Kubrick's research into how an environment in the title-giving year might look from the perspective of the late 1960s, *2010*'s set design has a much less timeless approach. The future presented in the later film, from 1984, looks even more dated today than the original 1968 film: the Apple IIc computer Dr. Floyd uses here (Fig. 3) appears to be only a clunky alternative to the slim, pad-like tablets onboard the Discovery (Fig. 4). HAL is even rebooted manually with the contemporary Kaypro II keyboard (Fig. 5) that was used by Arthur C. Clarke during production, but was never seen in *2001*. The HAL 9000 interfaces (Fig. 6) look cheap in comparison to the original minimalist, elegant elements. The communication screens in the spaceship, which had originally been produced as animated 16mm films projected onto the 'monitor' frames, are replaced in *2010* with cathode-ray tube screens that are fed with electronic video (Fig. 7). Finally, while Kubrick made use of a combined soundtrack of pre-existing classical and avant-garde music mainly by Johann Strauss, Richard Strauss, Aram Khachaturian, and György Ligeti, the film music score for *2010* by David Shire draws heavily on electronic synthesizers, which at that time had been only rarely used for Hollywood soundtracks. Again, today these aesthetic aspects make the sequel look dated.

Beside these obvious small intersections and great differences between *2001* and *2010*, one of the most striking variations is in the image of the astronaut. The two films provide astronaut figures that stand in opposition to each other, even marking two different ends of a scale. The astronauts of *2001: A Space Odyssey* are introduced and mirrored by the supercomputer HAL 9000. A transmission of a television interview on the fictitious BBC 12 channel evening news show "The World Tonight" is received onboard the Discovery spaceship as it travels to

Fig. 5: Kaypro II keyboard to reboot HAL 9000 manually in *2010: The Year We Make Contact*.

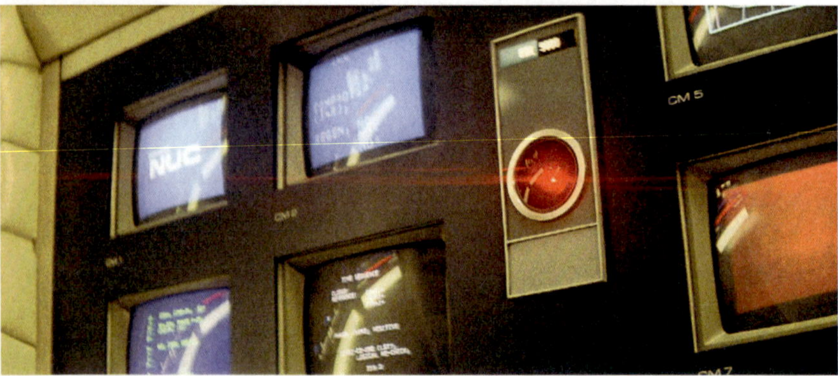

Fig. 6: HAL interfaces onboard the Discovery spaceship in *2010: The Year We Make Contact*.

Fig. 7: Electronic videos shown on cathode-ray tubes in *2010: The Year We Make Contact*.

its Jupiter mission. Interviewer Martin Amor characterizes the three protagonists of this chapter of *2001*: the astronauts Dr. David Bowman and Dr. Frank Poole, and the supercomputer HAL 9000. The so-called "foolproof" supercomputer-in-charge is introduced at the beginning of the Jupiter Mission sequence as "the sixth member of the Discovery crew".[3] (Three additional astronauts were put onboard the spaceship in hibernation.) In other words, it is like a human being of flesh and blood that not only shares an "enormous intellect",[4] but "enjoy[s] working with people",[5] considers itself to be a responsible "conscious entity",[6] and finds itself "having a stimulating relationship with Dr. Poole and Dr. Bowman".[7] HAL also reacts with quite lively human-like speech patterns, as Andrew Utterson has described: "[T]he voice of HAL suggests a blurring of the boundaries between human and computer; to the point where one cannot be easily distinguished from the other. HAL's voice is one of several characteristics that anthropomorphize the computer."[8] Or as summed up in a broader context by Vivian Sobchack in her discussion of the ironic use of language in *2001* as part of her genealogy of the genre:

> HAL's voice is ripe and soft whereas Bowman's and Poole's have no texture. In comparison to the astronauts, creating the context which emphasizes the lacklustre and mechanical quality of human speech spoken by humans, HAL–in the first part of the flight–can almost be regarded as a chatterbox, a gossip, emotional.[9]

HAL, with its striking ambivalence, is a new instance in the representation of Artificial Intelligence, which overcomes the simplistic, clichéd formulas of pre-*2001* film history of an either strictly evil or altogether useful computer. Its outstanding role has thereby overshadowed many computers that followed in popular culture since 1968. Utterson concludes:

3 Stanley Kubrick: *2001: A Space Odyssey* (GB/US 1968). Bluray edition. Hamburg: Warner Bros. Home Entertainment 2007, 1:00:54.

4 Ibid., 1:02:13.

5 Ibid., 1:02:20.

6 Ibid., 1:02:41

7 Ibid., 1:02:23.

8 Andrew Utterson: *From IBM to MGM: Cinema at the Dawn of the Digital Age*. London: Palgrave Macmillan 2011, p. 101.

9 Vivian Sobchack: *Screening Space: The American Science Fiction Film*. New Brunswick, NJ / London: Rutgers UP 1987, p. 177.

> Initially, HAL functions as a sixth member of the crew, performing tasks comparable with those undertaken by its human counterparts. On the voyage to Jupiter, the two conscious astronauts – the others are being suspended in hibernation – communicate with the computer as equals, on first-name terms. HAL appears both friendly and understanding, and is arguably more 'human' than its fellow crew members, whose demeanour is decidedly cold in comparison.[10]

While on the one hand a spontaneous and agile computer runs the mission with the characteristics of a human being that sometimes makes errors, the astronauts, on the other hand, appear dehumanized, almost animal-like. They are frozen in hibernation like animals in winter or like ice-cooled products from a refrigerator; the centrifuge of the Discovery spaceship is like a hamster wheel, on which they jog. Their space lunch is instant fast-food mush, differentiated not by texture, but only by color, and they eat sandwiches that they say "taste the same anyway [...] getting better at it all the time".[11] Furthermore, Dave Bowman and Frank Poole carry out tasks on the Discovery that could be handled, more or less, by a computer instead: they calculate, look for technical problems, and communicate in measurements and figures with the ground control on Earth, where ironically all the human decisions are constantly being backed-up by a twin 9000 series computer.

This technoid style of the astronauts' depiction is underlined throughout by the heavy use of technology that appears to be from the new millennium. The props and costumes provide further characterization of the image of *2001*'s astronauts, equipped with tools and gadgets that had been carefully developed and designed by Kubrick and his art department team in close collaboration with large brands at the time. These included Industrial Business Machines (IBM), Nikon Cameras, Pan American Airlines, Howard Johnson's Motels and Restaurants, Hilton Hotels, The Bell Telephone Company, and Hamilton Watches. The historic, often iconic corporate logos, integrated into the mise-en-scène of the middle scenes of the film, especially in the sequences in which we see space travel (within the spaceships or space stations), help to set up a realistic framework for the narrative, but also serve as a link between the technological future of this science fiction and the sponsoring corporations in an early form of cross-media marketing. This included special advertisements by various corporations that made use of

10 Utterson: *From IBM to MGM*, pp. 100–101.

11 Kubrick: *2001*, 0:47:24.

2001's imagery and products that were issued when the film was released.[12] The astronauts in *2001* thereby appear to be well equipped with a range of specifically designed visionary tools and gadgets (some that have not yet been invented today) that embody Kubrick's vision of the future. The astronauts use zero gravity toilets, wear special space suits with electronic inlays, which include buttons integrated into their clothing, and, most iconic of all, oval-shaped helmets that reflect the surrounding lights.

This vision of the future is most evident in the scene in which Bowman and Poole watch their initial TV interview on BBC 12 on small displays (Fig. 4). These screens are propped beside their meals on a table onboard Discovery, uncannily resembling the contemporary computer tablet. In fact, the prop was used as evidence in a lawsuit between corporate giants Apple and Samsung, in a dispute over the patent design rights for the iPad tablet. As part of their defense strategy, Samsung included Kubrick's film as evidence that Apple was not the first to invent the tablet computer, but that it had instead been envisioned by Kubrick's production as early as 1968, some half a century earlier. Needless to say, this was a rather unconventional case, in which a historic science fiction film served as evidence in a multimillion dollar lawsuit. It garnered the world's media attention, with explanations of the case alongside illustrations from *2001* in newspapers such as *Die Zeit*.[13] Yet despite the prominence of communication devices with only a seven-minute delay in transmissions between the Discovery and Earth, the astronauts hardly communicate. They rarely talk to each other and their pale faces, in contrast to HAL's glowing red eye, appear to be without feelings. The lack of emotional difference between the human astronauts and the calculating machine could not be starker, especially when Poole's parents on Earth send him a video message to congratulate him on his birthday. They have baked a cake and sing him *Happy Birthday*, the only other textually comprehensible vocals heard in the entire music score other than HAL's performance of *Daisy Bell,* but it produces no discernible emotional reaction at all from the astronaut, such as joy or homesickness.

Only Poole's chess game (with HAL, who wins, of course) and Bowman's drawings can be read as slightly exceptional cases of intellectual or artistic amusement outside the technical procedures of the astronauts' dehumanized, daily lives. Consequently, it is not the astronauts who are working on a psychograph

12 See Bernd Eichhorn: Branding 2001. In: Hans-Peter Reichmann (ed.): *Stanley Kubrick*. Frankfurt am Main: Deutsches Filmmuseum 2007, pp. 120–125.

13 See Marcus Rohwetter: Jäger und Trolle. In: *Die Zeit*, September 8, 2011, p. 38.

in *2001*, but the computer 'brain' HAL that undertakes this human endeavor, evidence of his "fundamental ontological ambivalence".[14] Not only does the computer appear more human-like in Kubrick, the astronauts, in turn, become dehumanized, machine-like characters and "indeed the humanization of machines and mechanization of humans is an important part of the theme of evolution that underpins the film".[15]

The astronaut in *2001* is therefore neither a lively, heroic, human individual, whose actions are set against an apparently evil machine, nor is he an android-like character of unknown origin and ontological status, like Rick Deckard in Ridley Scott's *Blade Runner* (US 1982). The astronaut in *2001* is definitively of human nature, but appears to be less humane in comparison to his computer counterpart, which is able to simulate human feelings throughout the film.

This ambivalent man/machine duality, established with the Jupiter mission, is further developed – and corrected, one might say – when HAL malfunctions and apparently goes insane. At this point, a new intimacy is developed between the two astronauts, as Bowman and Poole hide in their locked space pod and discuss in detail the concern and challenges they face in dismantling the machine. It is in this moment that the two astronauts are first surveyed, then overruled. HAL kills astronaut Frank Poole and three additional crew members that had been put onboard the Discovery in hibernation, so that the only surviving crew member Dave Bowman is finally forced to act willingly against it: HAL operates the whole Jupiter mission in the background and has an eye on Dave and Frank twenty-four hours a day. It kills Poole perfidiously while he is working outside the spaceship and the other astronauts, Kimble, Hunter and Kaminsky, before they even have a chance to wake up from hibernation. Ultimately, Dave Bowman finds himself the last surviving crew member of the mission. He has no alternative but to defeat the computer, which tries to persuade him not to disconnect it. HAL reacts in a human way one last time, taking offence, moaning and singing a good-bye song, *Daisy Bell*. This scene also shows the regression of the computer, returning to the evolutionary state of a young child, as Walter Filz has pointed out in his genealogy of talking computers in media history.[16]

Why does HAL kill Poole and why does the computer fear its disconnection? The answer to these questions could be found in a gender reading of the

14 Utterson: *From IBM to MGM*, p. 111.

15 Ibid., p. 101.

16 See Walter Filz: *Das Reden der Rechner*. Radio Feature, German public radio WDR: Cologne 2004.

astronauts and the machine as a triangular couple. Dominic Janes, in his article "Clarke and Kubrick's 2001: A Queer Odyssey", interprets the astronaut protagonists of *2001* in the framework of gender studies, providing additional depth in the consideration of their character. Janes bases his analysis on the fact that the film's co-author Arthur C. Clarke was a bisexual, probably homosexual, science fiction author, whose rich genre work from the 1950s onwards (following his divorce after a short heterosexual relationship) offers hints at his personal sexual desires:

> Even if he remained substantially in the closet, Clarke had, from his collaboration with Kubrick, begun to make increasingly open gestures towards homosexual themes in his fiction. [...] The appearance of explicitly gay or bisexual characters in Clarke's fiction occurred later in his life, hence the inclusion in the bibliography *Urian Worlds* (1990) of *Imperial Earth* (1975), *The Songs of Distant Earth* (1986) and *2061: Odyssey Three* (1987), the last featuring 'a sympathetic pair of emotionally stable gay male lovers, Floyd's oldest and closest friends'.[17]

Kubrick on the other hand, in whose many films "women play a negligible role",[18] "wrote extensively about homosocial environments such as the military"[19] and, in collaboration with Clarke, opted for ideas while developing their script for *2001* that can be read as assuring the film would have a certain ambivalent openness and queer potential.[20] Clarke, for example, wanted the alien life to be represented in the geometrical form of a pyramid in an early draft, but Kubrick opted for a phallic monolith, that "is always stiffly vertical when seen by humans [...]. It is possible to argue that this object is a kind of generic, modernist phallus".[21] Besides "a striking absence of heterosexual sensuality in *2001*" and no explicit sex scenes, there are not only phallic symbols found throughout the film; it is, in fact, "full of sexual imagery – uterine, ovular and phallic – from the arrow-shaped space-craft *Orion* landing inside the celestial wheel to the *Aries* sphere alighting on a circular base".[22]

17 Dominic Janes: Clarke and Kubrick's 2001: A Queer Odyssey. In: *Science Fiction Film and Television* 4:1 (2011), pp. 57–78, here pp. 59–60.
18 Ibid., p. 61.
19 Ibid., p. 57.
20 Ibid., pp. 67–74.
21 Ibid., p. 67.
22 Ibid., p. 58.

Kubrick, in an interview shortly after the release of his film, suggested that "it may be possible for each partner to simultaneously experience the sensations of the other [...]; or we may emerge into polymorphous sexual beings, with the male and female components blurring, merging and interchanging".[23] Therefore, it is no surprise that the two astronauts Bowman and Poole and the HAL 9000 computer have been described as "a sort of outer space *ménage à trois*".[24] This could be an answer to both the killing of Poole and the fear of being disconnected: HAL's jealousy about the companionship between Bowman and Poole leads to the isolation of the former by murdering the latter, but instead of successfully replacing Poole's role for Bowman to form a perfect relationship, the computer gets shut down. The final moments of the film that take place with Bowman inside the Louis XVI room can be read as a queer encounter and rebirth. Bowman is finally transformed from 'a representative masculine subject' into "an androgynous erotic object at the very end of 2001".[25]

In comparison, in Peter Hyams' *2010*, the astronauts are not really astronauts. In a basic sense, none of the characters, Dr. Heywood Floyd, Dr. Walter Curnow, and Dr. R. Chandra, are astronauts comparable to Dave Bowman or Frank Poole. Bowman and Poole carried out all their tasks without specialization. Dr. Floyd recast with Roy Scheider, to whom we were introduced as the coordinator of spaceflight operations rather than as an astronaut in *2001*, becomes here the powerful man-in-charge, who is not only hiding secrets from the Russians, but even from his own crew member Dr. Chandra: Dr. Floyd installs a power switch to deactivate HAL 9000 with a remote control, if necessary. Dr. Chandra, played by Bob Balaban, is more of a computer programmer and designer than an astronaut. The 'father' of HAL takes special care of his 'child' lost in space, but also displays some foolish behavior not worthy of a professional astronaut when reentering space at the exact moment the combined engines of two spaceships start. Dr. Walter Curnow, played by John Lithgow, wonders why he even ended up in space at all. He states to Dr. Floyd: "I'm not an astronaut, I'm an engineer, what am I doing here?"[26] The Americans therefore appear to be more of a mixed team of specialized non-professionals entering space for the first time, in comparison to the Russians, who perform their tasks in a stoical routine.

23 Janes: Clarke and Kubrick's 2001, p. 61.

24 Ibid., pp. 61–62.

25 Ibid.

26 Peter Hyams: *2010: The Year We Make Contact* (US 1984). Bluray edition. Hamburg: Warner Bros. Home Entertainment 2009, 0:42:29.

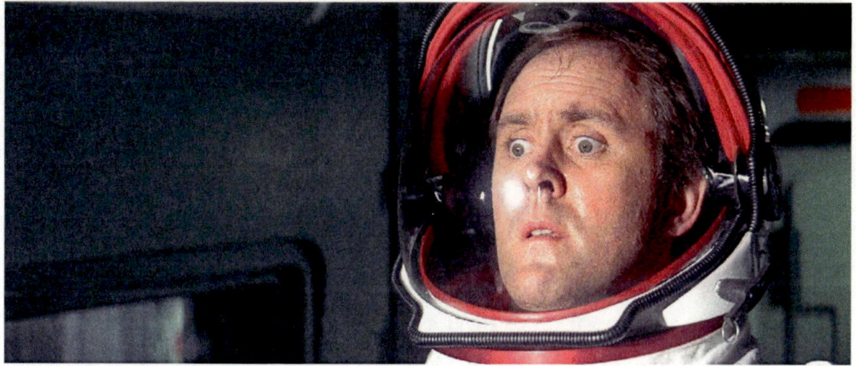

Fig. 8: Dr. Walter Curnow (John Lithgow) is afraid of his extravehicular activity outside the Leonov in *2010: The Year We Make Contact.*

Fig. 9: Cosmonaut Irina Yakunina (Natasha Shneider) joins astronaut Dr. Heywood Floyd (Roy Scheider) in his room in *2010: The Year We Make Contact.*

While astronaut Dave Bowman's deep breathing (performed by director Stanley Kubrick) in *2001* may mark the exceptional quality of the spacewalk he has to perform in order to check the presumably damaged AE35 unit of the ship's antenna, in *2010* Dr. Walter Curnow's breathing simply shows his physical instability. Dr. Curnow is afraid of heights and suffers from severe vertigo while carrying out his tasks on his way between the two spaceships (Fig. 8). The astronauts in *2010* not only show their emotions, they become emotionally overwhelmed by their surroundings. When the Russian spaceship Leonov maneuvers, cosmonaut Irina Yakunina, played by Natasha Shneider, joins astronaut Dr. Heywood Floyd in his room, first hugging and finally kissing him to overcome her fear and

stress (Fig. 9). Dr. Chandra appears to be the 'loving father' of his computer 'child' HAL 9000, deeply emotionally involved in the reboot and the final destruction of his creation. Thus the characterization of the astronauts as emotionless counterparts to the machine is reversed: HAL becomes a 'lame duck', who is no longer in charge of all the operations onboard the Discovery, who does not overrule the orders of the crew, and strictly follows Dr. Chandra's rules. When Chandra pretends that HAL will be of use for a new space station that has been built without its knowledge, the computer detects the lie and answers quietly: "I understand now, Dr. Chandra."[27] This is followed by its anodyne recommendation that stands in clear opposition to HAL's reaction in *2001*, when it murdered the crew to carry on the mission alone: "It is better for the mission if you leave."[28]
It is no problem in *2010* to install a "secure channel" for communication between Dr. Chandra and Dr. Floyd, whereas, in *2001*, Bowman and Poole struggled to prevent HAL from reading their lips. Furthermore, other troublesome technical features that caused some difficulty (such as the deaths of three astronauts in hibernation, who are obviously murdered by HAL) and thereby contributed to the action in Kubrick's film are solved in Hyams' film in a simple way: the hibernation cells are used again and this time the force of impact is the reason given in the film's dialogue when Dr. Floyd wakes up too early: "Don't worry, there's nothing wrong! Your government wanted us to awaken you."[29]
While Kubrick avoided the well-trodden path of the formulaic science fiction genre, *2010* makes a playful use of several clichés: here again, as in *2001*, a British actor plays a Russian character. This time it is not Dr. Smyslov, played by Leonard Rossiter, but Tanya Kirbuk, played by Helen Mirren with a strong Russian accent, her character's last name spelling "Kubrik" backwards. The Russian spaceship is named after Alexey Leonov, the first man to conduct extravehicular activity. The Russians onboard talk about *Pravda* magazine, while the Americans chat about whiskey from Kentucky and the best hotdogs. The Americans grumble about "the goddamn White House",[30] where "those sons of bitches"[31] reign. Russian cosmonaut Maxim Brajlovsky, played by Elya Baskin, is sacrificed to the mission – his brutal death while approaching the monolith mirrors the peaceful passing away of Dave's mother in her coma on Earth. The Cold War is heating up, as the television news from Earth received onboard the Leonov suggests.

27 Hyams: *2010*, 1:40:43.
28 Ibid., 1:40:56.
29 Ibid., 0:23:47.
30 Ibid., 1:15:49.
31 Ibid., 1:16:06.

The most obvious, but also most striking cliché is found in the battle of the Americans versus the Russians. What was once a minor side story in *2001*, when Dr. Floyd hid his knowledge about the excavation of the monolith on the lunar surface from his Russian colleagues Dr. Smyslov, Elena, Dr. Kalinin, and Dr. Stretnyeva, in *2010* the political affair becomes a main issue. The very first scene after the opening credits shows a long conversation between Dimitri Moisevitch, played by Dana Elcar with a strong Russian accent, and Dr. Heywood Floyd. The cosmonauts and the astronauts talk about their spaceship Leonov as "Russian territory" and the Discovery as "American territory" to underline the frontier battle in space. Steven Jongeward has hinted at this political sphere in comparing the scientific mission:

> The theme of community in science versus the factionalism of politics is constantly echoed throughout the film. Once aboard the *Leonov*, the Americans are treated like nothing more than unwelcome guests, but as the voyage progresses, political differences are set aside and the two crews become one in the face of the awesome events unfolding before them. Contrasted to this evolving unity is the growing hostility between the two governments on Earth. In fact, things get so bad that the two crews are ordered to separate and are given different flight instructions for the return home.[32]

The simple, obvious message of the film could be: 'Only together, with combined forces, can the mission be accomplished.' This is expressed most directly in the strong image of the combined power of the two spaceships, of both American and Russian origin, trying to help the Leonov to return to Earth, while the Discovery is left behind on Jupiter.

Last but not least, instead of developing its queer potential, as in *2001*, the classical heteronormative order is restored in *2010*. Hyams' film is largely structured through the off-voice commentary of Dr. Heywood Floyd, who addresses his wife Caroline and his son Christopher, both still on Earth. Floyd is shown in his private surroundings, having dinner with his family (Fig. 10), playing with his son and having a small, private argument with his wife, who is not amused by the thought that her husband is leaving for a space mission. The Floyds' home is shown before the flight to Jupiter, illustrating the personal, familial bonds of the character, which are enhanced by the contrast to the divide between the working NASA man and his daughter Squirt in *2001*, for whom he wondered about a birthday present. Dr. Floyd also carries a photograph of his wife and son onboard

32 Steven Jongeward: From Novel to Script. In: Arthur C. Clarke / Peter Hyams: *The Odyssey File*. London: Panther 1985, pp. 115–121, here pp. 116–117.

Fig. 10: The Floyd Family: Dr. Heywood (Roy Scheider), Caroline (Madolyn Smith) and Christopher (Taliesin Jaffe) in *2010: The Year We Make Contact.*

the Leonov; he dreams of being back in his home and prays for the mission, embodying the stereotypical heterosexual male, white, American Christian. Dave Bowman makes a surreal, quirky reappearance on his ex-wife's kitchen television set, which also features commercials for space travel with Pan American Airlines, bowing to *2001.* At this point, he is only worried about whether Betty got married again since he left. Thus, the film emphasizes both Bowman's heterosexuality and the approval of heteronormative marriage within the standard Hollywood mindset. Later on, when he reappears in different ages and is finally reborn as a star child once more, he has clearly lost his previous queer potential. Hyams' film is therefore not only much more of a product of its time, it also appears to be a more highly conventional Hollywood enterprise than Kubrick's experimental avant-garde. The future of yesterday from 1984 looks much more conservative and dated than the one from 1968: by closing unresolved questions with easy answers, instead of asking new ones; simplifying and ridiculing the estranged astronauts as overacting non-professionals; putting them back in charge of the machine; focusing on the national identity of the space travelers through a variety of clichés; and, finally, removing any hint of queer emancipation from the astronauts, Peter Hyams' film *2010*, although set nine years further ahead in the future than its predecessor *2001*, from today's perspective, appears to be a backlash against Stanley Kubrick's science fiction.

Marc Bonner

'Climb the Penrose Stairs to Merge with the (In)Finite'

The Astronaut as Reciprocal Posthuman

Introduction

In recent years, there has been a renaissance of (hard) science fiction films that focus on the astronaut's fate, current science discourses, and conventional technology.[1] With all the space opera heroes flooding the silver screen, one has to ask why the image of the astronaut is in vogue again? It could be argued that nowadays the ideological as well as symbolic relevance of the astronaut of the space race era is obsolete. Space exploration did not become what utopian futurism had imagined for it back in the 1960s; there are no colonies on the Moon or Mars. However, things are starting to get moving again: Elon Musk's SpaceX program has awakened NASA from a deep slumber and countries like China venture into orbit in order to re-enact, or reach beyond the American and Russian milestones of yesteryear. In this context and in light of current academic discourses like posthumanism, it is of interest to analyze the image of the astronaut in today's films. From the Cold War to the late 1990s and the post-9/11 decades, the cinematic, aesthetic, and political characteristics inherent in the image of the astronaut changed dramatically into a postmodern discourse beyond its two-dimensional patriotism. Stefan Brandt states in this context:

1 *Gravity* (GB/US 2013, D: Alfonso Cuarón), *The Martian* (US/GB 2015, D: Ridley Scott), *Passengers* (US 2016, D: Morten Tyldum), *Life* (US 2017, D: Daniel Espinosa) and *First Man* (US 2018, D: Damien Chazelle), to name but a few.

> Astronauts are often depicted in Western cultural imagery as postmodern migrants, independently traveling or rather floating towards new territories. [...] Astronauts are travelers not only in space but also in time. Instead of remaining within the geographical limits of cultural affiliation, the astronaut is searching for 'the final frontier' [...]. The postmodern subject has recognized in the metaphor of the 'new frontier' his and her own situation, which is equally marked by a multiplication and complication of life worlds. Due to fundamental changes in the ideological and social fabric of society in the course of the twentieth century, the postmodern individual learned to make adaptability part of his and her body scheme. The result of this development is, as Susan Bordo has demonstrated, a type of 'postmodern body' that builds its self-conception on a logic of constant transformation and assimilation.[2]

According to Dario Llinares, the astronaut embodies the "the central protagonist in a 'history' of 'factual' accounts reflecting a pivotal moment in human progress" and that "[s]pace histories whether textual, photographic, televisual or cinematic serve to naturalise the astronaut as a heroic masculine figure at the centre of modern Western culture".[3] Llinares summarizes the characteristics of these mediatized 'classical' images of the astronaut: "patriotism, family, democracy, capitalism, technology and religion".[4] He also states that "today's astronauts no longer symbolise the idealised masculinity of the Mercury and Apollo era".[5]
In order to understand the shifts and complex interrelations, it is necessary to approach this topic from within the context of postmodernism. Working independently from each other, Llinares and Andrew W. Butler[6] take French philosophers Jean-François Lyotard and Jean Baudrillard as well as American theorist Frederic Jameson into consideration. Both authors argue that such an approach offers an understanding of the construct of the astronaut:

2 Stefan Brandt: Astronautic Subjects: Postmodern Identity and the Embodiment of Space in American Science Fiction. In: *Gender Forum* 16 (2006), pp. 3–32, here p. 20.

3 Dario Llinares: *The Astronaut: Cultural Mythology and Idealised Masculinity*. Newcastle upon Tyne: Cambridge Scholars 2011, pp. 4, 6.

4 Ibid., p. 8.

5 Ibid., p. 196.

6 Andrew W. Butler: Postmodernism and Science Fiction. In: Edward James / Farah Mendelsohn (eds): *The Cambridge Companion To Science Fiction*. Cambridge: Cambridge UP 2003, pp. 137–148.

> [B]y the term 'postmodern', the astronaut, now a highly visible cinema spectacle, morphs into a site of increasingly explicit ambiguity. Socio-cultural shifts and aesthetic transformations, indicative of the latter half of the twentieth century, disrupt the rigid historical continuity of space exploration and man as the inevitable hero.[7]

From the micro level of the astronaut to the macro level of science fiction as a fictional mode itself, Jameson clarifies the postmodernist aesthetic inherent in science fiction:

> [S]cience fiction equally corresponds to the waning or the blockage of [...] historicity, and, particularly in our own time (in the postmodern era), to its crisis and paralysis, its enfeeblement and repression. Only by means of a violent formal and narrative dislocation could a narrative apparatus come into being capable of restoring and feeling to this only intermittently functioning organ that is our capacity to organize and live time historically.[8]

What Jameson calls the "narrative dislocation" of science fiction corresponds with Baudrillard's characterization of the "anti-gravitational" and "hyperreal". The latter contextualizes science fiction with postmodernism by referring to the novels of American writer Philip K. Dick and notes that within science fiction the distinction between the three orders of *simulacra* – (1) "natural, naturalistic simulacra", (2) "productive, productionist simulacra", (3) "simulation simulacra" – can be a medium of posthuman discourse (e. g. clones and AIs).[9] This corresponds with Marshall McLuhan's treatise on humankind's delusion with its technologies as one can consider that "[i]n the eyes of a hunter-gatherer, we might already appear 'posthuman'".[10] In the following analysis, I will focus on three astronauts who become posthumanistic entities within their diegeses, while arriving at points of cognition beyond their everyday work and environments, which in two cases are based on non-Euclidian structures: David Bowman in *2001: A Space Odyssey* (US/GB 1968, D: Stanley Kubrick), Sam Bell in

7 Llinares: *The Astronaut*, p. 151.

8 Frederic Jameson: *Postmodernism, or, the Cultural Logic of Late Capitalism*. Durham, NC: Duke UP 1991, p. 284.

9 Jean Baudrillard: Simulacra and Science Fiction. In: *Science-Fiction Studies* 18 (1991), pp. 309–313, here pp. 311, 313.

10 Nick Bostrom: In Defense of Posthuman Dignity. In: *Bioethics* 19:3 (2005), pp. 202–214. http://www.nickbostrom.com/ethics/dignity.html (accessed: July 3, 2017).

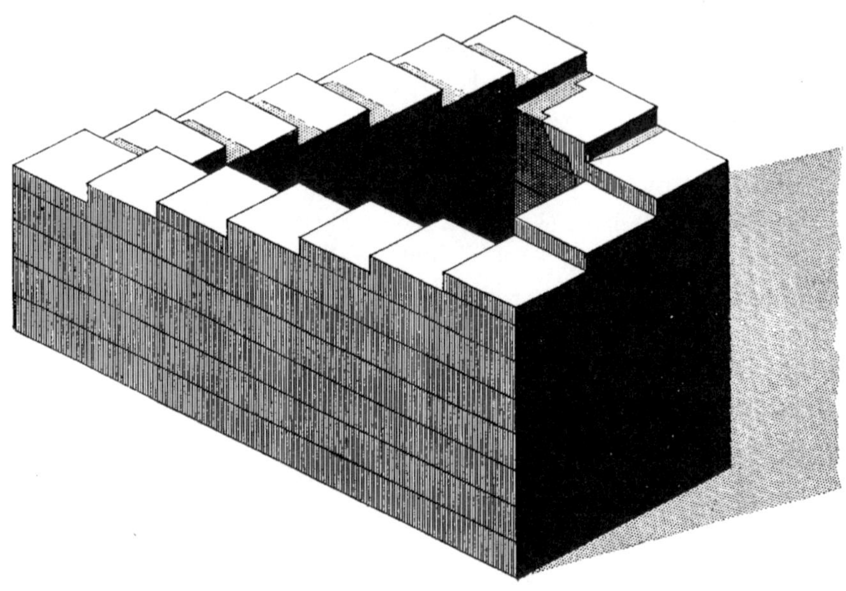

Fig. 1: L.S. Penrose / R. Penrose: *Penrose Stairs*, 1958.

Moon (GB 2009, D: Duncan Jones), and Cooper in *Interstellar* (US/GB/CA 2014, D: Christopher Nolan) all live and work at humanity's final frontier in order to exercise the effects of capitalism (Bell), or to gain new knowledge (Bowman, Cooper). In the beginning, all three are the perfect embodiment of what McLuhan calls the "gadget lover".[11] In reference to the Greek myth of Narcissus, McLuhan states that humankind is immersed in its prostheses (e.g. devices, tools, and convenience artefacts) so much that they delude themselves about the (metaphorical speaking) amputations that are inscribed in very same the technologies:

> By continuously embracing technologies, we relate ourselves to them as servo-mechanisms. That is why we must, to use them all, serve these objects, these extensions of ourselves, as gods or minor religions. An Indian is the servo-mechanism of his canoe, as […] the executive

11 Marshall McLuhan: *Understanding Media: The Extensions of Men* [1964]. London / New York: Routledge 2001, p. 45.

> of his clock. […] The machine world reciprocates man's love by expediting his wishes and desires, namely in providing him with wealth.[12]

Surrounded and deluded by an electro-mechanical and AI-controlled work life, the three depend on artificial anthropospheres, embodied by space ships and ground bases. Soon they come to ignore or counteract the directives of their companies and supervisors, represented by HAL 9000 or GERTY. They transcend their human borders in the climaxes of the films by freeing themselves from the said anthropospheres. Bowman, Bell, and Cooper become the hyperreal cause and effect of their fate and humankind's future. The plot twists – the process of cognition – of all three films can thus metaphorically be described as climbing the "Penrose stairs" (Fig. 1).

(In)Finite stairs

In 1958, Lionel and Roger Penrose published a paper on "impossible objects" as a special type of visual illusion.[13] Their intention was to illustrate geometrical structures like the "Penrose tribar" and the "Penrose stairs" that deny Euclidian laws and thus thematize physical and mathematic paradoxes. The authors show that "[t]wo-dimensional drawings can be made to convey the impression of three-dimensional objects. In certain circumstances this fact can be used to induce contradictory perceptual interpretations."[14] This is achieved by "false connexions of the parts" within the structure which leads the observers to the conclusion, that the "acceptance of the whole figure on this basis leads to the illusory effect of an impossible structure".[15] This is the case with the Penrose stairs. Observing the structure as a whole, the flight of stairs winds back to itself creating a loop in the sense of "a continually descending or ascending path".[16] Climbing these stairs in one's mind's eye means climbing infinitely. The Euclidian laws of gaining altitude are cancelled out. The two-dimensional illustration as a whole seems logical, but at the same time shows paradoxes within details when visualized as solid in three-dimensional space. Thus, the perception of the

12 Ibid., p. 51.

13 Lionel S. Penrose / Roger Penrose: Impossible Objects: A Special Type of Visual Illusion. In: *British Journal of Psychology* 49 (1958), pp. 31–33.

14 Ibid., p. 31.

15 Ibid.

16 Ibid.

structure in an isometric perspective is ambiguous and makes sense from this specific viewpoint only.[17]

These "impossible objects" can be specified as "multistable images". Swedish artist Oscar Reutersvärd pioneered their modelling in the 1930s by designing the tribar archetype and much more complex three-dimensional structures on paper. Such objects are perceived more broadly in the famous lithographs of Dutch artist M. C. Escher, such as *Relativity* (1953), *Belvedere* (1958), *Ascending and Descending* (1960) or *Waterfall* (1961).[18] The graphical simplicity of the Penrose stairs and Escher's intricate worlds of immersive impossibilities became pop-culture images. They entrench topics like media-specific self-reflection, geometry, spatial illusions, and perceptive awareness of the recipients not only in works of fine art but also in video game spaces, music videos and in cinematic spaces – especially the ones of science fiction.

In *Inception* (US 2010, D: Christopher Nolan), Arthur (Joseph Gordon-Levitt) teaches Ariadne (Ellen Page) the basics of constructing virtual places in another person's mind by climbing detached stairs in an airy entrance hall.[19] This architecture itself is fictitious, as both are phenomenologically present in Arthur's mind. With "paradoxical architectures", he wants to show her tricks to distract the targeted person they mentally intrude upon and "disguise the boundaries" of the trap. The establishing shot shows a Penrose stairs in isometric perspective. The following shots are on the stairs. After the characters circle it twice, the stairs are shown again in isometric perspective, albeit this time a dolly shot breaks the illusion, as the camera lowers its altitude, revealing a normal counter-clockwise ascending flight of stairs that ends in mid-air. The characters could therefore only 'ascend' in a loop as long as the camera does not reveal the truth – meaning that the dream world in one's mind is as fictitious as cinematic space

17 Nonetheless, there are researchers turning these "impossible objects" into three-dimensional 'sculptures'. For example, Kogichi Sugihara makes them calculable by a "'non-rectangularity trick', because those solid objects have non-rectangular face angles that look rectangular". These "solids" then exercise their effects only from one fixed viewpoint. Kogichi Sugihara: Spatial Realization of Escher's Impossible World. In: *Asia Pacific Mathematics Newsletter* 1 (2011), pp. 1–5, here p. 1.

18 The range of influence spans from multiple references in *The Simpsons* series (US 1989–, C: Matt Groening) to a steadily growing corpus of video games like *Antichamber* (Alexander Bruce 2013), *Monument Valley* (Ustwo 2014) or *Echochrome* (Sony 2008), which focus on solving spatial puzzle in non-Euclidean environments. For further reading: Thomas Hensel: PORTALe. Multistabil, changierend, paradox: Bild- und genretheoretische Zugänge im Computerspiel. In: *NCCR Mediality Newsletter* 13 (2015), pp. 3–14.

19 Christopher Nolan: *Inception* (US / GB 2010). Bluray edition. Hamburg: Warner Bros. Home Entertainment 2010, 0:40:30.

and spatial illusions can as easily confuse and be multistable as in the original two-dimensional graphic of the Penrose stairs.
Todd McGowan contextualizes this scene within the work of German philosopher Georg Wilhelm Friedrich Hegel's concept of infinity:

> This motion upward while remaining on the same path provides a visual image of Hegel's infinite of the Notion. The staircase itself indicates a movement toward the beyond but the perpetual circle makes clear that the beyond has already been attained.[20]

According to Hegel, the infinite always contains and is comprised of the finite. Thus, the infinite is a process that never leaves the finite:

> [T]he infinite is the transcending of the finite; according to its determination, it is the negation of the finite; the finite, for its part, is only that which must be transcended, the negation in it of itself, and this is the infinite. [...] Thus the finite and the infinite are both this *movement* of each returning to itself through its negation; they are only as implicit *mediation*, and the affirmative of each contains the negative of each, and is the negation of the negation.[21]

This "reciprocal exclusion"[22] of the infinite and the finite defines the very reversibility the Penrose stairs evokes. The tension between recognizing a looped staircase that ascends into the infinite and emphasizing the illogic of this possibility makes that the finite of the Penrose stairs becomes evident. Just as Nolan and Arthur use the Penrose stairs as metaphor to illustrate a rather complex state of mind in *Inception*, this paper will also use this "impossible object" to mediate the situation and agency of the aforementioned three astronauts. Bowman, Bell, and Cooper 'climb the Penrose stairs to merge with the (in)finite'.
In this context, the pictoriality of the Penrose stairs not only helps to clarify the understanding of the posthuman condition and postmodern reprimands the astronauts are embedded within, but also the shifting perspectives, states of knowledge, and spatial relations. This critical approach – the inclusion of the Penrose stairs and Hegel's concept – corresponds with science fiction discourses and the characteristics of science fiction as a fictional mode itself, since Simon

20 Todd McGowan: *The Fictional Christopher Nolan*. Austin: U of Texas P 2012, p. 155.
21 Georg Wilhelm Friedrich Hegel: *The Science of Logic*, transl. from the German by George di Giovanni. Cambridge: Cambridge UP 2010, pp. 114, 117.
22 Ibid., p. 138.

Fig. 2: A younger Bowman sees his older version in *2001: A Space Odyssey* (GB/US 1968, D: Stanley Kubrick).

Spiegel defines the staging of a "novelty" as reality-compliant in "naturalising the marvelousness".[23] According to him, multistable images by Escher or the Penroses are used to illustrate impossible or non-Euclidian cinematic worlds.[24] The recipients constantly desire to actualize their knowledge of a science fiction world due to the dichotomy of the 'marvelous' and the conventional state of physics and science.[25]

Bowman

While traveling to Jupiter in order to follow the monolith's signal, astronaut David Bowman (Keir Dullea) is forced to unplug the ethically and rationally conflicted AI HAL 9000, who killed his fellow colleagues. Bowman thereby overcomes his technically controlled existence and enters the stargate in the film's final chapter.[26] After transgressing the stargate, Bowman arrives in the non-Euclidean hotel room. He gazes with disbelief from within his space capsule. With its mixture of artefacts from the enlightenment era and light panels

23 Simon Spiegel: *Die Konstitution des Wunderbaren: Zu einer Poetik des Science-Fiction-Films*. Marburg: Schüren 2007, pp. 50, 197.

24 Ibid., p. 135.

25 Ibid., p. 145.

26 Stanley Kubrick: *2001: A Space Odyssey* (GB/US 1968). Bluray edition. Hamburg: Warner Bros. Home Entertainment 2007, 1:57:09.

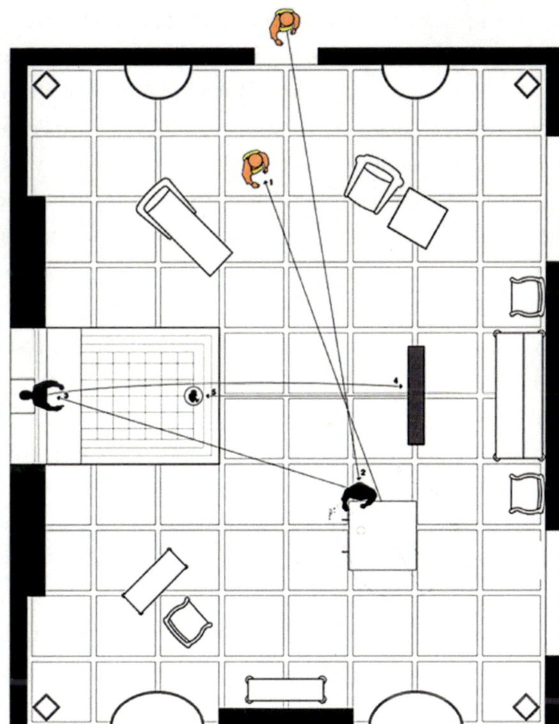

Fig. 3
Floor plan of
all four Bowman versions
within the hotel room.

from mid-century modernism on the floor, this place is reminiscent of a Las Vegas casino and feels surreal. As there are no windows, Bowman is not allowed to contextualize this space with a broader environment and thus the feeling of isolation and estrangement is increased. The artefacts refer to the French Revolution and are contextualized visually and cinematically by Kubrick's plot of human evolution. The Homo sapiens is an obsolete entity, which also needs to change or to transgress its bond with technical simulated reality. The hotel room embodies the "novelty" that is "naturalized" only in its interior parts. It evokes the liminal experience of astronaut Bowman in the final confrontation with the "marvelousness" represented by the black monolith.

This process of transgression of the once cold and emotionless Bowman – as an almost 'classical' image of the astronaut lacking the masculinity of a western hero topos[27] – is visualized by a shot-reverse-shot sequence. First, Bowman

27 See also the chapter by Nils Daniel Peiler "Backlash of the Future" in this volume.

strides aghast gazing and in full space suit through the hotel room. Bowman then beholds older versions of himself one at a time (Fig. 2). The viewer first gets the point of view of a younger Bowman and then that of the older Bowman, both from different places within the room. With this change in perspective, the former, younger Bowman is extinguished in the reverse shot. According to Ralf Fischer, there are four versions or incarnations of Bowman, who then gets rid of his space suit and accustoms himself more and more to this alien habitat (Fig. 3). During this process of looking at vanishing versions of himself, Bowman seems to forget his human ontology.[28]

He learns to see his older 'versions' as an identity that is being transformed into something new. In Baudrillard's sense, the semiotic system of reality is duplicated and thus Bowman seems to be the simulation of himself.[29] These jumps in aging denote the evolutionary jumps in earlier chapters of the film, from prehistoric man to Homo sapiens. Finally, the fourth and apparently dying Bowman transforms in presence of the monolith and, with another cut, into the floating "star child". The metamorphosis into the posthuman consciousness with Bowman's features traverses through the monolith back to near-Earth orbit. This whole scene can metaphorically be compared to climbing the Penrose stairs, as the dying Bowman merges into the posthuman star child and thus with the infinite. He sees his older 'versions' – finite entities of the human species – from different landings[30] within the loop of the Penrose stairs. Bowman's experience is due to his newly found knowledge and acceptance of his obsolete/finite state as a technologically induced space traveler. First, he is stripped of prosthetic technology and then stripped of body and mind. While Kubrick stages this climax with a stark cinematic rhythm, Arthur C. Clarke who wrote the novel simultaneously to the script, describes this metamorphosis as a fluid process:

> Even as one David Bowman ceased to exist, another became immortal. [...] The last links with Earth were gone, resolved back into their component atoms. His indestructible body

28 Ralf Michael Fischer: *Raum und Zeit im filmischen Œuvre von Stanley Kubrick*. Berlin: Gebr. Mann 2009, pp. 215, 287.

29 Jean Baudrillard: Simulacra and Simulations. In: J. B.: *Selected Writings*, ed. by Mark Poster. 2nd ed. Stanford: Stanford UP 2001, pp. 169–187, here p. 185.

30 I would like to thank Colleen Boyle (University of Melbourne) for the constructive discussion and suggestions helping me to clarify my intention of the Penrose stairs metaphor during the conference.

> was his mind's present image of itself; and for all his powers, he knew that he was still a baby. So he would remain until he had decided on a new form, or had passed beyond the necessities of matter.[31]

The infinite star child seems to be the posthuman future and perhaps a new kind of astronaut – if it succeeds in overcoming the finite imagination of the "gadget lover" and thus the hindrances and encumbrances of its old environment. Although this metamorphosis is only possible due to the alien monoliths, a technology denoting "marvelousness", Bowman had to overcome his simulated anthroposphere full of earthly devices. Thus, the astronaut of our current technological state is obsolete. David Roden defines posthumans as descendants of humankind enabled by technological advances (in this case the alien monoliths) – a new species that differs from Homo sapiens.[32] In contrast, transhumans are augmented or enhanced Homo sapiens.[33] Consequently transhumanism is anthropocentric while posthumanism is not.

Bell

While Kubrick stages a glimpse of a posthuman future to come, Jones thematizes the possible problems of a posthuman future in extreme isolation by clearly drawing inspiration from *2001*, *Silent Running* (US 1972, D: Douglas Trumbull) and *Blade Runner* (US/GB 1982, D: Ridley Scott) among others. Here the AI GERTY controls the Lunar Corporation base Sarang. Like Bowman, astronaut Bell (Sam Rockwell) is isolated from Earth and human civilization. In contrast to Bowman, Bell is a caring father and husband who counts the days of his three-year work contract and litters his bunk with pictures of his family. Hence he is a more humane image of the astronaut with a postmodern "'new-man' sensibility", as Llinares has argued in context of other films.[34] Bell has to supervise the automated factory and is reduced to engaging in little manual work. He builds models and talks to the plants he is nurturing.

31 Arthur C. Clarke: *2001: A Space Odyssey*. New York: ROC / New American Library 2000, pp. 291, 293.

32 David Roden: *Posthuman Life: Philosophy at the Edge of the Human*. New York / Abingdon: Routledge 2015, pp. 9, 14, 22.

33 Ibid., p. 9.

34 Llinares: *The Astronaut*, p. 153.

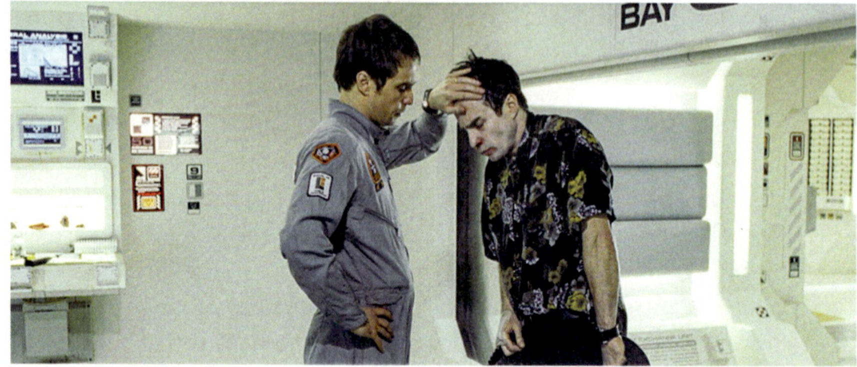

Fig. 4: Both Bell clones in one frame in *Moon* (GB 2009, D: Duncan Jones).

Fig. 5: The seemingly infinite corridor full of Bell clones in *Moon*.

The live broadcast to Earth seems to be out of order. In fact, it has been intentionally disabled, so that Bell only receives recorded video messages from his beloved wife Tess and little daughter Eve. As the "servo-mechanism" of his prostheses,[35] he does not scrutinize this ongoing outage. In one scene, he wakes to the Chesney Hawkes' song *The One and Only* (Chrysalis 1991).[36] At first this scene provides some dry humor, as he is the only responsible human at the Sarang base, but this then shifts into a grim critique of Bell's new condition towards the end of the film.

35 McLuhan: *Understanding Media*, p. 51.

36 Duncan Jones: *Moon* (GB 2009). DVD edition. London: Lunar Industries / Sony Pictures Home Entertainment 2009, 0:13:27.

On a routine inspection at a "Helium-3 Harvester", Bell crashes his moon rover and loses consciousness. He awakes in the base's infirmary with no memory of his accident and unstable walking skills. Later, he becomes suspicious when GERTY does not allow him onto EVA (extravehicular activity), even though the harvesters need to be drained. Bell manages to escape the base and finds the demolished rover and another bruised Bell at the crash site. Back at the facility, he asks GERTY about the other version of himself: "I found him outside. Who is he? You tell me who that is."[37] This is the moment of "novelty" where the "marvelousness" induces shock and awe. Several minutes later and after the bruised Bell has reawakened in the infirmary, the audience sees the other Bell standing in the distance with sunglasses covering his eyes. The bruised Bell also asks GERTY about the other guy: "Who is the guy that looks like me?"[38]

In the following two thirds of the film, the two Bells both ignore and confront each other, which cinematically is staged by the twinning effect of split-screen shots (Fig. 4).[39] The older, bruised Bell says: "GERTY says you're Sam Bell. I am Sam Bell, too."[40] The newer Bell later reflects: "Harvesters are fine. [...] Here, talking to a clone, that's slightly troubling." Here the older Sam reacts hysterically: "I'm not a clone. You're the clone." As they live side by side, both believing the other to be the copy, the alterity, they talk about the wooden model of their hometown Fairfield, recognizing and sharing their family memories. While the older Bell still reacts with disbelief, the newer one is crushed by the realization that they share the same identity.[41] The older, bruised Bell begins to look more and more unhealthy, as he exceeds his three-year working contract with Lunar Corporation and thus the life span of a clone.

After a fight between the two, the older, bruised Bell complains about the newer one to GERTY saying the "other guy" flies of the handle: "I see it now. What Tess was talking about."[42] At this stage, the older Bell demonstrates a form of self-reflection by observing the other Bell. Reflecting his shortcomings in context of his relationship to his wife, his sense of self also awakens by contemplating the

37 Ibid., 0:27:57.

38 Ibid., 0:31:00.

39 Since Georges Méliès and the early 1900s, there have been multiple strategies to duplicate an actor in cinematic space such as a doppelganger, double partial exposure of the film reel, green screen or the split-screen shot as used in *Moon*. For further reading: Graham Edwards: Seeing Double: Twinning in the Movies. In: *Cinefex*, 2014. http://cinefex.com/blog/twinning/ (accessed: October 4, 2018).

40 Jones: *Moon*, 0:33:30.

41 Ibid., 0:38:40.

42 Ibid., 0:46:30.

other Bell, as if he were his own mirror image. He beholds his own faults in the reciprocal Bell, not in himself but at this other place in time; that is and is not him. The incomplete, fragmented self of Bell only becomes a whole identity by observing his identical copy and provides him with a new perception of his body. Hence Bell also climbs the Penrose stairs seeing, interacting and reflecting with his identical copy from different landings. This marks an approach towards the infinite, as he gets an epistemic perspective on the finite posthuman iterations of himself (three-year life span).

Later GERTY reveals that both the older and the newer Bells are clones of a technician, Sam Bell, who lives on Earth, and that Tess and Eve are implants, uploaded memories, of the original one. Their fight over who is the original and who is the copy ends abruptly as they are both hyperreal. GERTY defies corporation directives and helps the older Bell to watch recordings of several deceased clones getting into the cryogenic protection pod that is supposed to bring them to Earth after completing the work contract, but is actually a death chamber.[43]

As every new clone wakes in the infirmary, both Bells find a seemingly infinite corridor full of stored clones (Fig. 5).[44] The red shining lamps show that six trays are already empty, which makes them realize that they are clone number five and number six. The "marvelousness" is "naturalized" by explaining the finite posthuman identities within the context of capitalist efficiency. This corridor complements the Penrose stairs metaphor as it is a seemingly infinite structure in itself, containing a seemingly infinite number of finite Bell iterations. It evidently broaches the issue of the hyperreal and the posthuman in the sense of Baudrillard: the semiotics of the real replace the real.[45]

The newer Bell, number six, finally returns to Earth in a Helium-3 Carrier, in order to reveal the unethical, immoral procedures of Lunar Corporation to the public. The AI GERTY voluntarily erases its memory and reboots once the newer Bell is on his way, in order to keep his plan secret. GERTY states: "The new Sam [iteration number seven] and I will be back to our programming as soon as I've finished rebooting." The newer Bell answers empathetically: "Gerty, we're not programmed. We're people, you understand?"[46]

43 Jones: *Moon*, 0:57:50.

44 Ibid., 1:03:00.

45 Baudrillard: Simulacra and Simulations, p. 170.

46 Jones: *Moon*, 1:24:50.

Through Bell's confrontation with his copy and the revelation that he is himself a copy, amongst an unlimited number of pre-packed Bells, director Jones thematizes the awakening of a person into a posthuman ontology without any 'real human' interference. Living three years, the posthuman Bell is, metaphorically speaking, ascending the Penrose stairs to merge with the (in)finite, by performing an ever-repeating three-year loop. Every finite clone is an iteration inscribed in the infinity of the corporation's capitalist efficiency. By having two clones confront one another, the issue of hyperreality becomes the "novelty". In this context, Jimena Escudero Pérez remarks:

> [T]he clone stands as a perfect discursive and biological exponent of the concept of alterity: a clone is an identical individual, one hundred percent human, who is nevertheless viewed as a subversion of the self. It is precisely the lack of difference here which constitutes the maximum threat to the cohesion of identity and ontology.[47]

Bell is the prosthesis of himself, the simulation of an original Sam Bell back on Earth. The perception of the self and the knowledge of the artificial posthuman condition is gradually validated.[48] Baudrillard writes: "When the real no longer is what it used to be, nostalgia assumes its full meaning. [...] There is an escalation of the true, of the lived experience."[49] *Moon's* discourse on identity, posthuman life and capitalist exploitation conforms with Baudrillard's remarks on cloning; humankind's DNA becomes just a code like any other and the act of infinite reproducibility degrades the clone to a finite organic entity of consumption without the rights of a human subject.[50] This can perfectly be visualized by the multistable image of the Penrose stairs and its (in) finite condition.

47 Jimena Escudero Pérez: Sympathy for the Clone: (Post) Human Identities Enhanced by the 'Evil Science' Construct and Its Commodifying Practices in Contemporary Clone Fiction. In: *Between* 4:8 (2014), pp. 1–24, here p. 5.

48 According to Pérez, the viewer's identification with the clones as protagonists is a difficult task of self-other relation in science fiction film. Nevertheless, it can be accomplished by a threefold process: first, the clone is introduced as human individual, second it will be objectified. Third, the clone is rehabilitated as person: Ibid., p. 17.

49 Baudrillard: Simulacra and Simulations, p. 174.

50 Maria A. S. S. Ferreira: *I Am the Other: Literary Negotiations of Human Cloning*. Westport: Greenwood 2005, p. 24.

Cooper

In a time of global drought, the skills of ex-NASA test pilot Cooper (Matthew McConaughey) are not useful anymore. He is 'reduced' to working as a farmer. Although he later traverses a black hole in search for a new home beyond the known solar system, Cooper never embodies the forward-looking cold astronaut of the Cold War era like Bowman. He is a caring father always looking back. Like the obsolete cowboys in revisionist western films like *Lonesome Are the Brave* (US 1962, D: David Miller), Cooper is the postmodern image of an anti-hero astronaut.

As with Bowman and Bell, the awakening of the (posthuman) self has its climax in a singular non-Euclidean space, the five-dimensional "tesseract". In order to let Brand (Anne Hathaway) safely use said black hole to reach another planet, Cooper detaches his shuttle from the main starship and dips into the black hole.[51] Cooper now has to eject from his shuttle and drifts, solely protected by his space suit, further into the black hole. Like Bowman, Cooper is forced to get rid of most of his prostheses.

He arrives in the tesseract, which seems to be the core of the black hole and provides Cooper with a liminal experience:[52] The tesseract is the enhancement of a three-dimensional cube into the fourth dimension of time and thus itself somewhat of an "impossible object" due to its ever-shifting solid structure. This hypercube has sixteen instead of eight angles and twenty-four instead of six square planes, which embody the spatiotemporal field of movement of a conventional cube. Christopher Nolan pushes the "marvelousness" of this setting even further in adding a fifth dimension, where the tesseract transforms the dimension of time into a spatial dimension.[53] Like the hotel room in *2001*, this is a singular space of maximum "novelty". In the diegesis, the tesseract is described as three-dimensional spatialisation of time, which henceforth becomes a navigable, physical dimension for Cooper.[54]

51 Christopher Nolan: *Interstellar* (US/GB/CA 2014). 2 Disc Bluray, Steelbook Edition. Hamburg: Warner Bros. Entertainment / Paramount Pictures 2014, 02:13:30.

52 For further reading: Marc Bonner: Interstellar Floating in Nostalgia: Christopher Nolans Dimensionen taktiler Retroästhetik. In: M. B. / Pablo Abend / Tanja Weber (eds): *Just Little Bits Of History Repeating: Medien | Nostalgie | Retromanie*. Münster: Lit 2017, pp. 53–75.

53 Marc Cotta Vaz: *Interstellar: Beyond Time and Space: Inside Christopher Nolan's Sci-Fi Epic*. London: Titan 2014, p. 131.

54 Ibid., p. 135; Bill Desowitz: Inside the Making of the Spectacular Tesseract in "Interstellar". In: *IndieWire*, December 10, 2014. https://www.indiewire.com/2014/12/inside-the-making-of-the-spectacular-tesseract-in-interstellar-189771/ (accessed: July 6, 2017).

Fig. 6: Cooper floating within the tesseract in *Interstellar* (US/GB/CA 2014, D: Christopher Nolan).

Fig. 7: Cooper sees his younger self due to the tesseract in *Interstellar*.

As Cooper floats within the tesseract, he disbelievingly gazes through the walls of time and space, recognizing his daughter Murph's room back at the farm. This room is copied infinite times and each copy is attached to another in spatialized time, that is to say all of the axis of the tesseract (Fig. 6). Each copy represents a different moment in time; it is an architectural notation of Murph's room in a grid-like structured timeline, very similar to the steel frame construction of skyscrapers. Cooper punches against the bookshelf and the young Murph (Mackenzie Foy) becomes aware of it.[55] This is a crucial moment, since it relates

55 Nolan: *Interstellar*, 2:17:48.

directly to several scenes at the beginning of the film where a ghost apparently seems to haunt Murph's room in particular, confronting father and daughter with a mystery. Very late into the plot it is revealed that Cooper's actions from within the tesseract affect the past back at the farm and thus the audience realizes that Cooper himself is/was the ghost. Consequently, he sees his younger self multiple times in his kaleidoscopic habitat (Fig. 7). Two finite moments in time (Murph's room during the farewell and Cooper's state within the tesseract's core) are spatially looped by the five-dimensional tesseract and thus correspond with the (in)finite of the Penrose stairs. Similarly to Bowman's and Bell's experiences, Cooper reflects his younger self as an alterity, as another Cooper from different landings of the Penrose stairs. In the re-enactment of his farewell from Murph, he has a first awakening of the self by realizing his failure when leaving his family. He shouts to his younger self: "Don't go, you idiot. Don't go!"[56] and "Make him stay, Murph.... Don't let me leave, Murph."[57] Meanwhile, time on Earth progresses in linear fashion and faster than for Cooper on his journey in space. Adult Murph (Jessica Chastain) finally recognizes that it was her father who sent the Morse code "Stay", which back in the past seems to have been formed by an invisible hand.

Cooper is then contacted by the robot TARS, who claims that aliens saved Cooper and himself in their fifth dimension. Here Cooper initiates his second awakening of the self: "I brought myself here."[58] He was able to induce the tesseract within the black hole. The five-dimensional tesseract allows Cooper not only to send a binary code of the TARS' processed quantum data of the black hole to his adult daughter by manipulating the second hand of a watch, but also to send his younger self the coordinates of the secluded NASA base. The moment adult Murph finalizes the scientific solution from the binary code, the tesseract collapses and Cooper is adrift in the solar system.[59] Cooper becomes an ephemeral ubiquitous posthuman astronaut. The tesseract here functions as a short-term prosthesis of Cooper who then leaves the infinite loop and, metaphorically speaking, exits the Penrose stairs again into a conventional linear corridor. He is his own cause and effect within the plot.

56 Nolan: *Interstellar*, 02:19:30.
57 Ibid., 2:21:31.
58 Ibid., 2:25:06.
59 Ibid., 2:27:28.

The "marvelousness" of the future Cooper contacting his younger self, his young as well as his adult daughter, is a nostalgia-inducing phenomenon in the sense of Svetlana Boym. The "marvelousness" is naturalized by fatherly emotions. The five-dimensional tesseract is "restorative nostalgia" materialized as architecture and prosthesis for Cooper in his most desperate moment: "[R]estorative nostalgia ends up reconstructing emblems and rituals of home and homeland in an attempt to conquer and spatialize time".[60] While in the tesseract, while being the tesseract, Cooper tilts between the infinite and its inscribed finite. As Llinares states, nostalgia is a

> [...] primary element in postmodern construction of the astronaut. [... A]n active process of making new meaning [...] It is a cultural longing for the astronaut to embody the 'symbolic repertoire' and thus provide a sense of historical continuity [...] In this sense, nostalgia represents a hyperrealisation of the past which is commodified as image, stereotype and pastiche in a depthless array of significations.[61]

This not only fits into the extradiegetic nostalgia of *Interstellar* itself, but also into the intradiegetic nostalgia of Cooper being a caring father, which can be understood as a critical commentary on Nolan's film itself. In its attempt to evoke a philosophical liminal experience of an astronaut, *Interstellar* uses a similar visual aesthetics to its antetype, *2001*, but falls short in addressing the complexity of posthumanism and postmodernism. It is therefore not on a par with *2001* or *Moon*.

Conclusion

The critical approach of merging the multistable Penrose stairs with Hegel's concept of the infinite and its inscribed finite ever-tilting into each other, helps to analyze and illustrate the intertwining postmodern and posthuman systems of meaning in these three films. To be more precise, the Penrose stairs, as spatio-temporal metaphor, clarifies the astronauts' liminal experiences of transgressions, metamorphoses and epistemic awakenings of the self in mostly non-Euclidean places. Escher's lithograph *Ascending and Descending* illustrates the astronauts' liminal experiences even better as all three see versions or copies of

60 Svetlana Boym: *The Future of Nostalgia*. New York: Basic / Perseus 2001, p. 49.
61 Llinares: *The Astronaut*, p. 199.

Fig. 8: M. C. Escher: *Ascending and Descending*, 1960. Lithograph.

themselves on different landings of the Penrose stairs (Fig. 8). Escher depicts the Penrose stairs as a cascading roof on top of a multi-story villa and fills it with several identical human figures circling in both directions. Most notably, Escher's world also imagines the recipients by the man that observes the activity on the impossible staircase from a lower balcony on the left. Clone, star child or transitory infinite being achieving a posthuman condition, Bowman, Bell, and Cooper metaphorically 'climb the Penrose stairs to merge with the (in)finite'.

Martin Butler

The Future That Never Was

Analogue Nostalgia and the Ambivalent Astronaut in the Songs of Man … or Astro-man?

Ignition sequence

Astronauts and space travel have been recurring topics in all kinds of popular music and have been dealt with in numerous ways and with a variety of different purposes. Indeed, as a simple search on the internet quickly reveals, there are plenty of songs from a range of different genres and historical contexts that articulate and regularly reaffirm the desire to go outer space, such as Frank Sinatra's well-known version of *Fly me to the Moon* (1964) or The Police's *Walking on the Moon* (1979). At the same time, we also – though not as frequently – find more skeptical and rather disenchanting titles such as *Space Travel is Boring* (1996) by the indie rock band Modest Mouse or the children's chant *I Don't Want to Live on the Moon* by Sesame Street character Ernie (1978).[1] Considering this engagement with space travel in various genres and sub-genres of popular music, ranging from affirmative voices celebrating the exploration of space to more humorous forms mocking this fascination, there seems to be comparatively little scholarly research on popular music's preoccupation with this topic.[2]

1 These songs (and many more) are listed by Tom Chao: The Astronaut's Playlist: Groovy Songs for Space Travelers. https://www.space.com/11037-space-music-playlist-astronauts-wakeup.html (accessed: July 16, 2017).

2 In fact, there are quite a number of studies that also touch upon images and ideas of space and space travel in their discussion of their material; yet there are fewer which *focus* on this topic. A more recent study of the latter kind, which indeed devotes a larger part of his argument to space travel, is Victor Kennedy's chapter "Science and Science Fiction in Rock" in his book *Strange Brew: Metaphors of Magic and Science in Rock Music.* Cambridge: Cambridge Scholars 2013, pp. 91–110. Another one is Michael Mooradian Lupo's Keeping Space Fantastic: The

Against this backdrop, this contribution sets out to add to the scholarly debate on popular music's concern with space and space travel by focusing on one particular sub-genre of rock music and its 'use' of the image of the astronaut. To be precise, it concentrates on representations of space travelers and traveling in a specific variation of US-American surf rock, which was particularly popular in the 1960s, re-emerged in the 1990s, and has seen yet another revival in recent years.[3] As a case study taken from this field of cultural production, my contribution will focus on the oeuvre of a band called Man ... or Astro-man?, which can be said to have contributed to this revival of surf rock in the 1990s and for which the references to space travel (on the verbal, the musical, and the performative levels) serve as an integral part both of the band's self-fashioning and of their song-writing. By analyzing a selection of examples taken from the band's discography, their live performances, as well as from the media discourse on the band, I would like to show that, in this branch of surf rock, the figure of the astronaut is often featured as the embodiment of a distinctly pre-digital era of technological development through a retrofied soundscape and what might well be called the 'nostalgification' of the visual inventory of mid-twentieth century science fiction. Taking into account the songs' lyrical and musical dimensions as well as the paratexts of their production and reception, my contribution proposes that these memories of past futures, revolving around the astronaut who is imagined as a signifier of 'past futures' and cast as an ideal observer due to its marginal position, potentially serve to sustain a notion of what could be called the 'authentic analogue' central to this genre's self-conception as a subculture.

Sounds of the past: on Man ... or Astro-man?'s "diachronic dialogue"

For a large part of their career, which reached its peak in the 1990s, the band Man ... or Astro-man? has drawn upon images and sounds which depict, or evoke, notions of space travel and 'outer space'. Already the band's name, with its question mark enigmatically indicating a state of in-betweenness, i. e. of being 'Man ... Or Astro-man?,' of being of earthly or non-earthly origin, programmatically hints at the band's thematic focus on space travel. Moreover, on the performative

Transformative Journey of Major Tom. In: Toija Cinque / Christopher Moore / Sean Redmond (eds): *Enchanting David Bowie: Space/Time/Body/Memory*. New York / London: Bloomsbury 2015, pp. 13–26.

3 Surf Music. In: *Wikpedia* [kursiv]. https: https://en.wikipedia.org/wiki/Surf_music (accessed: July 16, 2017). Of course, I am well aware that Wikipedia is not considered a scholarly source. However, with regard to its encyclopedic approach, it is a highly valuable resource especially when it comes to phenomena of popular culture.

Fig. 1: Man or Astro-Man? performing live at the Bottletree Cafe in Birmingham, Alabama on March 6, 2010.

Fig. 2
Front cover of Man or Astro-Man?: *Destroy All Astromen*, 1994.

and paratextual level, i. e. in interviews, in CD booklets or in promotional materials, the band has consistently fashioned itself as a team of astronauts. To be precise, they not only wear suits for space travel during their concerts, but also draw upon a specific set of images of outer space and space travel to frame their appearance as a band, combining 'authentic' space travel equipment such as the NASA space suit and elements taken from science fiction (Fig. 1 & 2).[4]

In this framing of their image as that of space travelers, Man … or Astro-man? frequently relies on a particular aesthetic which goes back to ideas about space exploration that were generated and disseminated in the middle of the twentieth century, when space travel was still considered to be a "giant leap for mankind" and, what is more, served as a prominent arena in which the Cold War between the United States and the Soviet Union was fought out in what would become known as the "space race". To be more specific, on the visual level, the band's outward appearance as well as the images used on record sleeves and tour posters feature an idea of space travel that amalgamates images from mid-twentieth century science fiction and encapsulates the promise of an emerging era of discovering 'outer space'. A vision of space travel, as one may argue, in which the astronaut still symbolized the peak of scientific and technological advancement and thus became the epitome of human progress, catering to the American dream of unfettered mobility as well as to expansionist fantasies even beyond planet Earth.[5]

Very much in line with this visual set-up, the musical level of the band's recordings and performances contributes to establishing this notion of the astronaut as

4 See also Shannon Finck: Man [Seeking] Astro-man? Nouveau Surf Rock and the Futuristic-Past Nostalgic. In: Alex DiBlasi / Victoria Willis (eds): *Geek Rock: An Exploration of Music and Subculture*. Lanham: Rowman & Littlefield 2014, pp. 119–134, here pp. 121–122.

5 For the formation of this image, see also ibid., pp. 119–120. Some of the aspects covered in this contribution are also discussed in Shannon Finck's highly illuminating essay, which unfortunately I only came across during the process of preparing this paper for publication. Finck, though with reference to other materials and with other areas of focus, also discusses the forms and functions of Man … or Astro-man?'s retrofuturism (on the lyrical, musical, and performative levels). Yet, her perspective, which is particularly informed by Svetlana Boym's ideas on nostalgia (cf. esp. ibid., pp. 119–121 et passim), predominantly sheds light on the critical momentum of the practices of nostalgic remembering in the works of Man … or Astro-man? (cf. e. g. ibid., p. 125). She discusses, among other things, the band's critical reflection on the "condition of communication in general" (ibid., p. 128) through their idiosyncratic and subversive appropriation of "space-age technology" (ibid.,p. 128) combined with "simple machines and consumer goods" (ibid., p. 130; cf. esp. pp. 128–132). Instead, my contribution sets out to highlight firstly, the band's fashioning of the figure of the astronaut against the backdrop of 'retrofuturism' and secondly, the affective dimension of the analogue vis-a-vis the digital created in and communicated through their songs. In parts, then, our arguments are complementary, in parts they overlap.

a cipher for a past vision of modernity characterized by the optimistic belief in scientific endeavor as the basis of limitless progress and territorial expansion. To be precise, the band regularly incorporates a range of sound samples from science fiction series into their songs and deliberately employs rather old-fashioned technologies of sound production and sampling to evoke the 'Golden Age' of space travel.[6] Moreover, their guitar-driven sound is modified with extreme reverb and echo effects, which contribute to rendering what could well be labeled a 'sonic space'. In other words, it produces the notion of endless space through specific sound modulations, which make the spatial expansion of sound waves perceivable for the listeners. Apart from these musical characteristics, the verbal dimension of the songs (whenever there is one, bearing in mind that the band's oeuvre is largely instrumental) adds to the emulation of space and space travel, for example, through references to outer space in the lyrics (e.g. in *Destination Venus*[7]), samples of allegedly authentic radio programs reporting about alien life (as in *Mystery Meat*), or sampled snippets of an interview, in which the band is asked how long they are going to visit planet Earth before going back to Venus again, thus highlighting the band's continuous space travel (as in *Destination Venus*). This visual and musical set-up, then, which the band employs to promote the image of space travel revolving around the astronaut as its main protagonist, refers to and pays homage to the surf rock of the 1950s and early 1960s, most prominently represented by bands such as The Astronauts and The Spotnicks. At that time, these bands not only conjured up the image and idea of space travel with their names, which were indeed highly indicative of the contemporary discourse on the exploration of 'outer space' as the ultimate frontier,[8] they also

6 See ibid., pp. 121–122, also p. 124.

7 This song is an adaptation of the eponymous song by a band called The Rezillos, recorded in 1978. cf. Derrick McMillon: http://www.whosampled.com/cover/486015/Man-or-Astro-Man%3F-Destination-Venus-The-Rezillos-Destination-Venus/ (accessed: July 16, 2017).

8 Surf rock was, of course, not the only form of music that reacted to and shaped the experience of space exploration. As Simon Reynolds points out with reference to avantgarde music: "[w]hen the space race actually kicked off with the 1957 Soviet launch of sputnik [*sic*] into orbit, composers jostled to title their works in reference to mankind's new frontier: Philips's sound researchers Tom Dissevelt and Kid Baltan rushed out *Song of the Second Moon* (a reference to the satellite), and Dissevelt reprised the idea with 1963's *Fantasy in Orbit*. Later in the sixties, inspired by cosmonaut Yuri Gagarin's first steps outside the Earth's atmosphere and the landing on the lunar surface of NASA's unmanned Surveyor, came Otto Luening's *Moonflight*, Musica Electronica Viva's *Spacecraft* and Subotnik's *Silver Apples of the Moon*. Simon Reynolds: *Retromania: Pop Culture's Addiction to Its Own Past*. New York: Faber & Faber 2011, p. 385. Reynolds also names a number of other popular musical examples of thematizing space exploration at that time (cf. ibid., pp. 385–386).

developed a specific sound, which was made possible through advancements in electric amplification that, in turn, were made affordable and popularized in different genres of rock music through companies such as Binson, Echolette, and Dynacord. Moreover, during the late 1950s and early 1960s, the Spotnicks in particular begun to wear astronaut suits on stage and established a specifically transmedial aesthetic on record sleeves and in promotion material and – very much in line with this agenda of self-fashioning – released their first LP *The Spotnicks in London Out-A-Space* in 1962. Considering the popularity of the so-called "space race" at the time, it perhaps does not come as a surprise that such a self-fashioning as astronauts, based on the band's 'space sound' and an equally distinct aesthetic, turned out to be particularly marketable and made the band and their sound a point of reference for ensuing generations of surf rock combos, including Man ... or Astro-man?

In this vein, then, Man ... or Astro-man? 'retrofies' the specific aesthetics of surf rock, nostalgically drawing upon and re-assembling different aesthetic references from the 1950s and 1960s, partly processed with the help of technologies from the same era. Employing a "repertoire" (in Diana Taylor's sense[9]) of images and sounds from the heyday of both space travel and surf rock in their own music and performance, the band thus establishes what Aleida Assmann has called a "diachronic dialogue" with the past.[10] By referring to these imaginaries of space exploration prevalent in those days, the band, at the very same time, also draws attention to a 'future that never was', which, as I would like to argue in the following, unfolds a specific ideological momentum in that it confronts the audience with the 'future that is'.[11]

9 Diana Taylor: *The Archive and the Repertoire: Performing Cultural Memory in the Americas*. Durham: Duke UP 2003.

10 Aleida Assmann: From the Printing Press to the Internet: From a Culture of Memory to a Culture of Attention. In: Natascha Gentz / Stefan Kramer (eds): *Globalization, Cultural Identities, and Media Representations*. Albany, NY: State U of New York P 2006, pp. 11–23. For a more detailed exploration of popular music's engagement with preceding musical developments, which also resorts to Taylor's concept of the "repertoire" and Assmann's notion of a "diachronic dialogue", see Martin Butler: Timeless Tunes, Immortal Voices: On the 'Historical Fate' of the Protest Song and the Musical Unconscious of the 'Other' America. In: Julius Greve / Sascha Pöhlmann (eds): *America and the Musical Unconscious*. New York / Dresden: Atropos 2015, pp. 51–64.

11 Cf. also Finck: Man, pp. 122, 124.

Man … or Astro-man? in the context of retrofuturism: on analogue nostalgia and the productivity of remoteness

With their aesthetics of nostalgia employed in the representation of the space traveler, then, Man … or Astro-man? can well be considered to represent a specific trend of revitalizing the past, which has become known as "retrofuturism".[12] Retrofuturism can be characterized as a revitalization of 'past futures' and manifests itself in a range of different cultural practices and forms of expression. These specifically draw upon utopian images and narratives of space travel from the 1950s and 1960s that, as I have already hinted at, feature the exploration of space as the basis of a "technocratic fantasy of global dominance based on […] scientific and technological achievements"[13] with the colonization of 'outer space' signifying the "ultimate territorial expansion".[14] Simon Reynolds describes this "retrofuturist emotion"[15] as "those sensations of wistfulness, mixed with irony, and amazement, offset by amusement, that are induced by old science-fiction movies, modernist cooking ware and furniture from between the two world wars, and images from the fifties and sixties World's Fairs, with their exhibitions of technological innovations and scientific breakthroughs".[16]

This 'retroification' of past futures is, of course, not a mere reproduction of these futures and their inherent ideological implications, but a process of productive appropriation, in which these past visions of the future are quite frequently employed to critically engage with contemporary discourses on technological development and progress.[17] Accordingly, the nostalgic invocation of the past, in this case of the golden "heady days of Sputnik and early manned spaceflight",[18] is by no means an exclusively aesthetic phenomenon, but also bears a particularly

12 The term "retrofuturism" or "retro-futurism" is said to have been used first by T.R. Hinchcliffe as the title of his 1967 book (Pelican), "[m]ost recent speculation has attributed the term to the writer, editor, and musician Lloyd Dunn, who coined the word and renamed his 'zine Retrofuturism in 1988". Elizabeth Guffey / Kate C. Lemay: Retrofuturism and Steampunk. In: Rob Latham (ed.): *The Oxford Handbook of Science Fiction*. Oxford: Oxford UP 2014, pp. 434–450, here p. 434. Guffey and Lemay provide a general definition of the term, as they contrast it with the notion of 'futurism,' arguing that "[i]f futurism is a term that describes our anticipation of what is to come, retrofuturism describes how we remember these visions" (ibid.).

13 Finck: Man, p. 119.

14 Ibid.

15 Reynolds: *Retromania*, p. 370.

16 Ibid.

17 Cf. also Finck: Man, pp. 120, 125.

18 Victoria Willis / Alex DiBlasi: Introduction. Q: Are We Not Geeks? A: We Are Geek Rock! In: V. W. / A. D. (eds): *Geek Rock. An Exploration of Music and Subculture*. Lanham: Rowman & Littlefield 2014, pp. xiii–xxi, here p. xx.

political or ideological potential, in that it, somewhat paradoxically at first sight, draws attention to the current (and perhaps also future) state of affairs by indulging in a mode of nostalgic remembrance. In other words and more generally speaking, narratives of the past and their specific sets of ideas about what constitutes 'history' are always formulated from a present perspective and are, in fact, much more indicative of the present than of the past. With regard to the retroification of past futures, then, Henry Jenkins points out that "past imaginings of the future need to be understood as historical artifacts of older ideologies about human progress and that their remobilization in the present can be used as a means of reflecting on the failures of those dreams to become realities".[19] Accordingly, the retrofuturism of Man... or Astro-man?, with its systematic invocation of past images of space travel, can also be read as a critical comment on the failure of a specific technology and its protagonist, the astronaut, which were once heralded as the vanguard of establishing a new frontier in outer space that would ensure the continuous evolution of the human species, in particular the US-American part of it. Furthermore, the band's invocation of the 'futures that could have been' do remind us of the fact that these futures are nothing that could have been predicted, determined, or controlled, and that even technology could not prevent these futures from 'not' happening. In this vein, then, the astronaut turns into the protagonist of a story of success that has not been too successful, of a narrative of longing and desire, which for the most part has remained a narrative and a somewhat tragic and frustrating one at that. This narrative, then, reminds us of the fact that in the era of space travel, the present day was imagined to be much more futuristic than it actually turned out to be:

> Switching from '19' (the numeric signifier for the twentieth century) to '20' seemed like it should automatically place us on the other side of a great divide, as if we'd made an abrupt leap into the future. But of course the new millennium has so far turned out to be barely different from the tail end of the last one [...]. This prosaic reality of something that once seemed fantastically advanced typifies the way that our ideas of the future have been gradually scaled down in the last three decades.[20]

19 Qtd. in Rebecca Coyle / Alex Mesker: Time Warp: Sonic Retro-Futurism in The Jetsons. In: K.J. Donnelly / Philip Hayward (eds): *Music in Science Fiction Television: Tuned to the Future.* New York / London: Routledge 2013, pp. 14–33, here p. 28.
20 Reynolds: *Retromania*, pp. 363–364.

Against this backdrop, one may indeed trace in the musical renderings of space travel a specific "nostalgia for the future", or "neostalgia", as Reynolds calls it.[21] Moreover, I would like to argue that – in the framework of this utopian narrative – the image of the astronaut produced by the band serves to denote a particular form of technology, i. e. analogue one, which was eventually outdated by the transition to digital technology. A transition that has, as we all know, affected technologies in all areas of life ever since the advent of the transistor in the 1960s, including the production, dissemination, and reception of popular music. While, as Johnston argues, "during the late 1960s is was [still] not clear if digital or analogue technology would be the way forward for satellite remote sensing"[22] and would thus find its way into the technologies of exploring space, the digital seems to have ultimately outdated the analogue. Paradoxically, at the same time that the digital has become the technological paradigm of the present and the future, there seems to be a growing tendency to revitalize the "aura" (in Benjamin's sense[23]) of authenticity attached to and dispersed by the idea of the analogue.

Indeed, as Coyle and Mesker observe, we nowadays tend to "construct a world in which technology is warm and personable", arguing that

> [...] while the sounds of technology have become transparent, we tend to reinsert 'the grain' of sounds from the past. Our modern approach to technological design concedes that, although digital technology is (most often) near silent, feedback in the digital world references the analogue. Historically, we learned through sensory feedback the nature of the state of the machine, and sound was a significant byproduct or result of the technology.[24]

As a consequence, then, digital technology is regularly employed to emulate the analogue, for example in the shape of a variety of old-fashioned ringtones from

21 Ibid., pp. 363; cf. esp. pp. 368–372.

22 Andrew K. Johnston: Exploring Planet Earth: The Development of Satellite Remote Sensing for Earth Science. In: Roger D. Launius (ed.): *Exploring the Solar System: The History and Science of Planetary Exploration.* New York: Palgrave Macmillan 2013, pp. 203–21, here p. 260.

23 See Walter Benjamin: The Work of Art in the Age of Its Technological Reproducibility: Third Version. In: W. B.: *Selected Writings*, vol. 4: 1938–1940, ed. by Howard Eiland / Michael W. Jennings. Cambridge, MA: Harvard UP 2003, pp. 251–283.

24 Coyle / Mesker: Time Warp, p. 29.

equally old-fashioned telephones, which are ready to be downloaded to replace the otherwise clean sounds produced by the digital interior of the cell phone.[25]

Through their use of tube amplification, extreme reverb and echo effects, feedback loops, and other noises and sounds generated by a variety of technological gadgets, Man ... or Astro-man? too embrace the analogue by exposing the materiality of the soundscape they produce in the very act of producing it. At the same time, they often feature analogue technology on record sleeves and tour posters as well as on stage. Accordingly, I would argue that, alongside their invocation of past visions of space travel, they also put forward a nostalgic approach to analogue technology, which is thus strongly associated with these early ideas of space exploration.

The figure of the astronaut can thus not only be understood as the protagonist of a futuristic utopia that has never become a reality, but is also turned into a signifier of an outdated technology. Indeed, by nostalgically embracing outdated technology in their music and performance, the band features the space traveler as the centerpiece of an image of a past, but 'authentic' technology, according to which technological investment and achievement are rendered as being directly interrelated to one another. This image of a past technology also brings forth notions of huge machines, incredible manpower gathered in equally huge control rooms, and enormous amounts of energy, which are imagined to be absolutely necessary in order to make space travel work in the first place. Its logic of equal proportions, then, stands in stark contrast to the story of digitization, which is a story of the reduction of size, of a race towards smaller and smaller units that are able to perform a myriad of calculations in a second. This development is perhaps epitomized by the microchip as the nucleus and catalyst of digital enhancement and progress, which has also affected the production, dissemination, and reception of popular music.

In this vein, then, one could even go so far as to argue that by explicitly exposing the materiality of their music as well as their appearance as 'astromen' on stage, the band emphasizes their own reliance on technology in their production of sounds in as much as they underline the astronaut's reliance on technology in his exploration of space, signified most prominently by the space suit enabling the survival of the astronaut 'outer space'. Against this backdrop, the 'authentic

25 The 'affective attributes' attached to these categories – with 'the analogue' being considered as a 'warm,' authentic and immediate, and the digital as rather 'cold' and remote – can not only be found in the transmedial discourse of retrofuturism, but also in other fields of popular culture, which especially in recent years can be characterized by what Simon Reynolds has called "retromania" and which nostalgically embraces the 'warmness' and 'immediacy' of analogue technology.

analogue' produced by the band – the "blast from the past," as Finck calls it, "a recycled form, and yet somehow also a raw one"[26] – can also be understood as unfolding a particularly self-referential momentum in that it sustains a specific notion of 'realness' so central for the genre's self-conception as part of a subculture. In other words, with its deliberate technological 'backwardness', the band caters to a narrative of the analogue as a mode of production and representation in which material input and output as well as signifier and signified are said to stand in direct connection to one another. Their narrative thus counters an equally well-established story of digitization, which is frequently told as a "process of deprivation and disembodiment",[27] and in which the mode of representation and articulation is at best indexical, in other words, only indirect or mediate, lacking the "grain"[28] of the voice and the sound, thereby suspending the human dimension of cultural production through mathematic interpolation.

To be sure, what matters in this juxtaposition of the analogue (as authentic) and the digital (as inauthentic) both in retro-culture in general and in surf rock in particular, of course, is not the actual "technical differences" between these technologies. In fact, space travel, from its very beginnings was partly digital already. Furthermore, the 1960s Apollo mission itself can be considered crucial to the digitization of space travel: as Dag Spicer has noted, "until Apollo, all computations for the equations of motion in these systems were performed by analogue computers" and it was already "in April 1961 [that] NASA contracted with MIT to study the feasibility of a digital control system for the Apollo program".[29] What matters instead is what Dominik Schrey has described as the "affective attributes"[30] afforded by and attached to these technologies, i. e., the ways in which they are *perceived* by their users as well as the specific discourses through which the categories of 'the analogue' and 'the digital' have been charged with normative connotations and implications over time. In this vein, Schrey also observes a "longing for what is assumed to be lost in the continuous process of digitization that accounts for contemporary media culture's romanticizing and

26 Finck: Man, p. 131.

27 Dominik Schrey: Analogue Nostalgia and the Aesthetics of Digital Remediation. In: Katharina Niemeyer (ed.): *Media and Nostalgia: Yearning for the Past, Present and Future.* Basingstoke / New York: Palgrave Macmillan 2014, pp. 27–38, here p. 29.

28 Roland Barthes: The Grain of the Voice. In: R. B.: *Image Music Text*, selected and transl. from the French by Stephen Heath. London: Fontana 1977, pp. 179–189.

29 Dag Spicer: One Giant Leap: The Apollo Guidance Computer. In: *Dr. Dobbs: The World of Software Development*, August 12, 2000. http://www.drdobbs.com/architecture-and-design/one-giant-leap-the-apollo-guidance-compu/184404139 (accessed: July 16, 2017).

30 Schrey: Analogue Nostalgia, p. 28.

fetishizing analogue media. Symptoms of this 'analogue nostalgia' in its broadest sense can be found in every area of culture and society."[31]

Seen in this light, the band's image of space travel can thus indeed be understood as a critical comment on the evolution of media, reminding us, at the same time, that "'before cyber space, outer space was the ultimate frontier', the mysterious expanse capable of embodying 'victory over the temporal and spatial limitations of human existence' and 'putting an end to longing'."[32] Indeed, with the popularization of the CD in the 1980s, the dramatic enhancement of computer generated images (CGI), as well as the advent of the World Wide Web in the late 1980s and early 1990s, it seemed as if the exploration of space would eventually be replaced by the exploration of virtual worlds of sight and sound constructed through digital media.

Yet in Man ... or Astro-man's oeuvre, the astronaut is not only featured as an emblem of analogue technology and a representative of the somewhat outdated and rather unsuccessful mission of exploring 'outer space', unfolding a particularly nostalgic and simultaneously critical momentum. The astronaut is also turned into a figure whose extraordinary vantage point qualifies them to be a specific well-equipped observer of earthly beings and doings. In other words, Man ... or Astro-man?, especially in their paratextual self-fashionings, usually render themselves as space travelers whose remoteness to the world ('remoteness' both in a literal and in a figurative sense) allows them to develop a particularly distanced perspective. This enables them to be both creative and critical in an extraordinary way, one which is only possible in 'outer space' and in the end benefits all humankind: on record sleeves, they identify as "mission astronauts" and, in a text promoting their most recent album *Defcon 5...4...3...2...1*, it is argued that

> Man or Astro-Man? have returned to Earth for the human masses and after years of hibernation they are now unveiling their finest recorded work to date [...]. The record combines ever-familiar Astro audio tones and the well-established playing ferocity that Man... or Astro-man? are known for, but yet now, there is an undeniably evolution to the band that is both intuitive, logical and well crafted.[33]

31 Schrey: Analogue Nostalgia, p. 28.

32 Finck, partially quoting Boym: Man, p. 119.

33 "Man ... or Astro-Man? Defcon 5, 4, 3, 2, 1". In: *Chunklet Industries: Blog*, February 5, 2013. https://www.chunklet.com/man-or-astro-man-defcon-54321/ (accessed: September 11, 2017).

Finally, the band promises that "the new album finds the band bringing their unique powerful style of Science Friction back to greater humanity in supreme form." As "Astromen," then, the band features itself as elevated – literally and figuratively – to a privileged position and perspective. One could indeed argue that in and through this self-fashioning, the figure of the astronaut is rendered as a variation of the topos of the itinerant man, the "homo viator", whose marginalized positions on the 'edge of the world' makes his (or her) view on this world particularly outstanding and productive. For this figure, as George H. Tucker argues, the margin that is his regular dwelling place turns into "an alternative, ever shifting, vantage point of critical freedom [...], enabling him continually to re-assess his own culture and to relativize the very perceptions of the world and habits of thought that he has inherited from it".[34] Being on the move keeps the itinerant man from being drawn into and absorbed by the centrifugal powers of the system (whatever this system might be). He – and it is mostly a 'he' – indeed "believes one must attempt the journey in order to assert autonomy, yet knows both that the struggle of this very journey leaves him equally uprooted and fragmented and that he will never achieve more than an illusion of such autonomy".[35] Against this backdrop, the move towards outer space as an exploration that necessarily includes a dramatic shift of perspective, may thus contribute to shaping the astronaut as an external observer, which in turn helps back up the band's critical stance on discourses and developments 'on Earth' and thus complements the ideological implications of the nostalgic turn to the era of space travel.

By way of conclusion: the astronaut as tragic and heroic figure

In the musical and performative self-fashioning of Man ... or Astro-man?, the astronaut is featured as the protagonist of a narrative on a 'future that never was', a narrative which revolves around the notion of 'the analogue' as an embodiment of what is generally felt to be a more 'authentic' and immediate form of technology. In so doing, the band's 'retromania', to quote Simon Reynolds' study on the

34 George Hugo Tucker: *Homo Viator: Itineraries of Exile, Displacement and Writing in Renaissance Europe*. Geneva: Droz 2003, p. 279. Cf. Martin Butler: Ramblin' Men: The Figure of the Hobo in Amercan Folk Culture. In: Alexandra Ganser / Katharina Gerund / Heike Paul (eds): *Figures of Mobility: Pirates, Drifters, Fugitives in the U. S. and Beyond*. Heidelberg: Winter 2012, pp. 155–175.

35 Todd Kennedy: *Hitting the American Highway: The Ontology of the Hobo-Hero in Twentieth-Century American Culture*. Unpublished dissertation, University of South Carolina 2007, p. 147.

self-referential dimension of popular culture again, can be understood as a critical engagement with the effects of media development in general and the process of digitization in particular, and thus on a more abstract level as a critical intervention into the surprisingly stable belief in 'progress-through-technology' that is characteristic of western modernity.

Moreover, the members of Man ... or Astro-man? use the aesthetics of past visions of the future to also position themselves in a particular genre and tradition of rock music, paying homage to the musicians and bands who emphatically embraced the figure of the astronaut and the idea of space travel as a frame of reference for *their* self-fashioning in the late 1950s and early 1960s.

The nostalgic move towards space travel and travelers can therefore be said to express both a fascination for the gigantic proportions of the idea and mission of exploring outer space and at the same time a fascination for the absolutely astonishing conviction of an entire nation at a specific time that this mission will, of course, be accomplished. As the nucleus of this narrative, which combines a "nostalgia for the future" as conceptualized by Reynolds with an "analogue nostalgia" in the sense of Schrey through the evocation of past futures as a comment on potential futures of the present, the figure of the astronaut is thus both a tragic and a heroic figure: tragic, as it is embedded in a vision of the future that, in retrospect, might well be referred to as a failure, as ridiculously idealistic; and heroic, perhaps, because the figure of the astronaut is still envisioned as a character with a particular point of view from 'outer space', which allows him or her to develop a privileged perspective from which to articulate social criticism through a distinct musical soundscape.[36]

36 Finck: Man, p. 122, argues along similar line with regard to the band's representation of space as "a kind of space that speaks of both possibility and failure, which we can only ever *almost* occupy but in which we might nevertheless find the resources to interrogate certain features of what we call the present".

Marc Bonner / Thomas Hensel

Astronaut and Avatar

Some Remarks about the Video Game as Outer Space

Introduction

The idea of space travel and video games being closely linked to each other is not as speculative as it may seem. In December 2011, scientists from the University of Freiburg in Germany put forward the idea that Nintendo's Wii home video game console, the Wii Balance Board and the Wii Fit Plus game software, could be used as a training device for astronauts during long-term space flights.[1] While many technologies and materials used in everyday life were developed in zero gravity laboratories orbiting Earth, now the reverse could happen: the Wii could be used in outer space in order to improve working conditions there. The scientists from the Department of Sport and Sport Science presented the results of experiments with a Wii Balance Board installed in a test aircraft of the type Airbus A300 ZERO-G.[2] This aircraft performs parabolic flight maneuvers and thus creates a short-term zero gravity environment, which is used to educate astronauts. With the Wii installed, it took off for a series of parabolic flights, which made it possible to examine balance training with the Wii Balance Board under zero gravity conditions. As is well known, gravity has a significant impact

1 Eine Videospielkonsole im Weltall. In: *Nintendo*, 2011. https://www.nintendo.de/News/2011/Eine-Videospielkonsole-im-Weltall-257653.html (accessed: October 4, 2018).

2 Ramona Ritzmann / Kathrin Freyler / Anne Krause / Albert Gollhofer: Auswirkung von Schwerelosigkeit auf den menschlichen Bewegungsapparat: Erfolgreiche Maßnahmen gegen Degeneration. In: *Flugmedizin Tropenmedizin Reisemedizin* 21 (2014), pp. 176–182. https://www.researchgate.net/publication/273322571_Auswirkung_von_Schwerelosigkeit_auf_den_menschlichen_Bewegungsapparat_-_Erfolgreiche_Massnahmen_gegen_Degeneration (accessed: October 5, 2018).

on the human body. Without specific physical training, astronauts lose about 10 percent of their muscle mass with each month they spend under zero gravity conditions in outer space.[3] In order to reduce these negative effects, the Wii was deployed; the Wii Balance Board and its accompanying game software were used to train the equilibrium of the astronaut body through its vibration mechanism. It enabled a sensorimotor workout to take place in zero gravity, thus training the whole body through motion sequences instead of just single muscles. The study and its positive results were immediately welcomed by the general manager of Nintendo Germany, Dr. Bernd Fakesch, who declared that Nintendo was very enthusiastic about the idea of testing the Wii Balance Board in outer space, stressing his own (and the company's) fascination for all things concerned with space.[4]

Using the arguments set out below, we would like to address the question of why science fiction as a setting or game world has been so closely related to video games since their beginnings in the early 1960s. Apart from the physiological reason indicated above, there are at least three other crucial reasons behind this relationship. The first two deal with the general coupling of space travel and video games on a macro-level. We will highlight aspects of both reasons by referring to and quoting from the preliminary work of Patrick Jagoda, who gives an overview of what he calls the "institutional and cultural" reasons, as well as the "technological" reasons.[5] The third reason is of a more specific nature and to explore this, we will examine the relationship between the astronaut and the avatar as the corporeal/intrinsic reason behind video games on a micro-level.

Institutional and cultural reasons

We have come a long way from the dawn of video games with the likes of *Spacewar!* (Steve Russell, MIT 1962), *Asteroids* (Atari 1979), and *Moon Patrol* (Irem / Atari / Midway 1982), which represent space travel and the astronaut with abstract spacecraft made from vector graphics and pixels, to modern video games and their non-linear, three-dimensional navigable space full of complex polygon meshes, such as the choice-based and dialog-heavy space opera trilogy *Mass Effect* (Bioware 2007–2013) and the space trading and combat simulator

3 Michael E. Long: Surviving in Space. In: *National Geographic* 199 (2001), pp. 6–29.

4 Eine Videospielkonsole im Weltall.

5 Patrick Jagoda: Digital Games and Science Fiction. In: Gerry Canavan / Eric Carl Links (eds): *The Cambridge Companion to American Science Fiction*. Cambridge: Cambridge UP 2015, pp. 139–152, here pp. 142, 143.

Fig. 1: In *No Man's Sky*, players are free to explore a seemingly infinite galaxy.

Star Citizen (Cloud Imperium Games), whose ambitious world depicting the whole Milky Way is still in development. Another recent example is the independent game *No Man's Sky* (Hello Games 2016–), which has created a galaxy of 18 trillion planets in stages, placing the players right in the vastness of outer space[6] to explore habitable and hostile planets, discover flora and fauna, mine minerals, and craft things in order to survive on the long journey to the center of the galaxy (Fig. 1). Loneliness at the 'final frontier', as well as an atmosphere of sublime transcendence are key features of today's science fiction video games, where astronauts and their intricately depicted spacesuits are directly seen on

6 In the context of video games, procedural generation is used in order to automate the building of game worlds by complex intertwining algorithms. *No Man's Sky* has no traditionally 'handcrafted' game world. Hello Games' galaxy is so vast that the small developer studio conceptualized some core aspects concerning physics, game rules, and aesthetics, and wrote a complex algorithm referencing fractal geometry using arbitrary numerical input. Thus, the layout of the world, its topology, and topography is generated in the process of playing instead of a prefabricated design. Every player experiences a different galaxy with another succession of star systems and combination of flora and fauna on the planets. Game Designer Sean Murray comments: "[T]he entire universe exists at the moment of its creation. In another sense, because the game only renders a player's immediate surroundings, nothing exists unless there is a human there to witness it." Sean Murray in: Roc Morin: Inside the Artificial Universe That Creates Itself. In: *The Atlantic*, February 18, 2016. http://www.theatlantic.com/technology/archive/2016/02/artificial-universe-no-mans-sky/463308/ (accessed: October 6, 2018).

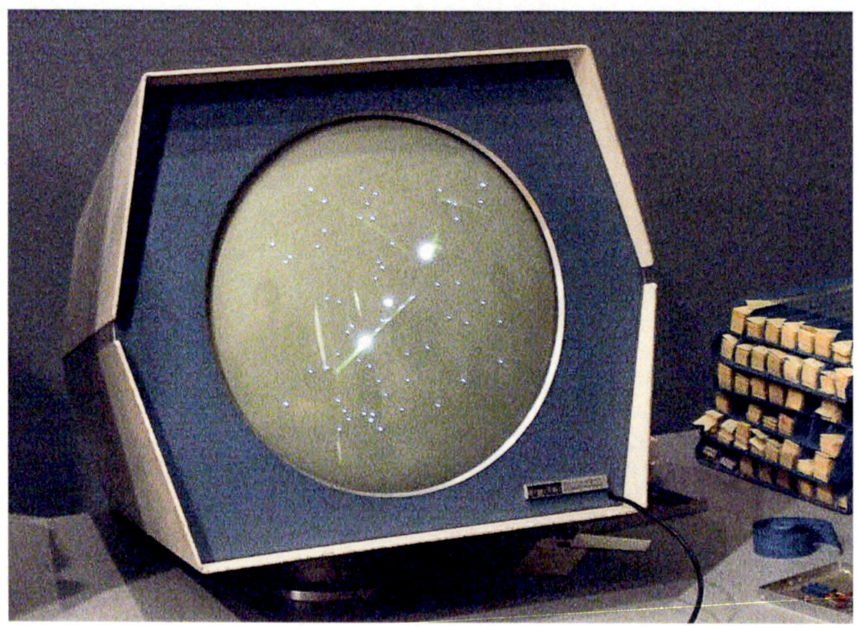

Fig. 2: *Spacewar!* was the first video game depicting outer space and spacecraft battles.

screen (from a third-person perspective) or controlled directly in first-person perspective. The experience from the perspective of the astronaut is crucial. Ever since the first video games, adventure and the exploration of the unknown and uncharted spaces have been crucial for making players feel involved, be it taking on the role of the cave explorer in the text adventure *Colossal Cave Adventure* (William Crowther 1975), or the idea of experiencing outer space and its physical peculiarities in *Spacewar!* (Steve Russell / MIT 1962). *Spacewar!* features two-player gameplay originally processed by a DEC PDP-1 computer and mediated by an Oscilloscope CRT monitor (Fig. 2). Both players must attempt to shoot one another, while maneuvering in the gravity well of a star and trying to avoid colliding with it. The ships fire missiles that are unaffected by gravity due to a lack of processing power. The spacecraft can move either clockwise or counterclockwise around the star and yaw within the enclosed game space, which is confined to the limits of the screen. Moreover, the players are confronted with a paradox in perspective due to the abstract vector graphics. Cult classics like *Pong* (Atari 1972) and *Pac Man* (Namco 1980) resemble medieval paintings, with the bird's-eye view and profile view of the avatar typically blending into a paradox of spatial representation.

Why did video games emerge in the era of the space age? In 1957, Sputnik 1 was launched into a low Earth orbit, thus marking the start of the space race to the Moon and the race for hegemony over a territory beyond Earth's atmosphere. By the time *Spacewar!* was developed in 1962 the idea of manned space travel still was regarded as pure science fiction by most people. It was not until 1968 that *2001: A Space Odyssey* (US/GB 1968, D: Stanley Kubrick) and its intricate depiction introduced new and believable forms of space travel. Eventually in 1969, actuality fulfilled some of Kubrick's visions of space travel with the manned lunar mission Apollo 11. Taking institutional and cultural reasons into consideration, it is significant that science fiction settings had a preeminent role in the emergence of video games in the 1960s. Jagoda observes that *Spacewar!* influenced game experiments as well as the emerging Western video game industry of the 1970s:

> [D]uring the first decades of digital games, science fiction became a core generic influence. [...] Following World War II, computers came to shape the ideological commitments, geopolitical strategies, and military systems that made up America's central role in the Cold War. As Paul N. Edwards contends, "Of all the technologies built to fight the Cold War, digital computers have become its most ubiquitous, and perhaps its most important, legacy." In the 1960s and 1970s, access to computers and nascent networks was limited to government research labs as well as universities such as the University of Utah, Stanford University, and MIT.[7]

Bearing this observation in mind, one can conclude that science fiction – as well as digital computers and their accompanying phenomena in the form of video games and several types of other software – was intrinsic to the Cold War era that rapidly developed in the wake of World War II. Game designer Anna Anthropy highlights the conditions that existed at that time in American universities when she writes:

> When computers were first installed in college campuses and laboratories, only engineers had the access to the machines, the comparative leisure time, and the technical knowledge to teach those computers to play games. It is not surprising that the games

7 Jagoda: Digital Games and Science Fiction, p. 142.

they made looked like their own experiences: physics simulations, space-adventures drawn from the science fiction they enjoyed.[8]

The emergence, form, and aesthetics of early video games in the United States of America were therefore not only heavily linked to the places where computers were installed for research purposes, but were also related to those people who could access them. Jagoda points out that engineers, physicists, and programmers working for the benefit of an "American Cold War research agenda"[9] shaped the mechanics and visual imagery of early video games, creating in the process a major cultural phenomenon that had become one of the biggest entertainment industries by the beginning of the twenty-first century. Hardware and software that were used to test, design, and compute spacecrafts, space travel, weapon systems, and overall modern physics research were converted into digital games like *Spacewar!*, which acted as a distraction from everyday research at the lab. Thus, video-game culture in the United States started off as a kind of playful practicing of scientific research. In Japan, however, the main other producer of digital games, video-game culture originated in toy-making companies like Nintendo, where video games were made by designers and artists from the outset. The development of digital computers and thus of software and its algorithms, of interactive vector graphics and human-computer interfaces, coincided not only with the emergence of the new-age topics of science fiction (e.g. robotics, post-humanism and the like), but also nurtured some of its fundamental themes: technological utopias, the time machine, the laser gun, and artificial intelligence. Jagoda concludes:

> It is perhaps unsurprising, then, that scientific and technological themes were so prominent in early games. Arguably, technoscientific change has always been a key subject of science fiction, dating back to the evolutionary and anthropological theories that influenced late nineteenth-century novels such as H. G. Wells's *The Time Machine* (1895), *The Island of Doctor Moreau* (1896), and *The War of the Worlds* (1899), as well as the work of Verne, London, and Doyle. Cold War culture, however, made technoscience an even more central dimension of American culture and geopolitical power.[10]

8 Anna Anthropy: *Rise of the Videogame Zinesters: How Freaks, Normals, Amateurs, Artists, Dreamers, Drop-Outs, Queers, Housewives, and People Like You are Taking Back an Art Form.* New York: Seven Stories 2012, pp. 5–6.
9 Jagoda: Digital Games and Science Fiction, p. 142.
10 Ibid.

In the wake of the successful manned lunar mission, space travel became a favorite topic in films and video games of the 1970s and early 1980s. In 1972, the first home video game console, the Magnavox Odyssey, could be bought and connected to TV sets.[11] The living room and its furniture had already been centered around the TV from the 1950s on. The home video game console was at first only a simple addition to the home and family entertainment sphere, until the Nintendo Entertainment System (NES) was launched between 1983 and 1986, enabling a new video-gaming culture that was independent from amusement arcades. The latter were already filled with science fiction games like *Space Wars* (Larry Rosenthal / Cinematronics 1977), *Space Invaders* (Taito / Midway 1978), and *Asteroids*, due to the overwhelming success of George Lucas' space opera *Star Wars: A New Hope* (US/GB 1977, D: George Lucas).

Science fiction and video games are still one of the most famous and successful couplings in the game industry today, despite the end of the Golden Age of space exploration, and when public fears of an escalation in the Cold War leading to nuclear strikes have largely disappeared. Besides adapting the long-established topics of exploration, colonization, trade, and spacecraft combat into three-dimensional game worlds, the idea of enabling players to experience navigating zero gravity in a spacesuit in outer space in a first-person perspective is a phenomenon featured in several recent video games. In the survival adventure *Adrift* (Three One Zero 2016), players float and move in any direction through the wreckage of a destroyed space station in the near future, which is reminiscent of the modular design of the ISS and the clean design style of *2001: A Space Odyssey*. Movement through outer space in the game is regulated by gathering oxygen tanks, collecting audio logs, and solving puzzles in order to piece together past events and thus find a way back to Earth (Fig. 3). *Adrift* also caused quite a stir in the gaming community as it can be played with the head mounted display device Oculus Rift to create a much more involving gaming experience thanks to the VR goggles. In the science fiction survival-horror game *Prey* (Arkane Studios 2017), the game world is a space station represented as a floating art deco skyscraper and the surrounding outer space. Players not only have to overcome obstacles in the complex yet coherent maze-like interior of the space station, recalling the classic *System Shock* (Looking Glass Technologies / Origin 1994), they must also navigate the exterior areas, such as venturing to abandoned space

11 Developer Ralph Baer worked as engineer for Sanders Associates, a company that developed electronic systems for the US air force and NASA. The home video game console was a side project of that company and was later sold to the entertainment electronics company Magnavox.

Fig. 3: While navigating in zero gravity, the player in *Adrift* has to find a way back to Earth.

Fig. 4: In *Prey*, outer space is even more hostile due to an alien bio-mass.

shuttles and parts of the station that are derelict, as well as secluded parts of the station. Meanwhile planet Earth and the Moon loom and glow in the blackness of virtual outer space (Fig. 4).

Both examples showcase the merging of what game theorist and designer Scott Rogers points out as two core design tropes of video game history, namely outer space and the space station.[12] When science fiction-based video games shifted avatar representation from spacecraft to playable humanoid characters, the astronaut as hero was born. From the very beginning, platforming games like *Major Havoc* (Atari 1983) or *Xenophobe* (Bally Midway 1987) mostly created space stations as abandoned dungeons full of structural or alien hazards. Players controlled the astronaut in profile view, while navigating through the space station as a constantly scrolling longitudinal section. Like the aforementioned *Prey*, they heavily drew inspiration from the film *Alien* (GB/US 1979 D: Ridley Scott). Prior to that, outer space mostly consisted of simple to compute starscapes and basic gameplay mechanics, which fitted in with early video games like *Spacewar!*, as well as the large group of arcade 'shoot 'em ups' like *Space Invaders* and *Defender* (Williams Electronics 1980). As we will now see, the development of outer space as a game trope largely developed in the way it did for technological reasons.

Technological reasons

As well as overlapping on an institutional and cultural level during the space age, the technology relating to the computer systems of that time and the following decades also had an influence on the close and clearly defined relationship between science fiction and video games. Jagoda gives the example of game designer Eugene Jarvis, who has observed "that science fiction space battles were so common in the games of the late 1970s and early 1980s because the abstraction of outer space 'covered up the inadequacies of [existing console] hardware.'"[13] This was not only due to limited capacities in the computation of graphics and sound, but also especially to the limited random-access memory (RAM), a data storage strategy that is still being used to store data (from the software's databases) and code (the software's algorithms). The architecture of computers, arcade games, and home video game consoles, including their techniques to compute data and algorithms into the audio-visually experienced game worlds on a screen, and their limited capacities in the early 1960s regulated the audio-visual aesthetics and gameplay mechanics of video games.[14] Thanks to advances in computing

12 Scott Rogers: Hell, Hyboria, and Disneyland. In: Christopher W. Totten (ed.): *Level Design, Processes and Experiences*. Boca Raton / London / New York: CRC 2017, pp. 101–120, here pp. 104, 117.

13 Jagoda: Digital Games and Science Fiction, p. 143.

14 Media theorist and artist Lev Manovich defines the process of algorithms gathering separately stored data and organizing them to a visual interface and/or images of software or game worlds as "transcoding". Thus, the "computer layer" becomes visible and interactable as

power and RAM capacity each decade, hardware is still a crucial agent in designing and "transcoding"[15] video games with their open worlds and photo-realistic graphics. That said, programmers of the 1960s and 1970s had to be creative to stage believable and easily understandable game worlds for players. Rogers remarks that depicting outer space on a cathode ray tube (CRT) was easy to manage by presenting the already black screen and only a few white pixels or light dots as distant stars.[16] The pointy and aerodynamic shape of spacecraft and rockets of that time could also be easily built by simple geometric vector graphics or a few pixels.

Spacewar!, Asteroids, Space Invaders, Defender, and *Galaxian* (Warren Robinett / Namco 1979) are accordingly as simple in aesthetics and as creative in mechanics as possible. For example, while the arcade game *Defender* has a colored starscape and a rudimentary planetary surface in the form of a single horizon line, it features a relatively complex control scheme, featuring a two-way joystick that sports five buttons for acceleration, shooting, changing directions, and altitude in the side-scrolling two-dimensional outer space. From the early 1980s onwards, numerous game mechanics and graphic design tricks allowed science fiction-based video games to branch out from simple arcade 'shoot 'em ups' in outer space to recreating the astronaut's numerous actions and tasks on alien planets and space stations. These include the aforementioned platforming games like *Xenophobe* and *Metroid* (Nintendo 1986), and strategy games where players have a bird's-eye view of isometric landscapes, such as *X-COM: UFO Defense* (MicroProse 1994) and its sequels, colony builder *Surviving Mars* (Haemimont Games 2018), and the world-famous real-time strategy game *StarCraft* (Blizzard Entertainment 1998). Space exploration simulations like *Nomad* (Intense! Interactive / Papyrus Design Group 1993) and *No Man's Sky* are also very distinctive in the way they stage science fiction, as well as more complex space trading and space travel simulation games such as *Elite* (Robert Holdstock 1984) and its numerous sequels. They also inspired action-adventure and role-playing games, such as Chris Robert's and Warren Spector's cinematic *Wing Commander* series (Origin Systems 1990–2007) and the *Mass Effect* trilogy (Bioware 2007–2012). In addition, survival-horror games such as the *Dead*

a "cultural layer" in the man-machine feedback loop. See Lev Manovich: *The Language of New Media*. Cambridge / London: MIT Press 2002, pp. 45–46.

15 Lev Manovich: *Software Takes Command*. New York / London / Oxford / New Delhi: Bloomsbury 2013, pp. 223, 300.

16 Rogers: Hell, Hyboria, and Disneyland, p. 104.

Space trilogy (Visceral Games 2008–2013) and *Prey* rely heavily on narrow maze-like level structures and suspense horror, while constantly confronting players with zero gravity and other hazards of outer space.
Since the early 1990s, the introduction of low-poly 3D graphics and of the CD-ROM as a digital data storage device has enabled bigger game spaces with volumetric objects, as well as higher resolution textures and sounds. Photorealistic graphics were written in the 1970s (for example by Henri Gouraud, James H. Clark, and Bui Tuon Phong) creating vast spaces to explore more elaborate algorithms for data compression and data streaming, as well as for simulated reflections and the surface characteristics of real-world materials. Since then they have been optimized for specific game franchises and graphic engines. Around the turn of the twenty-first century, the internet and social media not only enabled multiplayer gameplay, but also new modes of production and distribution, which called for new mechanics and algorithms and, as Jagoda states, extended the "scope of science fiction games":

> Massively Multiplayer Online Role Playing Games (MMORPG) have expanded multiplayer interactions and world making into huge virtual online environments, including fictional planets, galaxies, and cyberpunk cities. Science fiction instances with thousands of players such as *EVE Online* (2003) have experimented with utopian societies and collective forms of organization. Another experimental genre that emerged during this period is the Alternate Reality Game, which tells a transmedia story that includes online components while stretching out into offline environments. These games require players to adopt key roles in a narrative that they discover or help produce with the designers. During these years, mobile games also gained popularity, especially with the proliferation of smartphones and tablets.[17]

The dynamics of MMO game worlds rhythmize play sessions, generating new subcultures. Independent games, as well as art games by lone designers and small developer companies, reiterate established science fiction video games from the space age, however, they also introduce innovative concepts born out of temporal, financial, and technical restrictions, and therefore recall the video-game culture from the 1960s and 1970s described above. *Waking Mars* (Tiger Style 2012) with its flat profile view first reminds us of typical platforming games like *Xenophobe* and *Metroid,* but while exploring Martian caves in a traditional fashion,

17 Jagoda: Digital Games and Science Fiction, p. 146.

players have to build biomes, well-balanced ecosystems, in order to produce self-sustaining areas and thus the necessary biomass for survival. *Waking Mars*, *Tacoma* (Fullbright 2017) and *Planet Alpha* (Planet Alpha ApS / Team 17 2018) "run alongside and intersect with mainstream commercial production"[18] and stage topics other than alien invasions, shooting or gaining points.

Jagoda states that the hardware (limitations) and software (algorithms) of digital media have formed media-specific aesthetics of science fiction, separate from literature and film, and inherent to video games.[19] On a macro level, this has been a core discourse since the early beginning of Media and Game Studies. Like the modularity, variability, and automation of digital media in general game objects, level structures and game worlds are built from recombined and modulated assets, which are also present in quest design and game mechanics.[20] As the exploration and appropriation of space is the dominant agent of non-linear digital game worlds,[21] there is a very close relationship between science fiction's idea of an astronaut's role and its role in video games.

Corporeal/intrinsic reasons

Now let us turn our attention to the third argument in our analysis concerning the 'dispositif' of the video game itself. What do an avatar and an astronaut have in common? In relation to the video game, the term 'avatar' is well known as denoting the player's surrogate in the game world. Of course, there is an unbridgeable ontological difference between avatar and astronaut: while the astronaut is a human being trained for extreme conditions, the avatar in contrast is virtual and thus enables a potential play simulation ("Probehandeln") that could result in the numerous losses of the avatar, that reliably 'respawns'. However, there are nevertheless ontological analogies between the avatar and

18 Jagoda: Digital Games and Science Fiction, p. 146.

19 Ibid., p. 145.

20 Christopher W. Totten: *An Architectural Approach to Level Design*. Boca Raton / London / New York: CRC 2014, esp. pp. 41–160; Manovich: *The Language of New Media*, pp. 27–61.

21 Espen Aarseth: Allegorien des Raums: Räumlichkeit in Computerspielen. In: *Zeitschrift für Semiotik* 23 (2001), pp. 301–318; Manovich: *The Language of New Media*, pp. 78, 183, 214; Michael Nitsche: *Video Game Spaces: Image, Play, and Structure in 3D Worlds*. Cambridge / London: MIT Press 2006, pp. 51, 85; Stephan Günzel: The Space-Image, Interactivity and Spatiality of Computer Games. In: S. G. / Michael Liebe / Dieter Mersch (eds): *Conference Proceedings of the Philosophy of Computer Games 2008*. Potsdam: Potsdam UP 2008, pp. 170–189. http://pub.ub.uni-potsdam.de/volltexte/2008/2456/ (accessed: October 7, 2018).

the astronaut, at least on an aesthetic level. The avatar appears to be characterized by an ambiguity or, in other words, an ontological oscillation. However one might define an avatar – as a tool, a sprite,[22] a mythical figure, a prosthesis or a puppet[23] – it is ultimately characterized by a paradoxically dual function: it exists as the protagonist of a narrative on the one hand and functions as the player's tool, the point of action,[24] on the other.[25] Britta Neitzel clarifies this idea by stating that the avatar has factual and fictional facets and is affected by the paradox of representing someone who is both acting within and outside of the diegesis or the game world seen on screen.[26] Rune Klevjer talks of a video game-specific telepresence, a "*prosthetic* agency, which functions as an extension or a prosthesis of the player's body, a 'tactile motor/kinesthetic link', is a defining characteristic since *Spacewar!*"[27] The man-machine feedback loop enables real-time control or piloting of the avatar. Thus, the video game is an ergodic medium. Klevjer refers to Maurice Merleau-Ponty's *Phenomenology of Perception*[28] when he concludes:

22 The term sprite means a two-dimensional bitmap in computer graphics that is integrated into a larger scene, most often in two-dimensional side-scrolling video game. The avatar Super Mario was a sprite, a flat silhouette, up until three-dimensional polygon graphics made it possible to sculpt him plastically.

23 For a fundamental introduction, see Rune Klevjer: *What is the Avatar? Fiction and Embodiment in Avatar-Based Singleplayer Computer Games.* Dissertation, University of Bergen, 2006. http://folk.uib.no/smkrk/docs/RuneKlevjer_What%20is%20the%20Avatar_finalprint.pdf (accessed: October 4, 2018).

24 In order to analyze properly the agency and spheres of impact between the player and the avatar, point of view means the viewing perspective staged by the virtual camera, while point of action refers to the place in game space where the interaction takes place or where the avatar is situated. While in third-person perspective games the point of view differs from the point of action, in first-person perspective games point of action and point of view coincide. For more see Britta Neitzel: Point of View und Point of Action – Eine Perspektive auf die Perspektive in Computerspielen. In: *Hamburger Hefte zur Medienkultur* 5 (2007): Computer/Spiel/Räume: Materialien zur Einführung in die Computer Game Studies, ed. by Klaus Bartels / Jan Noël-Thon, pp. 8–28.

25 For more on this subject, see Britta Neitzel: Selbstreferenz im Computerspiel. In: Winfried Nöth / Nina Bishara / Britta Neitzel (eds): *Mediale Selbstreferenz: Grundlagen und Fallstudien zu Werbung, Computerspiel und den Comics.* Cologne: Von Halem 2008, pp. 119–196, here p. 170. The avatar in our study is regarded a crucial agent for the media-specific form of the video game, although there are many video games and game mechanics that function without an avatar as bodily prosthesis of the player in a narrower sense.

26 Ibid., p. 152.

27 Rune Klevjer: Enter the Avatar: The Phenomenology of Prosthetic Telepresence in Computer Games. In: John Richard Sageng / Hallvard Fossheim / Tarjei Mandt Larsen (eds): *The Philosophy of Computer Games.* Dordrecht: Springer 2012, pp. 17–38, here p. 19.

28 Maurice Merleau-Ponty: *Phenomenology of Perception*. New York: Routledge 2012.

> When we play, because the avatar extends the *body* rather than pure agency or subjectivity, screen space becomes a world that we are subjected to, a place we inhabit and where we struggle for survival. [...] The sense of bodily immersion that is involved in avatar-based play is rooted in the way in which the body is able to intuitively re-direct into screen-space a perception of itself as object, which is the perception of itself as part of external space.[29]

Gordon Calleja is more specific when he argues that widely discussed terms, such as 'immersion' or 'telepresence', do not go far enough in order to describe the dynamics of the media-specific relationship between players and their avatars in video games.[30] Calleja thinks the term 'incorporation' is more suitable for this phenomenon, an incorporation that is built upon six types of player involvement: "*kinesthetic involvement, spatial involvement, shared involvement, narrative involvement, affective involvement* and *ludic involvement*."[31] According to him, the incorporation of the player into the game space functions as follows:

> On the first level, the virtual environment is incorporated into the player's mind as part of her immediate surroundings, within which she can navigate and interact. Second, the player is incorporated (in the sense of embodiment) in a single systematically upheld location in the virtual environment at any single point in time. [...] [T]he player incorporates (in the sense of internalizing or assimilating) the game environment into consciousness while simultaneously being incorporated through the avatar into the environment.[32]

The incorporation is then defined as "*the absorption of a virtual environment into consciousness, yielding a sense of habitation, which is supported by the systematically upheld embodiment of the player in a single location, as represented by the avatar.*"[33] Astronauts can be conceived in roughly the same way: they also act as representatives or surrogates, not of players in game space, but of humankind in an outer space that is equally vast, empty, and alien to our understanding. They can even be thought of as puppets when we take recent developments in space technology into account: scientists of the German Aerospace Center (DLR) have developed

29 Klevjer: Enter the Avatar, p. 29.

30 Gordon Calleja: *In-Game: From Immersion to Incorporation*. Cambridge / London: MIT Press 2011.

31 Ibid., p. 38. Emphasis in the original.

32 Ibid., p. 169.

33 Ibid. Emphasis in the original.

a space robot called SpaceJustin,[34] which in future will replace astronauts when carrying out dangerous extra-vehicular activities (EVA) in outer space or on low gravity planetary surfaces. Instead of having to do risky spacewalks, the astronaut can remain in the space station or spacecraft and control the robot from there. Equipped with data gloves and arm cuffs, the astronaut, like a player, controls the movements of the surrogate SpaceJustin outside the station like a puppet attached to digital virtual strings. In December 2015, SpaceJustin functioned as a surrogate for the Russian cosmonaut Sergey Volkov on the ISS and back on Earth, Alin Albu-Schäffer (head of the DLR Institute of Robotics and Mechatronics) was able to sense the pressure and movement of Volkov's handshake via the robot and thanks to force-feedback systems.[35]

Astronauts, like the avatar, are also ambiguous figures. On the one hand, they are self-determined, autonomous actors in their usual habitat of outer space, but on the other hand, they are dependent on ground or mission control, which guides and supplies them with resources of vital importance. In other words, astronauts are also affected by the paradox of a 'double addressing', as people who are both acting inside and outside. Due to the ambivalence of their role as 'earthly' *and* 'cosmic' bodies, astronauts are thus also virtualized. Their reality floats between both roles.

Other analogies between astronaut and avatar can be found if one views the 'dispositif' of space travel and the apparatus of the video game as spheres of communication. In both cases, a dialogue between two communicating actors on a boundary between the inside and outside takes place. The astronaut can be characterized as an intermediary figure, just like the avatar. While the astronaut liaises between earthly space and outer space, the avatar liaises in a structurally analogous manner between the player's world and the game world, as was clarified by Calleja. Thus, both astronaut and avatar are characterized by a hybridity that is rooted in the idea of connecting heterogeneous worlds – on the one hand Earth and outer space, and the players' real-world environment and the digital game world on the other. Their intertwining of opposing characteristics – being

34 Roboter als virtuelle Marionette. In: *DLR_next*, September 20, 2010. https://www.dlr.de/next/desktopdefault.aspx/tabid-6946/11463_read-26642/ (accessed: October 8, 2018).

35 A 'Telehandshake' Between the ISS and Earth. In: *DLR*, December 18, 2015. https://www.dlr.de/dlr/en/desktopdefault.aspx/tabid-10261/371_read-16273/#/gallery/21499 (accessed: October 9, 2018).

both protagonist and tool at the same time – enables the astronaut as well as the avatar to function as a mediator or, put another way, as a medium.[36]

While the avatar itself (unlike the astronaut), as a perceptual prosthesis, does not embody a sentient being, it does offer a vicarious body through which the perception of the player is altered or re-wired. It is thus incorporation "as a sense of assimilation to mind, and as embodiment", incorporating the game world in the player's sole consciousness.[37] This incorporation is comparable with the astronaut altering or re-wiring the perception of humankind concerning outer (or inner) space.[38]

Through the mediation of an avatar, we are to a certain extent encouraged to re-center, to imagine ourselves as a subject within the world of the game, an imagining which is based on the extension and displacement of our locus of agency, via a puppet, any fictional subjectivity of which must be attributed to mental simulation. In a phenomenological sense, the meaningful actions that we perform when playing with (or through) our avatar are performed from outside the space that the avatar inhabits; it is from this detached position that we are able to see and hear what we are doing. This position is, we argue, structurally comparable with the figure of the astronaut when conceptualized as mediator (in the sense of a "figure of discourse, thinking and agreement", a "Verständigungsfigur") of human self-conception, as Henry Keazor terms it in his introduction to the present volume,[39] or on human imagination, as Colleen Boyle formulates it in her article "Through the Eyes of the Astronaut: Mediator of the Human Imagination" in this book.[40]

We would like to briefly clarify all of the above arguments by using two video games as examples, which in our opinion are self-reflective, insofar as they address both the astronaut and the avatar as mediators on a meta-level. In the independent puzzle-platformer *The Swapper* (Facepalm Games / Curve Studios 2013), players experience the game world in typical side-scrolling manner. The players control an astronaut stranded on a damaged space station and looking for means to escape. The astronaut acquires a hand-held cloning device early in

36 For further reading and in the context of the angel, see Louis Marin: *Das Opake der Malerei: Zur Repräsentation im Quattrocento*, transl. from the French by Heinz Jatho. Berlin: Diaphanes 2004, pp. 185, 167, 284; Sybille Krämer: *Medium, Bote, Übertragung: Kleine Metaphysik der Medialität*. Frankfurt am Main: Suhrkamp 2008, p. 137.

37 Calleja: *In-Game*, pp. 169, 172.

38 Inside SpaceJustin's 'helmet' is a camera through which the astronaut on board the space station can observe the actions of his avatar.

39 See pp. 32 of this volume.

40 See especially pp. 93–95 of this volume.

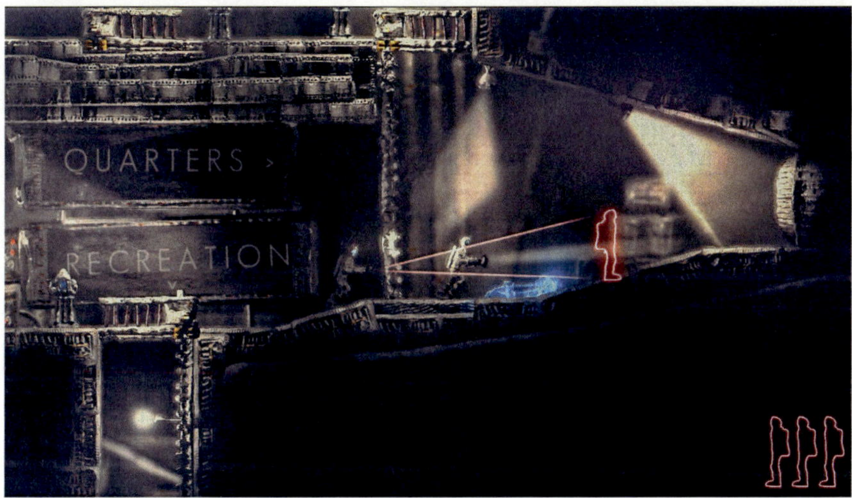

Fig. 5: Clones of the astronaut-avatar mirroring every move of the player in *The Swapper.*

Fig. 6: The astronaut-avatar creates a "magic circle" in *Astroneer* in order to interact with the alien environment.

the game, which is used to solve complex (spatial) puzzles. The device offers two functions: the ability to create simultaneously up to four clones of the astronaut-avatar and the ability to swap controls, and thus consciousness, to any of these clones, leaving the former avatar abandoned and hollow. Once created, the obedient astronaut clones will mirror every move of the players unless otherwise blocked by the environment. This allows the players to complete complex puzzles step by step, to activate doors and switches, and thus progress in the game world. Like the players, clones can also die by falling from a large height or from other environmental hazards. Clones are reclaimed if they die or if they physically move into the same space as the player. When using the cloning device, time slows down, allowing the players to execute even more difficult maneuvers involving the clones (Fig. 5). One example is scaling a vertical area by repeating the process of creating a clone higher than the currently active clone and immediately swapping control to the new clone while it is falling in mid-air, until a safe platform at the top of the area can be reached by a clone. Later levels include sections of the station where gravity has been reversed, increasing the difficulty of the puzzles. *The Swapper* examines many aspects of the science fiction trope of the clone conundrum. Furthermore, the video game raises ethical and metaphysical questions about the nature of consciousness, namely whether there would even be an original astronaut, a 'real' human being anymore.[41] This self-reflection is reinforced by the audio-visual aesthetics of the game world: the space station's eerie and at the same time brooding atmosphere. Indeed, it is not too far-fetched to interpret this cloning projection as a "mise-en-abyme" of the conception of both the astronaut and the avatar as mediators.

The name of the independent adventure game *Astroneer* (System Era Softworks 2016) is a hybridization of the terms "astronaut" and "engineer". We would propose that *Astroneer* stands in the tradition of reflection on the aesthetic boundary that marks the boundary between art and real space. Moreover, *Astroneer* might be considered self-reflective, in terms of how it incorporates and utilizes devices the avatar can play with within the game world. Even if it is not a so-called staged game, the avatar has an instrument that is designed like a stage and he/she can manipulate objects on this stage or platform (Fig. 6). In this way, *Astroneer* generates or implements what play theorist Johan Huizinga calls the "magic circle", the boundary separating the space-time of games from the space-time of everyday life.[42] This self-reflection is just one indicator for the omnipresence and for the significance of the figure of the astronaut for the video game – as a trigger not only for the self-conception of the human being, but also for the self-conception of the video game itself.

41 See also Marc Bonner's contribution, "'Climb the Penrose Stairs to Merge with the (In)Finite': The Astronaut as Reciprocal Posthuman" in this volume.

42 Johan Huizinga: *Homo Ludens: Vom Ursprung der Kultur im Spiel* [1956]. Reinbek: Rowohlt 2017, pp. 16–19, 22.

Table of Figures

Ansgar Oswald: The Space Traveler

Colleen Boyle: Through the Eyes of the Astronaut

Alexander Hauk / Sophia Hauk: Wall Calendar Journalism

Fig. 1: Sophia Hauk: *Climate Change*, 2015.
Fig. 2: Sophia Hauk: *Equity*, 2015.
Fig. 3: Sophia Hauk: *Peace*, 2015.
Fig. 4: Sophia Hauk: *Digital Change*, 2016.
Fig. 5: Sophia Hauk: *Drinking Water*, 2016.
Fig. 6: Sophia Hauk: *Overfishing*, 2016.
Fig. 7: Sophia Hauk: *Tax Fraud*, 2016.
Fig. 8: Sophia Hauk: *Nationalism*, 2017.
Fig. 9: Sophia Hauk: *Privatisation*, 2017.
Fig. 10 Sophia Hauk: *Tourism*, 2017.
All photos © Sophia Lukasch Photography / Sophia Hauk / www.Protestonaut.de

Jörg Hartmann: Female Space Travelers in Science Fiction Films 1898–2017

Fig. 1: Luna (Jehanne d'Alcy) as film's first female space traveler in *La lune à un mètre* (F 1898, D: Georges Méliès). © Flicker Alley, Los Angeles 2008.
Fig. 2: Film history's first female *and* human astronaut: Friede (Gerda Maurus), clothed like the real-life female aviators of her era in *Frau im Mond* (D 1928, D: Fritz Lang). © Friedrich-Wilhelm-Murnau-Stiftung, Wiesbaden 2001.
Fig. 3: Cora Peterson (Raquel Welsh) in a form fitting dress in *The Fantastic Voyage* (US 1966, D: Richard Fleischer). © 20th Century Fox, Los Angeles.
Fig. 4: Barbarella (Jane Fonda) helps an angel to regain his will to fly in *Barbarella: Queen of Galaxy* (F 1968, D: Roger Vadim). © Paramount, Los Angeles.
Fig. 5: A sentient ocean planet creates this 'female' cosmonaut (Natalja Bondartschuk) as a simulacrum in *Solyaris* (*Solaris*, SU 1971, D: Andrei Tarkovsky). © trigon-film, Ennetbaden.
Fig. 6: In space no one can hear you scream? Ellen Ripley (Sigourney Weaver) in *Alien* (GB/US 1979, D: Ridley Scott). © 20th Century Fox, Los Angeles.
Fig. 7: Ellen Ripley as mother and fighter. "This time it's war." Sigourney Weaver as Ellen Ripley on the movie-poster for *Aliens* (US 1986, D: James Cameron). © 20th Century Fox, Los Angeles.
Fig. 8: Compared to men, women are better at multi-tasking. Lindsey Brigman (Mary Elizabeth Mastrantonio) in *The Abyss* (US 1989, D: James Cameron). © 20th Century Fox, Los Angeles.
Fig. 9: The truth will not be televised. Dr. Eleanor Arroway (Jodie Foster) in *Contact* (US 1997, D: Robert Zemeckis). © Warner Bros, Burbank.
Fig. 10: How to cope with macho behavior at work? Lieutenant Starck (Joely Richardson) in *Event Horizon* (GB/US 1997, D: Paul W.S. Anderson). © Paramount, Los Angeles.
Fig. 11: That 'male gaze'. Mr. Hand (Richard O'Brien) in *Dark City* (US/AUS 1998, D: Alex Proyas). © Warner Bros, Burbank.
Fig. 12: Floating in inner space. Catherine Deane (Jennifer Lopez) in *The Cell* (US 2000, D: Tarsem Singh). © Warner Bros, Burbank.
Fig. 13: Don't panic. Dr. Ryan Stone (Sandra Bullock) presents a rare example of a strong female lead character in a Hollywood movie in *Gravity* (US/GB 2013, D: Alfonso Cuarón). © Warner Bros, Burbank.
Fig. 14: Empathy, intuition, and compassion as feminine traits: Dr. Louise Banks (Amy Adams) in *Arrival* (US 2016, D: Denis Villeneuve). © Universal Pictures, Universal City.

Marc Blancher: "Let's discover Space!"

Nils Daniel Peiler: Backlash of the Future

Fig. 6: HAL interfaces onboard the Discovery spaceship in *2010: The Year We Make Contact*. Screenshot from Peter Hyams: *2010: The Year We Make Contact* (US 1984). Bluray edition. Hamburg: © Warner Bros. Home Entertainment 2009.

Fig. 7: Electronic videos shown on cathode-ray tubes in *2010: The Year We Make Contact*. Screenshot from Peter Hyams: *2010: The Year We Make Contact* (US 1984). Bluray edition. Hamburg: © Warner Bros. Home Entertainment 2009.

Fig. 8: Dr. Walter Curnow (John Lithgow) is afraid of his extravehicular activity outside the Leonov in *2010: The Year We Make Contact*. Screenshot from Peter Hyams: *2010: The Year We Make Contact* (US 1984). Bluray edition. Hamburg: © Warner Bros. Home Entertainment 2009.

Fig. 9: Cosmonaut Irina Yakunina (Natasha Shneider) joins astronaut Dr. Heywood Floyd (Roy Scheider) in his room in *2010: The Year We Make Contact*. Screenshot from Peter Hyams: *2010: The Year We Make Contact* (US 1984). Bluray edition. Hamburg: © Warner Bros. Home Entertainment 2009.

Fig. 10: The Floyd Family: Dr. Heywood (Roy Scheider), Caroline (Madolyn Smith) and Christopher (Taliesin Jaffe) in *2010: The Year We Make Contact*. Screenshot from Peter Hyams: *2010: The Year We Make Contact* (US 1984). Bluray edition. Hamburg: © Warner Bros. Home Entertainment 2009.

Marc Bonner: 'Climb the Penrose Stairs to Merge with the (In)Finite'

Fig. 1: L.S. Penrose / R. Penrose: *Penrose Stairs*, 1958. Source: Lionel S. Penrose / Roger Penrose: Impossible Objects: A Special Type of Visual Illusion. In: *British Journal of Psychology* 49 (1958), pp. 31–33, here p. 32.

Fig. 2: A younger Bowman sees his older version in *2001: A Space Odyssey* (GB/US 1968, D: Stanley Kubrick). Screenshot from Stanley Kubrick: *2001: A Space Odyssey* (GB/US 1968). Bluray Edition, Stanley Kubrick Masterpiece Collection. Hamburg: © Warner Bros. Home Entertainment 2014.

Fig. 3: Floor plan of all four Bowman versions within the hotel room. From: Mehruss Jon Ahi / Armen Karaoghlanian: Floor Plan_1. In: *Interiors Journal*, 06/2012: 2001: A Space Odyssey, p. 4. http://issuu.com/interiorsjournal/docs/interiors0612 (accessed: July 12, 2017).

Fig. 4: Both Bell clones in one frame in *Moon* (GB 2009, D: Duncan Jones). Screenshot from Duncan Jones: *Moon* (GB 2009). DVD edition. London: © Lunar Industries / Sony Pictures Home Entertainment 2009.

Fig. 5: The seemingly infinite corridor full of Bell clones in *Moon*. Screenshot from Duncan Jones: *Moon* (GB 2009). DVD edition. London: © Lunar Industries / Sony Pictures Home Entertainment 2009.

Fig. 6: Cooper floating within the tesseract in *Interstellar* (US/GB/CA 2014, D: Christopher Nolan). Screenshot from Christopher Nolan: *Interstellar* (US/GB/CA 2014). 2 Disc Bluray, Steelbook Edition. Hamburg: © Warner Bros. Entertainment / Paramount Pictures 2014.

Fig. 7: Cooper sees his younger self due to the tesseract in *Interstellar*. Screenshot from Christopher Nolan: *Interstellar* (US/GB/CA 2014). 2 Disc Bluray, Steelbook Edition. Hamburg: © Warner Bros. Entertainment / Paramount Pictures 2014.

Fig. 8: M.C. Escher: *Ascending and Descending*, 1960. Lithograph. From: The M.C. Escher Company. http://www.mcescher.com/gallery/recognition-success/ascending-and-descending/ (accessed: July 12, 2017).

Martin Butler: The Future that Never Was

Marc Bonner / Thomas Hensel: Astronaut and Avatar

German National Library Cataloging in Publication Data
A catalog record for this book is available from the German National Library:
http://dnb.d-nb.de

Cover Design: Neofelis Verlag,
image by Vincent Fournier: General Boris V.,
Yuri Gagarin Cosmonaut Training Center (GCTC), Star City,
Zvyozdny Gorodok, Russia, 2007.
Courtesy by Vincent Fournier ©.
Editing & Typesetting: Neofelis Verlag (ag / ae)
Printed by PRESSEL Digitaler Produktionsdruck, Remshalden
Printed on FSC-certified paper.

ISBN (Print): 978-3-95808-213-7
ISBN (PDF): 978-3-95808-263-2